D1213421

# Motherhood at the Crossroads

## Meeting the Challenge of a Changing Role

# Motherhood at the Crossroads

## Meeting the Challenge of a Changing Role

### SUE LANCI VILLANI

with Jane E. Ryan, M.A., R.N.

 **INSIGHT BOOKS**

PLENUM PRESS • NEW YORK AND LONDON

Library of Congress Cataloging-in-Publication Data

Villani, Sue Lanci.
    Motherhood at the crossroads : meeting the challenge of a changing
  role / Sue Lanci Villani with Jane E. Ryan.
       p.   cm.
    Includes bibliographical references and index.
    ISBN 0-306-45566-8
    1. Mothers--United States--Psychology.  2. Housewives--United
  States--Psychology.  3. Mothers--United States--Social conditions.
  4. Housewives--United States--Social conditions.  5. Motherhood-
  -United States.   I. Ryan, Jane E.  II. Title.
  HQ759.V537   1997
  306.874'3--dc21                                                96-39451
                                                                     CIP

ISBN 0-306-45566-8

© 1997 Sue Lanci Villani and Jane E. Ryan
Insight Books is a Division of Plenum Publishing Corporation
233 Spring Street, New York, N.Y. 10013-1578
http://www.plenum.com

*An Insight Book*

10 9 8 7 6 5 4 3 2 1

All rights reserved

No part of this book may be reproduced, stored in a retrieval system, or transmitted
in any form or by any means, electronic, mechanical, photocopying, microfilming,
recording, or otherwise, without written permission from the Publisher

Printed in the United States of America

To my mother, Mary Louise Lanci, whose wisdom
and tenacity have guided me for 39 years

To my father, Joseph Lanci, whose faith in
me is endless

and to my son, Nicholas and my daughter, Francesca,
who have forced me to grow up

# *Preface* ∝

This book was written by Sue Lanci Villani with Jane E. Ryan, researcher and editorial assistant, whose 1978 undergraduate study served as the springboard for its main thesis. Their partnership was the result of a kinship that developed through the common bond of motherhood. Sue and Jane share a passion for inspiring social change so that women, as mothers, will be better understood and supported.

## JANE'S STORY

Twenty years ago, I came face to face with a desperation that I had never known before. Four challenging and sometimes out of control young children had truly gotten the best of me. I was the mother of three adopted children and one biological child, all about one year apart in age. For several years I had been frustrated, angry, frightened, and perplexed; I had no solutions to seemingly insurmountable problems. The challenges of motherhood were making me feel crazy. To find out if this feeling was a normal reaction to mothering, I decided to enroll in an undergraduate psychology course. Within a matter of weeks, my concept of myself as an individual and as a mother was shaken to its foundation. New information—facts and studies about adult psychology—forced me to take off the blinders that I never even knew I wore. Consequently, I had no choice but to reevaluate my entire belief system or continue to feel crazy.

Suddenly, I saw everything in a new light—relationships, choices, problems, decisions, solutions. But, most importantly, I saw myself differently as a mother. No longer could I define motherhood as something separate from myself. Who I was as an individual had to be integrated with who I was as a mother. My search for myself began with a term paper for which I interviewed a dozen mothers. Questions were designed to help me determine if I was "normal"; did other moms have the same feelings and experiences that I did? Did they feel afraid? Did they feel isolated and unsupported, guilty, overwhelmed, inadequate, unprepared? Meetings with the women turned out to be far more than standard interviews. They were passionate outpourings of each woman's experience as a mother. My findings elicited a profound reaction from my classmates and professor. They were spellbound by my results and asked questions I was unable to answer. Consequently, I was inspired to expand the study. With the help of my instructor, I developed a 50-question survey (see Appendix) that would become the foundation for two studies: one conducted in 1978 and the other in 1995. I distributed it to women across the United States—women who were home caring for young children, women who had given up their careers to care for their families. I reached them through a grassroots effort, through friends, friends of friends, sisters, and their friends. I followed up many with personal interviews. Despite the fact that I obtained a tremendous amount of new and significant information about women in their roles as mothers, I did not expand my findings. I was recently divorced at the time and a single parent of four young children, some of whom were having severe emotional problems due to the divorce and their adoptions. Still, I did not let go of the idea of someday turning my study into a book. Year after year, in town after town, job after job, I carried the study with me, so certain was I of its eventual relevance and importance.

Through the years I earned both a bachelor's degree and a master's degree in counseling, but never acquired the skills necessary to write a book on my own. In 1994, while on temporary assignment in Hawaii, I met Sue. It was a meeting that, in retrospect, seems utterly synchronous. I felt an immediate kinship to this woman. Before long, Sue was sharing information with me about her experiences as a mother. I knew instinctively that here was the person that I needed to make the book a reality. I knew it even before Sue showed me her work, before I had any evidence at all that she had the writing skills that I'd been seeking in a partner. Sue was a professional journalist who had a clear understanding of the issues presented in my study. A seemingly chance encounter had become the seed that would sprout into an auspicious future indeed.

## SUE'S STORY

Meeting Jane was like coming home through the back door. Immediately comfortable in her presence, I felt an attachment that was almost metaphysical in nature. Gripped in the confusion of new motherhood, I vented my frustrations to Jane, whose bland reaction to my troubles surprised me. As unique as my problems seemed to me, they were old hat to Jane. Her confidence and resolve that "this too shall pass," confused and unnerved me. I was sure that mothering was destined to remain the job from hell. I felt crazy and wondered how she had managed to stay sane throughout her early mothering years. When she told me about her study, I was both fascinated and relieved: fascinated because it tickled my journalistic fancy and relieved because it gave me hope. Finally! A woman I could connect with! Someone who took mothering problems seriously without dismissing them as the burden that all women must bear. When Jane approached me with the prospect of writing a book, I was excited, but cautious. I was comfortable in my role as a freelance journalist, but the idea of writing a book intimidated me. But because I've never backed down from a challenge—and this book was a challenge that had landed, unsolicited, right in my lap—I decided to write it.

It was at this point that the project seemed to take on a life of its own. Faith in a higher purpose, one that superseded our individual interests, began to sustain us. We were two spiritual warriors, albeit virtual strangers. Although we have markedly dissimilar backgrounds, a 13-year age difference, and had once had life goals that were diametrically opposed, the two of us met at a point in time when one of us was asking the same questions about motherhood that the other had asked nearly two decades ago. At the tender age of 12, each of us knew what she wanted to do. Sue was going to become a writer—marriage and children didn't enter into the equation. Jane was going to adopt children. In the end, we both ended up as professional women and mothers. Taking off our professional hats, we compared notes, woman to woman, mother to mother. It was interesting to us both that, after nearly two decades, women still seemed to be grappling with many of the same issues over motherhood—the isolation of staying home with a baby, the "correct" child-rearing techniques, the personal sacrifices inherent in motherhood, and the seemingly endless guilt. We wanted to find out why. Thus, a seed was planted. A series of brainstorming sessions followed that inspired us to resurrect the 18-year-old study that Jane had undertaken and to complement it with an updated study that utilized the same foundational material. Together, the two studies consist of interviews with some 300 educated, middle-class women, all of whom had given up their ambitions and careers to remain at home to raise their children.

# *Acknowledgments* ৫

Writing a book is a process that requires tremendous faith and a tolerance for delayed gratification. This project, my first manuscript, inspired me to seek more of both. I could not have put fingers to the keyboard day after day without the gentle prodding and loving support of my husband, Eric. I am overwhelmingly grateful for the help of Gail and Rob Caveney, two of my most cherished friends and the godparents of my children. They did far more than their fair share of babysitting during this strenuous undertaking. And to Kathy DeFoster, a wonderful friend and teacher, and Heather Cattell, who never once let me lose faith in myself. Another major contribution came from my mother, Mary Louise Lanci, who created the chapter-opening illustrations.

Paul LeClair, Assistant General Manager at Tony Honda Pearlridge Oldsmobile GMC, Inc., in Hawaii, and Mark Caliri, Vice President at Tony Honda Pearlridge, did their part in demonstrating how corporate America can support its employees and their families. Their ongoing support and flexibility could serve as a model for other corporations to follow. All of these kind, patient, and understanding friends allowed me to passionately and repeatedly bend their ears about the issues explored in this book for well over a year. A heartfelt thank you also goes out to the nearly 300 women, two generations of mothers, who provided Jane and me with intimate details of their lives. Their candidness was incredibly uplifting and added a richness to this book that would have been impossible to achieve otherwise. They have contributed greatly to what I hope will be a new understanding of women.

And then there's our editor, Frank K. Darmstadt, whose tireless encouragement to keep the faith, even when life's many challenges stood in the way of this book's progress, was more important than he might know. Many people helped Jane and me distribute surveys, both in 1978 and in 1995: Suzanne Ryan Inciong, Kathleen Ryan Martin, Trish Ryan, and Julia Ryan (Jane's sisters) hand-delivered surveys and made valuable contacts for us across the United States. Joshua and Brenda Daniel Lubrano were wonderful and willing research assistants. Mary James, founder of MOMS Clubs® and members of MOMS Clubs distributed questionnaires nationally and provided their most important input. Also, the mothers of FEMALE lent their invaluable help and enthusiastic participation to our newer study. The many women who helped Jane orchestrate discussion groups across the United States are also much appreciated: Brenda Murray Dye, South Carolina; Cynthia Evers, Nebraska; Tina Perelli, Pennsylvania; Carrie Slenkovich, Maryland; Ilana Fernandez, Florida; Bill and Kitty Manhke, Nebraska and California; Tina Murdock and Ellie Kurtz, Florida; Dawn Bernette, Pennsylvania; Susie Schmuckler, Maryland; Paula O'Brien, Minnesota; Sarah Lenz and Karri Knudtson, Wisconsin. After our interviewing, we had hundreds of hours of taped discussions and consequently hundreds of pages of transcripts to be typed. It was the nimble fingers of the following that struggled through a most tedious job: Joyce Underburg, Cindy Messenger, Beverly Major, Diann Kelilkoa, and Sharon Doughtie-Kramer. All the transcribers reported that they learned something about themselves due to their connection with this project. The staff of Copycat in Grand Island, Nebraska, were most helpful in making copies and facilitating the electronic communications between Jane and me when we were starting this amazing project long-distance between Nebraska and Hawaii. And then, just as important as the rest, are the many family members and friends who supported Jane emotionally, spiritually, and financially, during her painstaking efforts at research and data evaluation. She could not have done any of this without ALL of them: Peter Lubrano, Luke Lubrano, Gina Lubrano, Alexander Ryan Lubrano, Bev Major, Judy and Mike Murrell, Gail and Rob Caveney, Sandy

Noecker, William Brown, Robert DeBrandt, Cynthia Howe, Rose Kurz-Karor, and Kathy Lindstrom.

For these loved ones and anyone else whose name did not appear here, but who in some way participated in this amazing endeavor—Mahalo and Aloha.

—Sue Lanci Villani

The author gratefully acknowledges the following for interviews that took place between June and August 1995: Dr. Dyanne Affonso, Dr. Eleanor Morin Davis, Sally Dewald, R.N., Mary Hantske, R.N., B.S.N., I.B.C.L.C., Dr. Maisha Hamilton-Bennett, Dr. Leon Hoffman, Elizabeth Janeway, William Mattox, and Kim Miller.

# Contents ∞

# THE MOTHER CRISIS

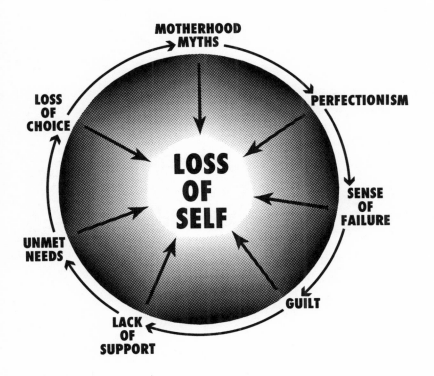

# *Introduction* ↻

*W*ebster's New World Dictionary defines crisis as "a turning point ... a decisive or crucial time, stage or event."[1] In the purest sense, that is what this book is about. Any woman who has ever confronted the idea or reality of motherhood, whether or not she chooses to have children, has had a crisis of identity, whether big or small. She has had to look deep inside herself, whether she wanted to or not. If she were honest with herself, she found some degree of conflict—over her feelings, her attitudes, her choices. For it is virtually impossible to exist as a woman in today's world without coming in contact with some myth or ideal that condemns one of the popular views of motherhood or that denounces the decision to not have children. As private a matter as motherhood is, the topic is fair game in a society that thrives in the midst of controversy. The unfortunate quarries of this sometimes ugly and increasingly public debate are women, mothers, and their children.

This is not a book about women as victims; it is about women as victors. It is about women who believe in one particular style of motherhood and have opted to live out that notion with conviction. These are mothers who have chosen to stay home with their children in a society that's still not certain how to characterize such a choice. The emotional distress that we have identified as *The Mother Crisis* appears in many individualized forms, but, in general, it is about mothers coming to terms with the cultural confusion surrounding motherhood and the inner turmoil that often erupts as a consequence. Specifically, it is about a point in time at which many mothers realize that their expectations of themselves as mothers don't quite match reality. In the pages ahead, I introduce scores of mothers who are busy doing what society says is best for its children and what the women themselves view as best for their offspring. But more importantly, I present women with the courage to scrutinize their own value systems by openly discussing the impact of their choice in terms of their own self-fulfillment and development.

The Mother Crisis as a phenomenon appears to be cyclic in nature. In the chapters ahead I will explore the following eight primary themes that constitute The Mother Crisis (see page 1):

- Motherhood Myths
- Perfectionism
- Sense of Failure
- Guilt
- Lack of Support
- Unmet Needs
- Loss of Choice
- Loss of Self

These themes are as timeless as motherhood itself. The same themes that prevailed in the 1978 findings dominated the 1995 results. They underscore virtually every aspect of mothering, from parenting practices and role identification, to family relationships, personal goals, and emotional health. Because the concept of motherhood is so poorly defined, a woman's success can be sabotaged from the moment she first brings baby to breast. Our society's failure to adequately define the mother role is the first theme and the catalyst that spurs the seven remaining themes. The Mother Crisis is a time when women experience tremendous guilt, shame, and anxiety over their performance as mothers, feelings brought on by both internally held and externally imposed myths concerning motherhood. It often includes conflict commonly experienced by women facing enormous pressure to live up to modern-day standards of motherhood—standards that often directly and indirectly conflict with self-fulfillment and development; standards that many women continually strive to meet despite an overwhelming lack of community and family support. Our research has shown that the crisis transcends cultural and geographical barriers; that collectively, those who experience its symptoms represent a universal phenomenon. Although an individual might not have a personal awareness of a crisis, she, nonetheless, lives amid its global existence simply because she is a mother.

The solution to The Mother Crisis can't be found in a psychological theory or in the pages of a law book. It can only be found in the hearts and souls of mothers. Women, as sisters, can accomplish a great deal by reaching out to one another in acceptance and support. But society as a whole also has a role in resolving this troubling issue, for much is at stake—the welfare of its mothers and children. Social workers, psychologists, and religious leaders can help our nation by abandoning mythical standards of motherhood and by determining family health according to individual function and merit. What can the rest of us do? We can listen to our mothers and support them. We can help them fill their needs. We can simply allow them to be who they are.

In 1978, Jane surveyed close to 200 women from around the United States and beyond, and interviewed more than 50 women in her quest for answers to the question that Sigmund Freud posed some six decades ago: "What do women want?" Jane's study, consisting of the comments of at-home mothers, asked that question and many others. What she discovered was startling. Despite the fact that all the women questioned lived lifestyles of choice rather than necessity—all of them could have worked and hired child care had they wanted to—a great many seemed truly vexed by the personal ramifications of their decision. Emotions ran high; there was a great deal to talk about. To help focus the study on the emotional and spiritual, rather than the economic or political aspects of motherhood, Jane established a set of criteria that would narrow her sample to include only women with post–high school education and who were married to professional men.

Jane's goal was to get a close-up look at mothers who were well equipped for careers but had chosen motherhood on a full-time basis, despite the fact that child care was well within their means. They did it because they thought it was best. Her assumption was that these at-home mothers possessed an array of skills and had access to more resources, contacts, and support systems than those who had fewer choices due to their financial status. By successfully performing a variety of roles, the women in our study have received validation and affirmation of their worth. As a consequence, they feel valued and have an added measure of self-esteem. If the self-esteem, then, of these advantaged women is shaken to the core by the challenges of motherhood, then what happens, asked Jane, to women who lack a strong foundation of esteem?

It is important to note that women who fall outside this circle of career moms have much to gain from observing their points of view. For once, they can see how women who have the luxury to strive for society's highest ideal of motherhood (staying home full time with the kids) face the same emotional demons as women engaged in different parenting styles (e.g., working full time with kids in day care) out of necessity or choice. In interview after interview in 1978 and 1995, women of many heritages, ethnic backgrounds, and talents talked about the joys and the frustrations of their role. Despite the fact that all the women participating were residents of the United States—twenty-four states were represented—many of them were born and reared in other countries including England, South America, Canada, and New Zealand. Although some women left the discussion groups secure in their decision, a great many others left questioning it. When it didn't meet with denial, our gentle probing opened a floodgate of contradiction and admission. Yet, all of it was good. The women did what few had ever been encouraged to do; they shared their uniquely individual points of view with two people who took them seriously. They felt validated, supported, understood.

"I think the process has been great because it has helped me rediscover a lot of things," said Carrie, from Rockville, Maryland. "I feel like I have a lot of things to say about motherhood because it's something that I don't always get to do. You've given me the opportunity to express myself, and it was nice to be honest and let it all hang out," echoed her friend Helen. Results of the study confirmed the suspicion that led Jane to conduct it in the first place, that hidden in the shadow of our nation's towering definition of the "Good Mother," lurk real women with real needs that cannot be met in the context of such an ideal. And these were the women who embraced it!

As Jane's 1978—and our subsequent 1995—study both demonstrate, women are still out there chasing after the same myth, the realization of the "Good Mother" personified. Not surprisingly, none of them ever catch up with it. Many times larger than life, the image is far too perfect and undergoes a subtle metamorphosis, generation after generation, along with society's changing values. What is "maternally correct," today might be condemned as bad mothering tomorrow. And while glorifying the image of the "Good Mother," society continues to repudiate at-home motherhood as an occupation requiring little intelligence and few, if any, marketable skills. Where does that leave today's mothers? Floundering about in search of a fragment of esteem.

There is currently hot debate over the impropriety of mothers who work outside the home. Much has been written about the negative impact of a working mother's absence on her children and, consequently, on society as a whole. Conversely, there are those who argue that the continuous presence of the full-time mother is stifling and breeds narcissistic adults with no potential for maturity. Neither side addresses whether the emotional well-being of the mother has anything to do with the well-being of her children. We neither advocate nor condemn either of the two approaches to mothering and feel that our culture's tendency to do so only serves to divide women when what they need most is unity. It is our hope that the information presented in this book will empower women to be comfortable with either choice; to allow them to give themselves permission to develop fully as women, whatever mothering path they choose. As long as society remains polarized over the issue, discussion will continue to be tainted with the generalizations and stereotyping typical of a subject that's painted only in broad strokes of black and white.

Little attention is paid to the gray area in between, where temperament, attitude, character, and individualized behavior comes into play.

The process of becoming a mother is a complex one indeed. A woman evolves into the role in much the same way that she develops as a person—sometimes in small steps, other times by leaps and bounds. But, change in a mother also means change in her children. Any alteration of her psyche will, like ripples in a pond, flow out to her children to be absorbed through a kind of emotional osmosis. Herein lies the rub. How can a woman be true to herself when what is culturally acceptable for a mother is so narrowly, albeit nebulously, defined?

American women of recent history have been culturally pigeonholed into one of four acceptable images, chiefly that of "Loyal Wife," "Good Mother," "Sex Kitten," and "Old Maid." A woman who digresses from any one of these impressions is often greeted with derision, not to mention confusion. First Lady Hillary Rodham Clinton is a classic example of a woman who refuses to be stereotyped by a myth or ideal. When Bill Clinton was accused of philandering during his campaign for the Presidency, Ms. Clinton—lawyer, feminist, mother—stood firmly by his side. Yet, when criticized for stepping outside the boundaries of the "Good Mother" construct, the First Lady uttered her now infamous remark about not wanting to stay at home and bake cookies. The popular press just can't figure her out! Still, not all women have the fortitude to withstand such societal pressure. And in their roles as mothers, many find it particularly easy to succumb. Women are subject to intense public scrutiny when their personal style of mothering fails to live up to the "Good Mother" image. Such pressure is a real double whammy to the mother already consumed by self-doubt, for motherhood is the kind of job that can challenge even a strong woman's sense of adequacy. Sometimes even the slightest external criticism can push a woman into the abyss.

The issues that emerged in the 1995 study were identical to those that were revealed in the 1978 study, and altogether just as relevant. Moreover, discussion about them was as explosive in

1995 as it was nearly 20 years ago. Both studies revealed that lack of self-esteem is the core of The Mother Crisis. In both studies, the majority of the women reported that they had expectations of themselves as mothers before having children.

"I guess I saw myself as more of a fairy-tale image, but I'm not as patient and understanding as I thought I would be," noted Bernadette from Rhode Island, a 35-year-old mother of two. Becky, a 31-year-old teacher from South Carolina, said, "I swore I would never raise my children as my mother raised me. Well, hello, mother!" When asked to reflect on the reality of motherhood, a great many of the women saw their former self-images shatter into pieces. Thirty-four-year-old Louise, an inner-city schoolteacher with two children, admitted, "Before the children came along, I envisioned myself giving top priority to them, but I don't always do so. I tend to get bogged down with studying or housework." "I was very naive [about motherhood], even though I was older, and you would have thought I'd known better," said Nancy from Nebraska, a 32-year-old mother of four. "I imagined myself as a good mother with lots of love and patience. Well, I love them with all my heart, but I do lack a lot of patience and understanding." Twenty-eight-year-old Crystal, from Florida, tearfully admitted: "I can't tell my daughter that I love her; I don't know why. So she can't tell me. I don't know if she loves me or not."

Despite the discomfort of such wide-open introspection, the women seemed relieved to be discussing feelings that had been previously repressed. But how unsettling it is to have an idea that's wrapped up all neat and tidy suddenly scattered about. It is precisely at this point in time that a woman's sense of self becomes the casualty of awareness; she begins to question who she is. The Mother Crisis is the dilemma of the woman who has allowed her own personal growth to be stunted. But there's no reason for such a woman to be ashamed. The myths and standards attached to the concept of motherhood are so powerful that even an individual with a fully developed sense of self has difficulty standing firm in their wake.

Thirty-two years ago, in her book, *The Feminine Mystique*, Betty Friedan shook up the nation by attacking the validity of the

1950s-style ideal of a woman. Since then, there has been great discourse, and discord, over what is right, what is wrong, what is good, what is bad, what is shameful, what is not, in relation to women in their roles as mothers—identified by the mystique as a woman's primary function. Unfortunately, little, if any, concrete understanding of the issue has managed to rise above the din. The end result is a great deal of conflict and controversy in motherhood.

During the 1995 murder trial of football legend O. J. Simpson, Deputy Prosecuting Attorney Marcia Clark commanded bigger headlines for her predicament as a divorced working mother than she did for her performance as a lawyer. Struggling to retain custody of her two preschool-aged sons, the accomplished Los Angeles attorney was forced to defend herself against accusations of neglect. In short, her performance as a mother was questioned. The most troubling fact of the event is that so few people asked whether her children were content. That the lawyer did not fit the image of the "Good Mother" implied all the damage that her critics needed to convict her. Any mother knows that even the consummate Clark must have felt the sharp pang of parental guilt. But if time spent home with the kids is the primary measure of a mother's worth, then why do stay-at-home mothers experience so much of the same tormenting guilt? The problem lies in the myths that define women and in our culture's fanciful view of motherhood.

The solution lies within mothers themselves, and in everyone else who has a role in supporting them. In our search for a solution, we discovered some startling truths. Primarily, mothers of today are no better off than their mothers or grandmothers in a cultural and social context. Many of the changes that women have experienced in the past 50 years are simply window dressing. Society still expects women to be responsible for child care, even when they work outside the home. Women still do most of the housework. Salaries for women are still not equal to those of men who are employed at the same job. Despite the lip service that society pays its mothers, in actuality, full-time career moms are often treated as second-class citizens. Observed Maryland mom Ginny, "We're doing a 1950s thing in the 1990s." This point, and others, is illustrated in the chapters ahead.

In stark contrast to Betty Friedan's assertion that the "problem which has no name," stems from a chronic sense of nonfulfillment among at-home moms, our research indicates that the real crisis has its roots in different soil. Many of today's at-home moms by choice—as well as those in the 1970s—report that career mothering is a good fit, that lack of fulfillment is not the issue. Rather, it's a vacuous feeling of inadequacy, caused by a lack of support, feedback, validation, and affirmation that work together to undermine their self-esteem. Women from both generations fell into their own disfavor in the role of mother, despite having ample intelligence, skills, material assets, and options. Motherhood, it seems, is a profession that destroys its own. Although exalted by our culture, it is simultaneously devalued. This is the paradox that breathes life into The Mother Crisis.

# PART I

# *Motherhood in the 1970s* ⁊

# *A Lack of Identity* ❧ *Women without a Strong Sense of Self Are High Risk for a Mother Crisis*

*T*he 1970s were a time of great enlightenment for women. Conflict and controversy abounded, from the beginning of the decade, when 50,000 women's rights activists marched down New York City's Fifth Avenue in the first annual nationwide Women's Strike for Equality, to its stormy conclusion, when Phyllis Schlafly hosted a victory party in Washington, D.C., celebrating "The End of an ERA." Throughout this turbulent, exciting time in U.S. history, women were doing what they have always done—work, love, raise children, mold

families, share ideas, and speak out for what they believe in. The events of the 1970s, and those of the decades that preceded it, provided an appropriate backdrop for the women in our 1978 study so that we could view them in a social context. Although the lion's share of our data consists of information about the women as mothers, a relevant portion of it includes their perceptions of themselves as individuals, before motherhood. Presenting a picture of the women as individuals allows us to compare their premotherhood personas to the women they become after having children. Examining this decade was great fun for Jane and me, since we were at such different points in our lives at the time and, therefore, influenced by its events in distinctively separate ways.

Despite the sheer massiveness and unbridled passion of the women's movement, it seemed to have little influence over the women in our study. In stark contrast to the feminists of the time, who embraced individualism, advocated freedom of choice, and exuded a remarkable sense of self-confidence, given the existing social climate, our women appeared passive and indecisive. Many seemed to experience a vague lack of purpose and lacked an awareness of their innate talents and abilities. There was also much floundering about by respondents in their searches for a life path or goal. Although a great number of the participants reported having feelings of pride and a sense of accomplishment in their jobs or careers, many of these same women also experienced a sense of incompleteness and confessed to having little or no ambition or desire to move up to a higher position. Still others found their careers to be too difficult to endure and viewed the promise of motherhood as an attractive fallback position that was less competitive than the marketplace.

"I went to New York to become a world-famous model, and I was there for a year, but I wasn't aggressive enough," noted Janet, from upstate New York. Our purpose here isn't to pit career women against at-home moms, but rather to shed some light on how and why women become so polarized once they make a choice. One reason is that the limitations set by the roles and character traits deemed culturally acceptable for women have worked to snuff out the spirit, dim the aspirations, and inhibit the contributions of women to American society. Women who want to contribute, and can't, often become frustrated and defensive. Women who strive for worldly success anyway often demean those who don't.

The jobs and careers represented in the pool of nearly 100 women amounted to no more than nine, the majority being in traditional "women's" roles or in the helping professions— including teacher, nurse, secretary, student, speech therapist, dental hygienist, florist, proofreader, and social worker. By contrast, a total of twenty-six professions were included in their husbands' profiles, ranging from businessman, CPA, medical doctor, journalist, and college professor to real estate developer, clergyman, engineer, philosopher, and football coach.

The majority of the women appeared to be stunted in their goal setting by the assumption that a pregnancy would naturally result in termination of employment. "I went as high as I wanted to go, knowing that when the children came, I'd quit," wrote one mother, Kathy, 32, a former secretary and administrative assistant, and the mother of two children, ages 8 and 4. A great many of the respondents went to college or to work to find a husband. "I went to a junior college, and it was strictly to get a husband; that's why my parents sent me," recalled Janet, a former teacher and a mother of two. Among the women as a whole, the career choice of motherhood was frequently arrived at by default. "I wanted to have a family because it would give me something to do," admitted Pat, a 33-year-old Canadian mother of three with a bachelor's degree in political science. Such responses caused us to wonder why the characteristics of these women are so markedly different from that of feminists. Where is their drive to succeed as individuals? Why are they not demanding a place of their own in the world? Why do they have such a vacuous sense of self? As staid observers of this phenomenon, we were driven to find answers to these questions. Some explanations could be found in the surveys and transcripts, mostly by reading between the lines. We were sensitive to innuendo and took note of the cross talk between the women who took part in discussion groups. Finally, after determining that the attitudes and self-images of the women were formed long before the explosion of ideals that took place in the 1960s and 1970s, we turned to history for an explanation. "What kind of messages about womanhood did our participants receive throughout their formative years?" we wondered. Exactly what kind of models and influences were they surrounded by that caused them to think of themselves in such dubious, limited terms?

## *WOMEN ARE SOCIALIZED TO BE PASSIVE, NOT AMBITIOUS*

History alone tells us why all women of the social-minded 1970s were not dauntless feminists. Indeed, even a superficial look at our nation's recent history gives reason to wonder how modern women manage to muster up any true sense of self at all. Before she can even begin, a woman must first possess the wherewithal to challenge the ideals of authority figures in her life, the lives of the women in her life who serve as role models, the messages she hears, and the images she sees regarding how a woman should exist in the world. For more than a few women, this is a tall order indeed. Most of the images that women receive throughout their lives negate any holistic view of the female persona. A woman is either smart or she is pretty, but never both. She's either athletic or she is feminine; she's either kind or she's ambitious. Women are socialized to believe that one set of character traits contradicts, rather than balances, another. Any trait that's not passive, and therefore feminine, in nature is designated as taboo.

In 1979, anthropologist Margaret Mead observed society's tendency to squelch women's talents, warning that "we run a great risk of squandering half our human gifts by arbitrarily deny-ing any field to either sex or by penalizing women who try to use their gifts creatively."[1] Confirms Maxine Harris, in her book *Down from the Pedestal*, "Most of our popular folk tales present us with only a narrow range of female possibilities."[2] For example, Shake-speare's *The Taming of the Shrew*, written in 1595, introduces a lively young woman, headstrong and willful, who marries a young adventurer. The comedy is about their struggle—her will against his. When tamed, she becomes "a loving and obedient wife."[3]

The surveys revealed that most of the women in our study had a positive view of themselves as individuals before having children—positive by modern standards, that is. The majority of respondents described themselves as "independent." Other de-scriptions included adjectives such as "headstrong," "risk-taking," "hardworking," "stimulated," "mature," "secure," "energetic," "sensitive," "extroverted," "experimental," "curious," "self-assured," "popular," "professional," "organized," and "content,"— words that suggest anything but a passive, capricious nature. In an effort to interpret this paradox, we asked ourselves the follow-ing questions: What have women been told about themselves through folk tales and otherwise throughout the decades? How has history contributed to the shaping of their identities and self-perceptions? What goals have they been coached by society to abandon or pursue? Why is career motherhood chosen by so many with so little conscious thought?

The answers to these questions come in many forms. In the early 1900s, President Theodore Roosevelt painted a glorious, albeit narrow, portrait of the "good woman," presenting her as the foundation upon which a strong nation is built. "There are certain old truths which will be true as long as this world endures and which no amount of progress can alter," wrote the nation's leader. "One of these is the truth that the primary duty ... of the woman is to be the helpmate, the housewife and the mother. The woman should have ample educational advantages; but save in exceptional cases the man must be, and she need not be, and generally ought not to be, trained for a lifelong career as the family breadwinner."[4]

Mr. Roosevelt deified the role of mother proclaiming

> The woman's task is not easy—no task worth doing is easy— but in doing it, and when she has done it, there shall come to her the highest and holiest joy known to mankind; and, having done it, she shall have the reward prophesied in Scripture: for her husband and her children, yes, and all people who realize that her work lies at the foundation of all national happiness and greatness, shall rise up and call her blessed.[5]

One can almost hear the angels sing when listening to this speech. What woman wouldn't want to revel in the sanctity of such a noble pursuit? Women of the time were dignified by such remarks, which validated their worth and gave them a sense of power. After all, they were pleasing the President of the United States!

Long before Mr. Roosevelt felt the need to espound on woman's highest and best purpose, other men of power exerted their influence, with the Bible in one hand and the rod in the other. One early nineteenth-century American minister counseled brides as follows:

> Bear always in mind your true situation and have the words of the apostle perpetually engraven on your heart. Your duty is submission—submission and obedience are the lessons of

your life and peace and happiness will be your rewards. Your husband is, the laws of God and of man, your superior; do not ever give him cause to remind you of it.[6]

The messages were consistent and came from the highest authority figures that our culture has to offer.

## *"EXPERT" OPINIONS OF WOMEN DIMINISHED THEIR INDIVIDUALITY*

In the late 1800s, popular medical theory reduced women to a collection of body parts, introducing the concept of the battle between the uterus and the brain. This fanciful, yet widely accepted, belief was used to explain countless ailments among women who were obviously not emotionally or intellectually suited to the confines of traditional women's roles. Treatment for a woman who exhibited any symptoms of distress was to suppress the use of her intellect so that her uterus could resume its natural, dominant place, which would allow her to heal. If a woman was academically or artistically inclined, she was advised either to cease or decrease all such activity. Dr. S. Weir Mitchell, a popular Philadelphia physician of the time, advised his patients to "Live as domestic a life as possible.... Have but two hours of intellectual life a day. And never touch pen, brush, or pencil as long as you live."[7] When one of his patients, Charlotte Perkins Gilman, attempted to follow his counsel she reported, "I came perilously close to losing my mind. The mental agony grew so unbearable that I would sit blankly moving my head from side to side ... I would crawl into remote closets and under beds—to hide from the grinding pressure of the distress."[8] To Mitchell, a woman was designed for one purpose—reproduction. A successful man could have no better ornament than a wife who embraced the womanly "virtues" of delicacy and ignorance. A "lady" could be charming but never brilliant, animated but never ardent.

The theories that guided doctors' practices from the late nineteenth century to the early twentieth century held that woman's normal state was to be weak and that a pregnant woman should avoid all forms of stimulation, intellectual or otherwise. The sexual woman was viewed as a sperm-draining vampire. Young girls were warned that too much reading or intellectual stimulation could result in permanent damage to the reproductive organs and sickly babies. In his book *Sex in Education, or a Fair Chance for the Girls*, Dr. Edward H. Clarke concluded that higher education would cause a woman's uterus to atrophy. Consequently, many doctors argued against education for women. Or in the words of R. R. Coleman, M.D., of Birmingham, Alabama, "Science pronounces that the woman who studies is lost!"[9] One man who recognized the waste of women's tremendous resources, the Reverend Theodore Parker, was, in 1853, a lone cry in the dark. "To make one half of the human race consume its energies in the functions of housekeeper, wife and mother is a monstrous waste of the most precious material God ever made," he proclaimed during a speech in Boston.[10] The empathetic minister was obviously way ahead of his time.

## SOCIETY WANTED WOMEN TO STAY HOME

In addition to being medically humiliated, women were also socially and politically suppressed. In 1900, only four states gave ballot privileges to women—Wyoming, Colorado, Idaho and Utah. "Sensible and responsible women do not want to vote,"[11] stated former President Grover Cleveland, who smugly declared that God himself had worked out a social and political hierarchy with men on top. Astonishingly, many wives and daughters dutifully agreed. Yet the status of women was changing rapidly. By 1900, as many as 700,000 young women had hung up their pots and pans and gone to work as teachers, sales clerks, or office assistants.

Despite this mass exodus out of the kitchen, the early 1900s were also the springboard for the romancing of the home as evidenced by President Roosevelt's manuscript. Like Roosevelt, clergymen, popular magazines, and other politicians continually raved about the sanctity of the home and the dangers assailing it. The 1909 White House Conference on the Care of Dependent

Children declared, "Home life is the highest and finest product of civilization."[12] Women, of course, lay at the center of it. It was also at this time that domesticity emerged as a science and gained popular support. By 1916, 20 percent of the public high schools offered courses in domestic science, or home economics, as it was more commonly referred to at the time. At the college level, home economics made spectacular gains: from a total of 213 home economics students in the nation in 1905 to 17,778 in 1916, most of them preparing to be home economics teachers. In 1909, the American Home Economics Association had 700 charter members.[13]

Ironically, one of the most receptive and supportive groups standing firmly behind the new science was the women's movement. The Woman's Suffrage Association steadily adopted the ideas of home economics leaders. It should be remembered, however, that the women's movement at the turn of the century was not based on a feminist ideology. The ideology of the movement was sexual and domestic romanticism—women deserved the vote *because* they were homemakers, not in spite of it. The focus was on getting the vote and getting women into college. Domestic science soared in popularity because it lent credence to both activities. Given this curriculum, higher education would not "de-sex" women, or destroy them, it would actually make them "better" women.

The romance of the home was an enduring one. Through both World Wars, when women were encouraged to replace their aprons with coveralls in war-related efforts, it persisted. Once the wars were over, women's boundaries were put staunchly back in place. Mother blaming, Freudian style, began about this same time in American history, when women were beginning to actually use their rights of emancipation, to go in increasing numbers to college and professional schools, and into the professions to compete with men. The neuroses of children were blamed on the independence and individuality of this new generation of women, traits the housewife–mothers of the previous generation did not possess. The press picked up and headlined any study that implied working mothers were responsible for juvenile delinquency, school difficulties, or emotional disturbance in their children. The studies that showed working women to be happier, better, more mature mothers did not get much publicity, even though, as one Stanford University psychologist, Dr. Lois Meek Stolz, declared, research that supported both sides of the debate could be found in abundance.[14]

For those who feared that women's infatuation with home and hearth should dim, the love affair was reignited in 1946 by a powerful spark. Dr. Benjamin Spock, a New York pediatrician with a background in psychology, wrote his guide to raising children for an enormous and receptive audience: young married couples wanting to put the war behind them and start a family. The book sold some 750,000 copies in its first year and became a perennial best-seller. *The Common Sense Book of Baby and Child Care* changed the nation's ideas about raising children. The premise that most affected women, however, was his strong belief that a mother's place is in the home, particularly during the first three years of a child's life. The spark for the romance was mothers' guilt.[15]

## *WOMEN STAYED HOME TO PROVE THEIR FEMININITY*

The messages aimed at American women in the 1950s had a major impact on the women taking part in our 1978 study. It was a decade when questioning the dual roles of wife and mother was tantamount to challenging the culturally defined concept of true femininity. Any form of overt doubting cast a dark shadow on one's private life as well. The women bold enough to even consider alternative roles for themselves during this time in American history invited public scrutiny of both their sexuality and their motives. They paid a huge price. But so, too, did those who didn't.

Women who had children after the war were caught up in the movement that drove them back to the home with little or no domestic help, strongly supported by government policy, using the current psychological theories that idealized motherhood. Whether they worked in or away from it, millions of American women heeded the call home. A new way of life emerged in the

1950s, with sterile, planned communities called *suburbs* replacing crowded, dirty cities. Of the 13 million homes constructed in the United States in the 1950s, 11 million sprang up on the fringes of city limits.[16] Home life was glamorized by all kinds of experts—doctors, statesmen, politicians, and religious leaders alike. But most of all, it was glamorized by the media. Advertisers of home-use products spent millions of dollars convincing homemakers that a pristine home was among the loftiest of pursuits. A marketing study conducted in the mid-1950s concluded that marketing aims should be to

> capitalize on housewives' guilt over the hidden dirt. She then will rip her house to shreds in a deep cleaning operation which will give her a sense of completeness for a few weeks. The seller must stress the joys of completing each separate task, remembering that nearly all housekeepers, even those who detest the work, paradoxically find escape from their endless fate by accepting it—by throwing themselves into it.[17]

As small as it was, a woman's domain was simultaneously and mysteriously defined as a tremendous responsibility requiring monumental talent and ability. Housewives were urged to express themselves through product buying for home and family. Any other form of expression was discouraged, provoking guilt. The result? Housework expanded to fill time available.

In the early 1960s, feminist and author Betty Friedan identified these widespread marketing practices as a national conspiracy and hoax on American women. Her book, *The Feminine Mystique*, released in 1963, challenged the myth that the only truly feminine women were mothers and homemakers, dismissing it as bunk. Nonetheless, women bought it. By the end of the 1950s, the average marriage age of women in America dropped to 20 and was still dropping into the teens. The proportion of women attending college in comparison with men dropped from 47 percent in 1920 to 35 percent in 1958.[18] By the end of the 1950s, notes Friedan, 60 percent dropped out of college to marry, or because they were afraid too much education would be a bar to marriage. By the end of that same decade, the U.S. birthrate was surpassing

India's. There was a fantastic increase in the number of babies among college women. Women who had once wanted careers were making careers out of having babies. At a Smith College commencement, Adlai Stevenson reminded young women of their duty "to restore valid, meaningful purpose of life in the home and to keep their husbands truly purposeful."[19]

Because the cultural stereotypes received such rigid support from all segments of society—industrial, political, social, and so on—many women who had a problem living with the status quo in the 1950s or '60s were convinced that something must be wrong with either their marriages or with themselves. Friedan identified the fallout resulting from this faulty deduction as "the problem that has no name"—or the vague sense of hopelessness and despair being experienced by millions of housewives nationwide. The reason so many women were suffering, declared Friedan to the dismay of the nation, was because of our culture's insistence that women be pigeonholed *en masse*. Dubbing this narrow definition of womanhood "the feminine mystique," the author contended that American society was infatuated with a totally unrealistic view of women that was, at best, unnatural, and at worst, fatal.

The feminine mystique says that the highest value and the only commitment for women is the fulfillment of their own femininity. It says that women envied men, women tried to be like men, instead of accepting their own nature, which can find fulfillment only in sexual passivity, male domination, and nurturing maternal love. According to the author, the mystique is so powerful that women grow up no longer even knowing that they have the desires and capacities the mystique forbids.

Although the mainstream press had a field day with *The Feminine Mystique*, the book emerged as a landmark essay on collective social consciousness and served as the catalyst for the women's movement of the 1960s and '70s. In 1966, three years after its release, Friedan cofounded the National Organization for Women (NOW). But while this housewife and mother of three was struggling to write her now infamous book, she found herself drowning in the same river of misinformation that was sweeping away the very women about which she wrote. The messages directed toward women by the media were as ubiquitous as air and just as pervasive.

In the early 1950s, *McCall's* magazine declared that adult women could find their deepest satisfaction by marrying at an early age and rearing large families. Fewer than one in ten Americans polled answered "yes" to the question of whether an unmarried person could be happy.[20] Friedan rallied against a notion that, to her, was painfully obvious—that the prevailing beliefs about what was proper conduct for a woman barred women from the freedoms of human existence and a voice in human destiny. "The feminine mystique permits, even encourages, women to ignore the question of their identity." she asserted.[21] Friedan surmised that the heart of women's problem in America was a lack of a private image. "Public images that defy reason and have very little to do with women themselves have had the power to shape too much of their lives,"[22] she said, maintaining that such images would have little influence if women were not suffering a crisis of identity. It was the author's main thesis that identity is the core of the problem, represented by a stunting or evasion of growth that is perpetuated by the feminine mystique. The feminist revolution had to be fought simply because women were stopped at a stage of evolution far short of their human capacity.

Friedan noticed that feminists had to fight the conception that they were violating the God-given nature of women. She also noted that many of the college women she observed in 1959 were afraid they'd be typecast as "unfeminine" if they took themselves or their studies too seriously. Freidan concluded that it is a sick and immature society that chooses to make women housewives, not people, and that it is sick or immature men and women, unwilling to face the great challenges of society, who can retreat for long, without unbearable distress, into that "thing-ridden" house and make it the end of life itself. Her convictions sent a shock wave through mainstream America.

Prior to *The Feminine Mystique*, there were few signs that women's roles would become a heated issue in America. A 1962 Gallup Poll found that three out of five women were at least "fairly satisfied" with their lives.[23] The controversial book changed all that. Once again, the pursuit of women's rights was making headlines. In 1964, a woman reporter helped women attain one important legislative breakthrough, the inclusion of women into the 1964 Civil Rights Act. Television journalist May Craig was interviewing Rep. Howard W. Smith of Virginia on "Meet the Press" when the civil rights bill was in congressional committee. Would he, she asked, consider revising the bill to include women? Yes, he said. In fact, Smith hoped to defeat the bill by adding women to the list of minorities it covered. When Smith proposed the inclusion of women in the bill before the House, laughter broke out on the floor. The process, in all its hypocrisy, sent a message with which feminists would become increasingly familiar—campaign all you want, but don't expect the powers that be to take you seriously. The Civil Rights Act of 1964 passed and Title Vll prohibited discrimination in employment on the basis of sex. The Equal Employment Opportunity Commission (EEOC) was set up to enforce the law, but it would be another eight years of legal maneuvering before the Equal Employment Opportunity Act (EEOA) was passed and the EEOC had any power.

If history wove the fabric that formed the mind-sets of the women in our 1978 study, then current events provided the stitching that held the entire tapestry together. At the same time that feminists were waging war on behalf of women to obtain equal rights, societal messages about women's roles and accepted behavior were as restrictive as ever. Many women who were in leadership roles were incredibly outspoken against a patriarchy that refused to budge from its ideals. The public conflicts in which such women found themselves in the 1970s presented a gruesome picture to the many other women who, intimidated, stood securely on the sidelines. The women in our study could be counted among the bystanders. For them, the mystique provided a much safer playing field. While they were retreating to the safe harbor of home and hearth, their feminist counterparts were relentlessly stretching the very boundaries that served as their shield and braving the ensuing storm.

For example, when Katherine Graham, publisher of *The*

*Washington Post*, allowed her reporters to pursue their investigation of Watergate, John Mitchell retaliated with typically derogatory verbiage: "Katie Graham's gonna get her tit caught in a big fat wringer," he said. [24] In 1973, responding to questions about including women in the NASA space program, astronaut James Lovell stated innocently, "We've never sent any women into space because we haven't had a good reason to. We fully envision, however, that in the near future, we will fly women into space and use them the same way we use them on Earth—and for the same purpose."[25] That same year, Spock renounced his earlier sexist views on child care and revised his classic work. On January 22, 1973, the: *Roe v. Wade* decision was handed down by the court, claiming that the right to privacy is broad enough to encompass a woman's decision whether or not to terminate her pregnancy, yet a mere 4 years later, Rosie Jimenez died as the first victim of the restriction of Medicaid funds for abortions. Curiously, in a June 1979 Gallup Poll, 70 percent of Americans agreed that Medicaid should pay for abortions for poor women "under all circumstances."[26]

There were many subtle messages regarding the parameters of acceptable behavior for women as well. Wrote Gail Rock in the December 1973 issue of *Ms. Magazine*:

> Mary Richards of the Mary Tyler Moore Show is over 30, unmarried and not the least in a panic about it, actually appears to have a sex life, and is neither stupid nor helpless. Still, she has her problems. Mary is supposedly the associate producer, which would make her second in command on her evening news show. Yet she addresses the producer (the dominant male) as Mr. Grant and he calls her Mary.... Mere writers on the show call him Lou. They, of course, are men, so it's okay.[27]

Crusading feminists of the time acknowledged these parameters and addressed them head on. "Any woman who chooses to behave like a full human being should be warned that the armies of the status quo will treat her as something of a dirty joke; that's their natural and first weapon," said women's rights activist and author Gloria Steinem.[28] "A man has to be Joe McCarthy to be called ruthless. All a woman has to do is put you on hold,"[29] echoed feminist actress Marlo Thomas, who starred in "That Girl," a 1960s sit-com about an unmarried actress living alone in New York City. Ironically, Marlo Thomas's character married her boyfriend at the end of the 1966–1971 series.

## THE WOMEN'S MOVEMENT CHALLENGED SOCIETY AND CONFUSED WOMEN

Whether entertainer, activist, educator, student, or writer, everyone seemed to be putting in their two cents during the increasingly heated public debate over women's rights. No matter how controversial or private, no subject was sacrosanct. In a 1976 article entitled "Phallic Imperialism," *Ms. Magazine* correspondent Andrea Dworkin addressed our society's practice of defining women as the producers of babies, then took the subject one step further. "Once the baby is born, this product of the mother's labor, made from the raw materials of her body, does not belong to her. It belongs to man," she reminded her readers.

> It belongs to one who did not and cannot produce it. This ownership is systematized in law, theology and the national mores; it is sanctioned by the State, sanctified in art and philosophy, and endorsed by men of all political persuasions. A baby who is not owned by a man does not have a legitimate civil existence.[30]

Still, there were many gains for women in this tumultuous decade. In 1974, the Supreme Court outlawed mandatory maternity leave for teachers and a year later prohibited the automatic exclusion of women from jury duty. New York state outlawed sex discrimination in insurance coverage in 1975, the same year that the Working Women United Institute was created to fight sexual harassment on the job. *Time* magazine broke its tradition of naming the Man of the Year by designating ten women for cover honors. Awareness in the business arena was also heightened. The National Advertising Review Board issued a position paper in 1975 on "Advertising and Women," which pointed out that it is "a counterproductive business practice to try to sell a product to someone who feels insulted by the product's advertising."[31] In 1977, AT&T announced that it was ready to allow dual listings of married people in phone books. A year later, Congress passed a bill requiring pregnancy disability benefits for pregnant women and allocated $5 million to the Department of Labor to set up centers for displaced homemakers.

As enlightened as we had supposedly become, the long-enduring concept of "superwoman" was spawned in the 1970s by a media that seemed obsessed with the idea that, for women, having it all also meant doing it all. Speaking before the Association of National Advertisers in November 1978, newspaper columnist Ellen Goodman addressed it tongue-in-cheek:

> Superwoman gets up in the morning and wakes her 2.6 children, feeds them a grade-A nutritional breakfast, and then goes upstairs and gets dressed in her Anne Klein suit, and goes off to her $25,000-a-year job doing work which is creative and socially useful. Then she comes home after work and spends a real meaningful hour with her children because, after all, it's not the quantity of time, but the quality of time. Following that, she goes into the kitchen and creates a Julia Child 60-minute gourmet recipe, having a wonderful family dinner discussing the checks and balances of the United States government system. The children go upstairs to bed and she and her husband spend another hour in their own meaningful relationship. They go upstairs and she is multi-orgasmic until midnight.[32]

At the opposite end of the spectrum were women who, threatened by feminist ideals, refused to believe that there was anything wrong with the status quo. "The claim that American women are downtrodden and unfairly treated is the fraud of the century," declared antifeminist Phyllis Schlafly. "The truth is that American women have never had it so good. Why should we lower ourselves to 'equal rights,' when we already have the status of special privilege?"[33] A woman couldn't open a newspaper without observing the rampant cultural confusion over twentieth-century womanhood. The results of this confusion were measurable. Of prescriptions written in 1975, 80 percent of amphetamines,

67 percent of tranquilizers, and 60 percent of barbiturates were prescribed for women.

The women taking part in our 1978 study were as diverse as snowflakes, with every bit as much character and individuality. Some were traditional in their thinking; others viewed themselves as feminists. There were artists, hobbiests, students, teachers, and academics among them. They were all passionate about their role as mothers yet had few other life paths to pursue in which they received as much encouragement and support. When passion existed elsewhere, it was neatly channeled into the culturally exalted roles of wife and mother. It is our premise that the absence of a strong identity is one of the primary conditions of The Mother Crisis, that motherhood undermines individuality, and that women lacking either knowledge of or commitment to their own wants, needs, and ideals fall quickly into a crisis of self-esteem. We observed that women with strong identities fell more slowly but still tended to decline. In introducing the women in our study, we explore the various ways they embrace their allotted role and how they fare on the oftentimes perilous journey from womanhood to motherhood in their own uniquely personal ways.

## CHAPTER 2

# *Embracing the Myths of Motherhood* ⌘
## *Women with a Mythical View of Motherhood Are in Stage One of The Mother Crisis*

*L* *acking a clear idea of who* they were in the world and where they were going, the women in our 1978 study clung to mythical and sentimental views of motherhood that inspired them to get married and have children. When asked why they decided to have children and to stay at home with them full time, more often than not, their answers were thin and vague. They either loved babies, were at the "right" age, or had nothing better to do. The majority of women said they believe that females are best equipped for the job of child rearing, regardless of

their makeup, citing religious or social tenets to support the absurd premise.

"There is no higher calling for a woman than to be a wife and a mother," noted 32-year-old Karen from Texas. "Procreation is one purpose of marriage. This is why I was created. To not stay home with my kids would have been cheating them as well as myself." Imelda, a mother of three from Rhode Island, simply declared, "A mother's place is in the home." Dianne, also from Rhode Island, believed that she was "predestined from childhood" to assume the role of mother and had her first baby "to prove that I could conceive and deliver a child." Twenty-five-year-old Andrea wanted to have a baby to please her husband, so they would "be more of a 'real' family."

While society was discouraging women to ignore or sublimate their own passions and needs, it was also encouraging them to put the wants and needs of others before their own. They were handed a culturally imposed blueprint for a woman's success and expected to follow it without hesitation or doubt. Whether they had either the aptitude or desire to do so, was a point that was considered moot, if not completely irrelevant.

Even if a woman hinted that she might be happier or better suited to another task, the convictions of Freud and Spock won out in the end. However obligatory, career mothering loomed large as the only proper choice. Elizabeth, a 32-year-old medical secretary from New York, who had her first child out of boredom, said that she opted to stay home with her three children because "I feel it is my job." Judy, a nurse from Nebraska echoed, "My job is here." Another nurse, Anna, 35, said she stopped working outside the home because "they [the children] are my responsibility." Some of the 1978 women were motivated to stay home by fear. "I wouldn't trust anyone else [to take care of them]," admitted one 27-year-old graduate student. Only a handful of the women seemed to think through their decision to give up outside employment. "The initial years a child is home, a mother's influence is essential," maintained Maria, 30, originally from Argentina and a mother of three. She failed to explain, however, where that belief originated or why it translated into a decision to stay home all the time. Another woman approached her options from a practical angle noting, "I really feel capable of doing only one full-time job at a time and don't think I could do a good job of raising a child and holding an occupational position too." It never occurred to her to challenge the idea that child care was a responsibility that only mothers should bear.

Many women assumed that a pregnancy would naturally result in an end to their careers. Combining the roles wasn't considered as a valid option. "I went as high as I wanted to go, knowing that when the children came, I'd quit," wrote one respondent. Another young mother, Becky, 29, a Rhode Island mother of a 4-year-old and 3-year-old, admitted that she had already reached her aspired goal—obtaining a master's degree—and that having children of her own represented a new challenge in life. Among all the 1978 women, expectations of motherhood were unrealistically high. Whatever the reason, total immersion into family life was overwhelmingly viewed as the final wellspring of fulfillment. These women were not encouraged to be responsible for their own happiness. Perhaps that's because women who grow up in Western society are taught since childhood that only good things come from mothering. They're introduced early to a sentimental view of motherhood characterized as Madonna-like. The real experience of motherhood, with all its inherent ambivalence, is not readily or openly discussed. In all our research, in fact, no clear definition of motherhood has ever emerged. It is precisely this deficiency that begins the downward spiral of The Mother Crisis, with its inevitable culmination in a loss of self-esteem. Motherhood as nirvana is perhaps our most powerful societal myth, one that serves to funnel women's aspirations into a solitary field that promises great rewards for selflessness and virtue. A great many of the 1978 women grew up clinging to this idea, a concept of maternal altruism that, however obscure, is reinforced by family, culture, and society. It dominates the value systems of the majority of the women we interviewed. Motherhood, they believed, is a glorious means to a variety of fanciful ends. Such is a mind-set that's nothing short of delusional, one that sets up every mother-to-be for feelings of tremendous disappointment.

What are some of the myth-based reasons women gave for starting a family? "The idea of being married and having a child was thrilling to me," declared one. "Fulfillment in our lives as people," stated another. "It would be a satisfying and fulfilling experience; it would give purpose to our lives," gushed a third.

Although some responses were intellectual and rational in nature, they were nearly always presented amid the romantic assumption that bringing children into the world is forever a natural, positive, universally appropriate undertaking. "We were ready for something more than the 'egocentric' existence we had had up to that stage," noted a mother of four preschoolers. But this same woman also explained, "We wanted an extension of the love process which had developed." One mother sought "fulfillment and a closer bond with my husband." Another woman, a teacher, saw children as a way to "complete our marriage." The sentimental view of motherhood glorifies the mother role, and society reinforces it in two powerfully influential ways—by upholding the myth of total fulfillment as true and by discouraging women from pursuing other aims. Most of the women in our study felt the full impact of both messages. Jane asked all those who had once worked outside the home if they had viewed their job as a filler of time until marriage and children. The majority responded "yes." "I met my husband when I was 15, and I knew we were getting married when he got out of college," noted Anita, 34, a mother of three from Warwick, Rhode Island. "That was at the time when it wasn't that important for a woman to go to school, so I wasn't pushed—it wasn't an important goal; I wasn't encouraged to go on." Her friend, Doreen, 30, originally from Pennsylvania, was actually quite ambitious. Still, the knowledge that she would someday be a wife and mother compelled her to reevaluate her goals. "I wanted to advance as far as I could, yet I knew it wouldn't be forever," she said. "I couldn't see a married woman with children having the type of job that it was. In other words, I knew it would end, but I wanted to make the best of it."

According to Alison, who had her first child at 23, any role divorced from mothering is totally inappropriate for women. "I really feel that it is God's prime calling for womanhood in general.... I think our personalities, our temperaments, just the way we are built inside, is geared toward being with children," she said. "I get the impression that women's lib seems to think [men and women] are all the same, that we're all equal. I'd like to know what makes people think that. I think there's an inborn difference."

Pat, on the other hand, was conscious of her social conditioning and challenged it. "I feel very definitely that I was brought up with the expectation that I would be a [wife and mother] someday, that it would be my role, that I should finish college so that I would have something to fall back on if my husband ever died," she said. "I was training to be a teacher. I didn't really want to be a teacher, but this was one of the things that you could do if you were a woman." In retrospect, Pat admitted that she "feels cheated ... that all through my life I had everything planned out for me. I'm not really sure that I wanted to be a wife and mother," she confessed. "If I could go back and look at things differently, I would have chosen something for a career that I really loved and really wanted to do."

According to sociologist Jessie Bernard, who is cited in Judith D. Schwartz's, *The Mother Puzzle*, the role of full-time mother is the product of an affluent society. "In most of human history and in most parts of the world today, adult, able-bodied women have been, and still are, too valuable in their productive capacity to be spared for the exclusive care of children," states Bernard.[1] "If an exclusive mother relationship were, in fact, essential, we would have to conclude that except for a brief period in the fifties, most cultures produced damaged people."[2] The sociologist specifies the fifties as a unique point in history, when the majority of women in America stayed home to raise their children. Shari Thurer, author of the *Myths of Motherhood*, broadens this view even further, reinforcing Bernard's assertion that full-time mothering is a cultural and historical anomaly.

> Wet nursing was popular in Europe until the nineteenth century, suggesting that many mothers did not even see their own children for two years. Certainly preindustrial mothers were too busy cultivating or preparing food to lavish round-the-clock attention on their offspring. And even bourgeois Victorian mamas relegated the task to servants.

Overall, the women in our 1978 study were generally content with their jobs or professions, yet the majority still had no desire to advance. Of those who responded to the question about outside employment, 59 considered their positions worthwhile and only

9 did not. Fifty-seven reported that they were pleased with their jobs; 7 were not. Yet only 16 acknowledged a desire to achieve more in their work role; 51 did not (see Appendix).

Clarissa, a 29-year-old mom from Colorado and a former linguist and language teacher, reported that she was once highly ambitious, but that her mother discouraged her from pursuing her goals. "My original goal was to go into the state department—the foreign service or something—but my mother kept coming up with other ways to go so I could get married," she recalled. "She would say, 'Play the piano well so you can teach it,' or 'Learn to iron so you can bring in laundry if you ever get stuck.'" Erma, who had once aspired to be a doctor, admitted that she was immediately sidetracked from her goal when she met her then husband-to-be. "Up until I met Henry I was dead serious about being a doctor," she said. "Before I met him, I never once thought about marrying anybody." Missy, who got married right out of college, worked as a secretary for 4 years to put her husband through law school. She loved her job and stayed in it until two days before her first child, Angela, was born. "I could have kept moving higher in what I was doing, but I chose not to because I felt that it would be unfair, because I knew that as soon as [my husband] was ready, I'd have children," she said.

Although occurring nearly 20 years later, the phenomenon of embracing a culturally-defined identity, rather than developing one's own, is reminiscent of Betty Friedan's feminine mystique and is a critical prelude to a crisis that is remarkably similar to her "problem which has no name." Although the "problem," as identified by Friedan, certainly caused women much tribulation, The Mother Crisis is a distinctly separate ordeal with causes and conflicts that bear a drama all their own. The "problem that has no name," is fed by a sense of unfulfillment; the heart of The Mother Crisis is guilt, invalidation, and lack of support. Our data indicate that some women are totally fulfilled by mothering yet still experience The Mother Crisis in some way, shape, or form. It begins with the myriad of myths that society injects into the concept of motherhood—myths that serve to sabotage any concrete or realistic definition of the role.

## *"GOOD MOTHER" IDEALISM PUSHES WOMEN INTO THE MOTHER CRISIS*

Virtually every myth about motherhood works toward the creation of a venerated ideal, known commonly in theory, but much less so in person, as the "Good Mother." Just who is this good mother, anyway, and what exactly does she look like? According to Thurer, the "Good Mother" is continually reinvented as each age or society defines her anew. She asserts that contemporary myths in Westen society set standards that are unattainable and self-denying, that propel women into a life of self-sacrifice. Motherhood in our society, she says, excludes the experiences of the mother. Rather, mother plays a supporting role in her child's drama, in which the child is the star of the show. Given this prerequisite, mother's needs as a person become "null and void," maintains Thurer. Paradoxically, mother is simultaneously viewed as all-powerful, with any mistake or deficiency on her part having a disastrous effect on the child. This idea of maternal omnipotence leads to a wide array of presumptions. One, says Thurer, is that full-time, stay-at-home mothering is a necessary practice. This myth also remains intact, she surmises, mainly because ambition is still largely considered suspect. "There is no getting around the fact that ambition is not a maternal trait. Motherhood and ambition are still largely opposing forces,"[4] she contends. "If we are ambitious, or even if we work outside our homes out of necessity, we are afraid of what our distraction will do to our children."[5]

Dianne reported, "It would be a guilt-trip for me to leave my kids with others. Call it ego, call it whatever, but I think my kids need me or their Dad to be here." Thirty-five-year-old Marisa, also from Rhode Island, said that her children deserve the security of having a parent available at all times. "I do use sitters a lot," she admitted, "but never on a 'day care' basis." Andrea was afraid that any distraction on her end would somehow cause the family to deteriorate. She took full responsibility for its continued well-being. "I believe that the family is very important and that the only way it will hang together is with my full-time attention," she said.

A full 60 percent of the women interviewed in 1978 reported

that they chose to stay home full time because it was the best thing for their children. Only 16 of the 71 survey respondents who broached the subject actually wanted to do it. In her book, *Inventing Motherhood*, author Ann Dally noted that the total and exclusive exposure of mothers to their young children has never existed on a wide scale in any other society since civilization began, and it does not exist in many societies today.[6] It arose out of the social changes of twentieth-century America. The justification of the idea is based on psychoanalytical theory, she asserts, a theory that has itself influenced some of the social changes that led to the binding together of mothers and children in relative isolation. In short, the theory says that young children who don't receive the exclusive and continuous care of their mothers are at high risk of possessing a permanent sense of insecurity and ability in later life to form warm and loving relationships. Yet, in 30 years of intensive research, this theory is still unproven. According to Dally, what has been shown is that young children need a central, permanent person in their lives to whom they can become attached, and this is usually the mother.

Gail, a mother of two from Boston, wanted to return to work at least part time after having kids but talked herself out of it with a host of rationalizations. "What I'd be doing would be escaping," she confessed, adding, "I would feel as though I was cheating them [the children] and, in the long run, my husband. I'd be so frustrated and my husband would be frustrated." She had an all-or-nothing attitude about mothering that surfaced when she talked about eventually leaving her kids as they grew older. "I think that [working] is just avoiding the issue," she said. "Either you can do it or you can't do it. And I do feel strongly that no one is going to love your children the way you do or really be patient." Only one mother in 1978 seemed to dismiss the myth that mothers who work damage their offspring, believing instead that her children might actually benefit from her absences. Nevertheless, a variety of obstacles prevented her from acting on her conviction. The first was the widely accepted notion that child care is the responsibility of mother and mother alone. "I think my children will fare better if I went back [to work] and did what I want to do

... but when I sit down and think about how I'm going to arrange everything, that stops me, and I think that some of the time I feel very frustrated because I'm saying, 'Why am I the one who has to figure this whole thing out?' " The logistics of child care weren't the only blocks to a brief break from home life, however. She felt that any steps she took toward personal fulfillment away from the nest would threaten her husband's self-esteem. "If I was working, it would probably put Charlie and me on a more ·equal level, which is a weird thing ... and I think Charlie would react to that. He would feel like he was no longer able to solely support us," she explained.

At the same time our society bombards women with messages about what a mother should not do, it shells them with edicts outlining exactly how they should look, be, and behave. Indelibly implanted in the minds of most of the 1978 mothers is the unremitting image of what we will refer to throughout this work as "martyr mom." In the popular television program, "The Adventures of Ozzie and Harriet," (1952–1966) Harriet Nelson was perhaps one of the most resilient and long-suffering of television moms. "The oft-heard joke about the show was that cardigan-sweatered Ozzie puttered around and never seemed to go to work, but that Harriet was always working—cleaning house, making dinner, settling squabbles, and then finding time to stand in the back of the room at the sock hop and bask in the screams of teenage girls.... where TV Ozzie was scatterbrained and excitable, TV Harriet was commonsensical and calm. Harriet Nelson was always more intelligent and ambitious than the woman she played on television, but her serene TV persona radiated a soothing grace that many of us cherish."[7] Other popular television characters, such as June Cleaver on "Leave It To Beaver" depicted mothers as perfect, possessing almost superhuman abilities, juggling all domestic duties while maintaining a pristine, immaculately groomed appearance. Another program characterized the mother persona as the stable, steadfast hub of the family. On "The Andy Griffith Show," a widowed and lonely Andy Griffith struggled to raise his only son Opie. His aunt, matronly Aunt Bea, represented the glue that held the family together, yet when presented with any dilemma outside the realm of domesticity, she somehow couldn't manage to cope. The 1978 moms based their expectations of themselves as mothers on many of these media images.

## MOTHERHOOD AS AN IDENTITY IS A WORLDWIDE PHENOMENON

Despite the prevalence of its media images, the West isn't the only society to deem motherhood the sole source of a woman's identity or her only area of capability. Traditionally, a Japanese woman's *ikigai* (life's worth) has been associated with her motherhood over all other roles. Only after giving birth to a child does a woman become a fully tenured person in the family.

> First priority goes to her relationship with her child, and within that context she develops self-confidence as a competent mother and her validation within the domestic sphere. Even if she does engage in non-domestic activity, that activity is usually secondary to and compatible with motherhood.[8]

On the other hand, many other countries have well-established child-care policies that indicate these cultures view the needs of the parents both inside and outside the home as important. In Spain, Greece, Belgium, Portugal, and France, women with children are more likely to work than married women without children and enjoy ample government and community support. Sweden's policies acknowledge the importance of personal parenting to children, the importance of work outside the home to adults, and the importance of both to the whole society, by making the care of their children something that parents do within their ongoing outside work. Parents do not give up work; they take parental leave. Parental leave is like the temporary assignment of a professional or the sabbatical of an academic. Every baby born brings an entitlement of eighteen months of parental leave. That leave can be taken by either parent or shared between them. There are other societies that protect the earnings of parents, but they do so at the expense of their active parenting. China, for example, expects parents to continue working as if they were childless and thus provides universal, publicly funded day care—even residential care or boarding school if work involves travel or irregular hours. In the Western world, the designation of the mother as the total source of child care eliminates the need for society to provide such alternatives.

## *MYTH VERSUS REALITY: FEELINGS ABOUT MOTHERHOOD ARE NOT ALL POSITIVE*

Contrary to popular belief, women's experience of the mother role is not universally positive. Our research shows that the real common denominator among mothers is ambivalence. Furthermore, women report that they experience far more negative effects of motherhood than our cultural stereotypes would lead us to believe. Much of the impact is felt right away. Seventy five percent of the 1978 women studied described themselves in positive terms before having children, yet, after becoming mothers, only 50 percent reported that they enjoyed an upbeat state of mind. The reality of motherhood quickly shattered any myth-based images they had of the role and of themselves. The ensuing disillusionment became the genesis of The Mother Crisis.

"I don't think you really know what it is all about until you have kids,—whether you are going to like it or not—and that goes for men and women, but by that time it's already too late," noted 28-year-old Jean. Her friend Gloria, a mother of three, acknowledged that she had a commonly held image of what it would be like after giving birth the first time and that it was a set-up for disenchantment.

> I really feel that people have this image that they will have this baby and for the first couple months it is going to sleep, sleep, eat, sleep and eat. That's really their image, and when things go wrong, it's always the woman's fault. It's like people say, "Poor Gloria, she is just falling apart with this baby." They just don't have any sympathy for the fact there are many other factors involved.

Elaine, 26, a Massachusetts mother of three who thought she had the work "bug" out of her system because she had taught school for 2 years before having children, was surprised by the feelings that surfaced after becoming an at-home mom.

> I still feel like there is something lacking in me, as far as, you know, being ... probably selfish about it ... but there has got to be more to life for me than washing clothes and taking care of children—although I love my children and I wouldn't change that and I couldn't have somebody else raise my children, but I still have that need to go out and do the things I want to do.

Another mom felt that she was completely blindsided by the totality of her new role, as well as others' expectations that its duties should, and must be, all consuming. "The mother is constantly making the arrangements and working herself around everybody else's schedule," she complained. "Not only the children's but the husband's also, and sometimes it is just too much." Betty, a mother of two, was at her wits end over the same dilemma:

> I resent the fact that my husband can come and go—totally— he can come home, have dinner, but if the kids are annoying him and making a lot of noise, he says, "After you get them in bed, I'll come home." I can't do that, although I've thought about it. I never told him that I'd like to give him a taste of his own medicine. It seems so unfair.

Dr. Eleanor Morin Davis, codirector of the New Center for Modern Parenthood and Psychotherapy in New York, is visited by scores of women grappling with a host of conflicting feelings that have erupted as a consequence of motherhood. Interestingly, it doesn't seem to matter whether the women work inside or outside the home. According to Davis, the myths about motherhood that our culture embraces represent a dichotomous view of motherhood that prevents women from making a smooth transition into the mother role, whether they choose to stay home or not. "There's such a split—the ideal view [of motherhood] and a very demeaning view of it, and women have to reconcile that within themselves," she asserts. Davis, who specializes in the field of psychobiology—the interaction between biological and psychological processes—says the "split" exists in women because society refuses to allow a bridge to form between the two views of "perfect mother," and "demeaned, no good mother." Perfect mother, she says, possesses all the Madonna-like, nurturing, caregiver qualities. Demeaned mother is assertive, creative, and striving. "Women have to be taught that it's OK to be both, that what makes a full person is a full range of human emotion and capacity to develop all aspects of themselves," she explains. "Those who come to me have this conflict because they're not able to be comfortable with both these sets of feelings. They're having big trouble with it." Unfortunately, she declares, when women become mothers, society forces them to choose between these two different "psychological syndromes," or "senses of self." Women, particularly after motherhood, are denied access to themselves as whole human beings.

Lynn, a mother of two, admitted that she felt a real sense of loss after giving up a career as a nurse, even though staying home had been a conscious choice. "I really felt more important working," she said. "Not that I was a 'big wheel' or the 'big fish,' but I felt good about myself working. It didn't bother me to leave except that I feel now that I should be out there changing the world. But that's only on the bad days." Debbie, who also worked for several years before marriage, described her transition into at-home mothering as smooth, but also acknowledged that the experience wasn't what she'd thought it would be. "Oh my gosh, I felt so busy at first, but I had very few people that I knew, so it was very boring. At that time I thought, 'Wouldn't it be nice to be back working'—I quit working to sit home. I felt really complimented that I was called and asked to go back [to work] because it bolstered my ego ten times." Another professional caregiver was actually delighted to give up her career but was unprepared for the feelings that surfaced once she no longer drew a paycheck. "I wasn't crazy about work to begin with, so it wasn't a big decision to give up work before I had children" declared Kathy. "But I think right away you have to realize that you are dependent when you don't work. I think if you fight that feeling you just make yourself miserable. I think you just have to live with that feeling." Dana, on the other hand, reacted physically to the change in her life.

> I was thinking that it didn't hit me right away—losing ground in intellectual stimulation—because I still kept

abreast of things. I took a course after my first was born. I pursued my field and that kept me in touch with the real world, but then as soon as we moved, 1 didn't pick up anything. I put on weight, I got very nervous, I was tired, my face was drawn. I had ailments all of a sudden; ailments I never even knew I had—arthritis—all those tacky little things.

One of the most dramatic ways a woman can enter into The Mother Crisis is when the disappointment over failed myths combine with a plummeting hormone level to bring about a severe postpartum depression (PPD). The biological processes involved in pregnancy and childbirth couple with a woman's overnight loss of identity, thrusting her into despair. According to Carol Dix, author of *The New Mother Syndrome*, a woman's biological makeup undergoes massive upheaval after childbirth and can, if subjected to other overloading factors such as relationships or expectations of herself as a mother, lead to a temporary breakdown in the normal flow of chemicals in the brain that creates our natural state of mental balance. "The person we used to be seems to have vanished, almost overnight. Even if we have not experienced emotional swings or depression before, we may be subject to them once we become mothers,"[9] notes the author. Unfortunately, despite the fact that some 400,000 women in the United States each year suffer mild to moderate PPD,[10] the medical community has done an abysmal job of addressing the condition, she maintains. Most obstetricians don't talk to their patients about PPD during prenatal exams, and few hospitals have specialized programs for treating women who are afflicted by the condition. If a women does experience a severe case of PPD, her obstetrician will, more than likely, refer her to a mental health professional, few of whom have any clinical understanding of the ailment. According to Dix, knowledge about PPD

> is so widely scattered and unevenly shared among doctors at large that women still tend to blame themselves for their condition. "She is weak, dependent, unable to deal with change or lack of control, hates her mother, hates children, was obviously the depressive type or a latent schizophrenic anyway" are all common arguments used to explain mothering reactions that are not viewed as normal.[11]

The real tragedy is that women remain silent about their suffering, she says. But is it any wonder? asks Dix. "Not only are they ashamed, guilty, and isolated, but they are downright afraid of being classified as insane."[12]

Jeanne Watson Driscoll, a master's-level nurse and an expert in pregnancy, childbirth, and postpartum depression, explains that pregnancy and motherhood are irreversible processes that change life in all domains: physical, psychological, and spiritual. Driscoll's "transition" theory correlates with our own data, which demonstrates that women undergo an initial crisis of identity that, if not resolved, has the potential to mushroom into a full-blown Mother Crisis. According to Driscoll, there is a natural process of disorientation and reorientation after a woman gives birth that marks the turning point on the path of emotional and spiritual growth. Each woman must muddle through a period of time in which she feels lost and empty before she can begin life anew and experience a rebirth or new sense of self. If a woman is supported by others, she asserts, change can lead to growth, development, and a sense of renewal. Being a parent is a dynamic process that requires information, validation, and support, she reminds us. The Mother Crisis is perpetuated by a lack of all three. Although, as noted by Davis, society's demeaning of the mother role is usually subtle, sometimes a woman is directly invalidated. Recalls Mindy, a mother of three, "I once sat and talked with this guy—he was a professor at Brown [University] and he told me, 'You have got to get out and do something. Anybody can be a mother, anybody can bring up kids. What you work at is going to be your mark in the world, not bringing up a bunch of brats.'"

The women from our earlier study enjoyed little, if any, information, validation, and support as they made the transition into motherhood. Consequently, they held firm to the only safe pillars they could find—the myths with which they had grown up. But when they did so, they also embarked on a path that would lead to The Mother Crisis—the destruction of their complete selves, demoralization, and the diminishing or loss of their self-esteem. They mounted the first steed on a treacherous merry-go-round and started the ride on a horse named Perfectionism.

## CHAPTER 3

## The Mother Crisis ∾ When Mothers Sacrifice Who They Are for Their Children

*E*very woman who raises children wants to be the perfect mother. We have yet to speak to one who doesn't strive toward this goal. While intellectually she might understand that perfection is impossible to achieve, there are a thousand unseen demons that drive her to pursue it on an emotional level. We've talked about the myths; we've talked about the messages. But one of the fiercest demons that women face is the one that blames mothers for everything that goes wrong with the children. It lurks deep inside a woman's psyche and perches on her shoulder, ready to strike at the first sign of impropriety or doubt. When it does strike, the wounds are deep. The aftermath of battle brings with it a deep sense of failure, shame, and guilt. Women fear mother-blame so much that they'll do virtually anything to evade it. Most of their efforts are in vain, however, because anything a mother does that's less than perfect is an excuse for the demon to attack. The internal and external forces of mother-blame prompt a woman to view any mothering mistake as a failure and to fear that it will cause irrevocable damage to her children. A mother's intense love for and instinct to protect her children further exacerbates these feelings, emotions that often overwhelm her.

"I saw Abigail Van Buren on "Donohue" one day, and she said that to spank a child perpetuated violence," recalled Carol, a mother of four from Texas.

> I tried. I read all those things before I had children about talking to your children instead, but it seems that they push you and push you until you just have to spank them. When I smack the kids, I feel guilty about it and say to myself, "There should have been another way." So I agree with her in theory, and yet I don't do it in practice.

Perfectionism bred guilt among the majority of the 1970s moms. Many of them admitted that many segments of society, directly and unapologetically, perpetuated the emotion.

"It comes out every day in just the little things," noted Jennifer, a mother of two who was pregnant with her third child. "For example, in my mom's day, if something happened at school, the teacher would send the kid home and my father would say, 'You did something wrong.' I think the guilt I feel today is a result of the books I've read, so it's the psychologists' fault, not mine." Another young mother, Delores, 29, formerly a history teacher, said her own mental picture of "perfect mom" stems from childhood fairy tales that have stuck. "It's that image of not allowing yourself to have any feelings but just being able to talk things out all the time, and being rational all the time, and being able to smooth out everyone's problems. From very early on, little girls hear that's how motherhood should be," she explained. "That they won't make the same mistakes that their mothers did; that somehow they are just going to be able to handle it; that there's something about having a baby that's presto-chango, now you're a different person. I don't know why that is." The prevailing view that a child's success is the total responsibility of the parent is yet another guilt-provoking mechanism, noted Sally, a mother of two, who once worked as a medical secretary. "When you first have this little immobile individual, you don't realize this person comes with its own personality," she said. "I think you begin to feel guilty when you can't produce an intelligent, well-rounded child that's going to do everything and behave and follow directions." Victoria, a mother of three and a former high school teacher, pointed to education as another guilt-inducing culprit. "Education has something to do with it, because we know of a lot of the psychological problems that we can create. I just assume that someone without that much education wouldn't care one way or the other," she said. "I feel the guilt, because I think that my daughter's psychological makeup when she's older will be the result of something I did while disciplining her."

## SOCIETY BLAMES MOTHERS FOR ALL CHILDHOOD PROBLEMS

Since early in the twentieth century, mental health professionals have legitimized the tendency of laypeople and experts alike to blame mothers for whatever goes wrong with their offspring. In 1985, an article entitled "Mother-Blaming in Major Clinical Journals" in the *American Journal of Orthopsychiatry* tracked the incidence of mother-blaming in major clinical journals for the years 1970, 1976, and 1982, largely to determine whether any reductions had resulted from the efforts of the women's movement. What they discovered is significant. The authors of the 125 articles read for the study blamed mothers for a total of seventy-two different kinds of psychopathology in children, naming everything from arson, depression, incest, homosexuality, and moodiness to narcissism, phobias, schizophrenia, sleepwalking, tantrums, timidity, and transsexualism! Mothers were by far the most likely to be discussed in relation to child behavior problems, followed by parents as a couple. Fathers, individually, were least likely to be discussed. In other words, when authors wanted to illustrate some problem or other, and when they used only mother or father for this purpose, they chose father only 17 percent of the time.[1] In no article was the mother's relationship with the child described as simply healthy, nor was she ever described only in positive terms. Judgmental terms were used by the authors to describe the mothers in 74 percent of the articles and the fathers in only 41 percent.[2] The most striking pattern reflected in the study's results, noted the authors, is that mothers always emerged in a far less favorable, more "blameworthy light" than fathers. "The attribution of offspring's problems to the mother is, of course, profoundly misogynist,"[3] wrote the authors. The mother-blaming attitude pervades everyday life and language as well, they claimed. "A nasty woman is a 'bitch,' but a nasty man isn't nasty in his own right: he's a 'son of a bitch,' or a 'bastard,' both words reflecting badly on his mother."[4] According to the authors, psychiatric and psychological theories of the 1940s and 1950s claimed that children need intensive and exclusive female mothering, whereas the mother is expected to provide total physical and psychological care. "She has the responsibility for bringing about, in perfectly timed and graduated sequence, the healthy degrees of her child's separation and independence from her. She is to do all of this without either providing too much care or too little."[5] Claims such as these, when added to society's tendency to have women do most child rearing, provide powerful support for the belief that women's physiology and hormones—but not men's—naturally suit them for child rearing. Why then, asked the authors, do women create such a wide range of emotional disturbances in so many of their children if they come by child-rearing skills so naturally? It's a curious dichotomy indeed.

In their insightful conclusion, the researchers point out that the increasing number of single mothers, whether due to separation, divorce, or personal decision to raise children on their own, make them easy targets for blame because they are, above all, there.

> They are there for the professionals who assess and treat their children; they are there to be identified, studied, and questioned by these professionals; and they are there for the general public to see, raising their children. It is easier to attribute a child's problems to the behavior of a parent who is present than to the imagined or suspected behavior of a parent who is no longer on the scene.[6]

To a certain extent, the same is true for at-home, career moms, where the father's presence at home is limited for financial reasons.

Society's propensity to blame mother for the problems of its children is merely the tip of the iceberg, declare some experts. The practice of finding fault with mother, they argue, is culturally indigenous. Morin Davis claims that society has the dual need both to deny the power of motherhood and to demean it. This need, she asserts, stems from each individual's unconscious hostility toward his or her own mother. In Davis's view, each of us is angry about past unmet needs, anger that grows out of a primitive sense of entitlement that mother should have met all our needs. "We're very goddamned angry about it, and we're going to stay that way until we mature and recognize the reality of the situation," she declares. The reality, of course, is that no one person can meet all of another person's needs, not even mother. Some people grow into an understanding of that reality, explains Davis. Others spend time in therapy to arrive at the same conclusion.

This collective form of mother-bashing is precisely what keeps the myth of "Perfect Mother" alive. Observes Judith D. Schwartz in her book *The Mother Puzzle,*

> Just as the individual projects his needs and ideals on his own mother, society does the same thing on a massive scale, imbuing the institution of motherhood with a series of attributes that keeps the prevailing culture feeling safe.... The essential paradox is that while we accept the fallibility of the individual, we expect one half of the human race, by dint of its reproductive capacity, to be beyond reproach.[7]

This cultural disillusionment perpetuates The Mother Crisis on a global scale and explains why women need not experience a crisis personally to feel its effects. Since women as well as men bring the disappointment of being imperfectly mothered into adulthood, they, too, are a factor in this global equation. But since they, and not men, are the ones who may eventually become mothers, their conflict is doubly pronounced. According to Schwartz, the challenge for each woman then is to resolve those feelings before becoming a mother herself so that she might pull free from the internal drive toward perfection.

As women, and as actual or potential mothers, we need to separate our assessment of motherhood from the rage we still feel
from being imperfectly (i.e., humanly) mothered. We need to distinguish our ideas of maternal responsibility from the disappoint-
ments in life we still feel our own mothers are responsible for.[8]

Penny, 33, a young mother of two from Ohio, illustrates how
unresolved mother-blame caused her to doubt her own performance as a mother: "Sometimes I find myself doing things that
[my mother] did that I didn't like, and I feel I can't be this way,
because this was the way my mother was and I didn't like it," she
admitted. Another 1970s mom, Mary, says that, rather than being
spawned by anger, her own perfectionism stems from a need to re-
create the childlike illusion that she was perfectly mothered. "We
have this internalized idea that is too perfect and that we can
never live up to; even though our mother might not have been that
great, we just remember it that way," she said. "Maybe it has
something to do with returning to the womb, where life was so
perfect when you were a child and you just can't get back to it."
Gloria, a mother of three from rural Rhode Island, observed that
mother blaming is blatant in our culture, and that messages from
the media and elsewhere are causing an entire generation of
mothers to buy into the notion of perfectionism and experience
the subsequent remorse. Whereas Eve was responsible for original
sin, she surmised, the image of the failed mother is responsible for
original guilt. "People grow up messed up, they go through anal-
ysis, then we hear it on a talk show that it was their mother's
fault," she declared. "Then we'll read about how a psychotic
person murdered all these people, and they'll talk about it being
the mother's fault. I think that's where this whole guilt thing
starts, with this general attitude."

## *MOTHER GUILT: THE CATALYST FOR A FULL-BLOWN MOTHER CRISIS*

A topside view of the vicious cycle we've entitled the Mother
Crisis (see page 1) shows that perfectionism breeds a sense of
failure that, in turn, breeds feelings of guilt. If not resolved, this

guilt has the potential to blossom into a full-fledged crisis, in which a mother deteriorates into a pattern of continual self-effacement. If she does so, as so many of the 1970s mothers tended to do, and also fails to receive adequate nurturing and support, she stands in grave danger of collapsing into a state of complete loss of self. Of the 71 women who answered the question about whether they continually feel guilty about their child-rearing performance, 58 reported that they did. Responses ranged from a woman's guilt over losing her temper or not having a spotless house to guilt over reading a book, taking a class, spending money, or having children who don't behave appropriately all the time. The phenomenon is particularly threatening to the emotional well-being of at-home moms, since they have no other yardstick upon which to measure personal success. Ann Dally, author of *Inventing Motherhood: The Consequences of an Ideal*, asserts that when women discover that the idealized version of motherhood does not exist, they usually go one of two ways—they either idealize it further or they have a nervous breakdown.[9] Since both paths lead to feelings of entrapment and a perceived loss of choice, a woman can take either one and still experience the Mother Crisis. The woman who continually feels like a failure as a mother hurts. What she needs most is reassurance and support. Our research has shown us that, in the 1970s, mothers got little, if any, of either. Women across the country hoed their rows alone. Although the majority of the women we interviewed were able to acknowledge the pain of their aloneness, many of them didn't know what to do, or to whom to turn for relief. Most were stuck in the assumption that suffering in mothering is something they must, and more importantly, should be able to endure on their own. Many reported feeling ashamed and weak in their inability to cope by themselves. A prevailing belief was that any acknowledgment of discontent in the mother role somehow meant the woman was a bad mother or a misfit.

"There is a built-in guilt for mothers," stated Melinda, from Nebraska. "For a mother, raising a child is your top job, so you feel as if you should be able to cope. Is there any built-in guilt for fathers?" Nancy, from Rhode Island, felt tremendously guilty for not enjoying playtime with her children. "I hate myself. I'll sit down and tell myself, 'OK, Nancy, all these other people play with their kids, so you're going to do it too.' I last five minutes and I quit. I'd rather empty out the dishwasher than sit down and play with blocks," she admitted. "Now how awful is that? I feel terribly guilty because I'm supposed to like it."

In her second landmark book, *The Second Stage*, released in 1981, Betty Friedan asserted that at-home mothers of her generation—the 1960s—used perfectionism to seek out power.

> That control, that perfection demanded of home and children, that insistence that she be always right, was her version of machismo—her supervirtuous equivalent of male strength and power, which she used to counter or mask her vulnerability, her economic dependence, her denigration by society and denigration of herself. Inauthenticity was bred into women by weakness. Lacking male power in society, which was the only power recognized then, she got power in the family by manipulation and denying the feelings of men and children, and her own feelings, behind that mask of superficial, sweet and steely rightness.[9]

Although Jane didn't observe much "steely rightness" among the 1970s moms that she interviewed, she did notice a lot of denial or doubting of feelings. "I think that a lot of the time I wonder if I'm being too selfish, which I'm petrified of," mused Tonia, a 26-year-old former secretary from Wisconsin.

> I wonder why I'm not content. Why can't I just say I've got this nice home and nice husband and beautiful children and that I'm lucky? Why can't I just like to sew and cook? But then there's another part of me that says, 'What is the matter with you? You are as smart as anybody you know and you've got all this talent.' It's like there are two people inside of me. So that's what my guilt is about.

*LACK OF SUPPORT—FROM SOCIETY, FROM THE FAMILY, FROM ONE ANOTHER—CAUSES MOTHERS TO DESPAIR*

Perhaps the best way to understand how our culture fails to support its mothers is to take a close-up look at the role from the vantage point of women themselves. Some details of their daily lives must be examined. Where do they live? Are they near their extended families? Who do they turn to for help? From the 1950s until today, the majority of women in America did their child-rearing work in relative isolation, rarely asking for help, even when they had family members living nearby. One of our primary goals was to study exactly how women got their needs met from the confines of their homes while they were busy meeting the needs of their offspring and their spouses. What the data revealed is that, more often than not, even their most basic psychological, spiritual, and emotional needs were often left unmet. Discussions with the women disclosed that they had a tremendous need to be listened to, to be recognized, to relax, to play. They had no time to pray or for solitude of any kind. There was no opportunity for them to affiliate with other adults or to challenge their intellect. There was nothing in their situation that affirmed their individual existence, apart from mothering. According to Dr. Sandra Scarr, author of *Mother Care, Other Care*, however, this type of existence is okay for some moms. "Many mothers in traditional families thrive on their children's dependence. Because their primary role is in child care, traditional mothers need to be needed. Their role is to serve the family. Clearly, young children need caring, attentive adults. Traditional mothers often fill this role well," she insists, "and young children meet their needs well."[11] Scarr is describing what psychologists refer to as psychological or emotional *sym-biosis*, a state in which mother and baby still retain a mystical oneness, in which they are not really separate beings. Symbiosis, as interpreted by many modern psychologists, implies that the constant, loving care of the mother is absolutely necessary for the child's growth for an indeterminate number of years.

Nevertheless, the women in our initial study found this type of relationship grossly inadequate. Perhaps that's because mothers, like everyone else, require autonomy in order to develop into healthy adults. Notes Herta A. Guttman, M.D., "[Autonomy is] the development of a sense that one has separate needs and goals, that one has the freedom and capacity of taking a course of action and making decision in the light of one's own judgment, and that one is responsible for one's behavior and enterprises."[12] It's no secret that being a mother means giving up many things that may be important. But lack of suitable stimulation is unbalancing, even when one is doing what one most wants to do. In her book *Juggling: The Unexpected Advantages of Balancing Career and Home for Women and Their Families*, author Faye J. Crosby explores why:

> Imagine a buffet table with meats, vegetables, fruits and breads. Now imagine that the host decrees that all the guests in one corner of the room must eat meat and nothing else while all the guests in the second corner must eat vegetables and those in the third corner fruits, and the last corner bread. Imagine that the banquet goes on continuously, so that all their lives each group could only eat the meat, the vegetables, the fruits or the breads. Such a scheme is boring and fundamentally unhealthy. One does not have to be a nutritionist to know that the body needs variety in food. It is the same with psyches.[13]

Despite the fact that the women in our study had both the intellect and the skills to seek out ways to meet their own needs, many of them failed to do so. Furthermore, a full 63 percent reported that they were not experiencing autonomy. The isolation of spending countless numbers of days alone with young children was often more than they could bear. It drained them of any number of life-affirming qualities, leaving them confused, frightened, and impotent. The fact that most women are conditioned to be dependent made it even more difficult for them to exercise their own God-given free will. According to Guttman,

> They must work very hard at developing a sense of self-determination to overcome this conditioning.... Women must either capitulate to or struggle against this definition, not only on a rhetorical and intellectual level but also on an emotional and behavioral level.[14]

To do so in the face of almost total daily seclusion was impossible for the majority of the mothers interviewed.

Martha, a Nebraska mom and LPN who stayed home with her kids because "That's what I was supposed to do, so that's what I did," felt the shock of isolation right from the start. "The only thing that bothered me after I had the baby in the beginning was the fact that I felt cut off from the world," she recalled. "There wasn't time to read; there wasn't time to concentrate. I felt as though my mind was slipping. My memory was slipping too." One of her neighbors, Marianne, a 28-year-old mother of two, concurred. "I was pretty unhappy just because there wasn't enough hours for me because of the environment. We were isolated and I would not have chosen that." Like many of the mothers interviewed, Marianne was quite fulfilled by motherhood but found the self-denying aspect of the role overwhelming at times. "There was no opportunity for me to get away by myself to do anything unless I went through all kinds of shenanigans to get a baby-sitter. You couldn't just call up and have someone around the corner come, because we were living way out in the country."

## LOSS OF SELF: THE CORE OF THE MOTHER CRISIS

One of the questions Jane posed to the at-home mothers in 1978 dealt specifically with self-esteem. What has happened to your self-image since becoming a mother, she asked? There was a fascinating correlation between a woman's level of self-worth and the degree of isolation she experienced. Without any form of feedback about her performance, or external validation of her existence, apparently a mother's self-esteem begins to drop. This lack of positive reinforcement only exacerbates a woman's self-doubt about a position that's already been devalued by society. In 1850, early feminists wrote, "The isolated household is responsible for a large share of women's ignorance and degradation. A mind always in contact with children … whose aspirations and ambitions rise no higher than the roof which shelters it, is necessarily dwarfed in its proportion."[15] But such lack of support and subsequent neediness among mothers is often overshadowed by the myth that portrays their situation as maternally correct. After all, isn't "martyr mom" one of the primary images of the good mother?

Prominent 1940s-era psychologist Erich Fromm, however,

paints a less-than-glorious picture of unselfish mother love. A mother who sacrifices her autonomy to fulfill her obligations to her children does a great disservice to them both, he asserts.

> The children are affected by their mother's hidden hostility against life, which they sense rather than recognize, and eventually become imbued with it themselves.... If one has a chance to study the effect of a mother with genuine self-love, one can see that there is nothing more conducive to giving a child the experience of what love, joy and happiness are than being loved by a mother who loves herself.[16]

The 1970s moms claimed to have lost a wide variety of positive character traits due to their total immersion into motherhood, the result of which was an eventual loss of self-love. "I feel like I have lost my self-confidence; I feel inferior," confessed Deborah, a former teacher.

> My whole day is absorbed in a child's world. I'm not using my mind like I used to, and I think I have lost a lot of it. I find sometimes that I just have to sit there and be quiet, because I feel stupid. I really feel that I have lost my intelligence. Really, how much intelligence does it take to clean a house, to do the ironing and washing and all that?

Elaine, a New Hampshire mother of six with tremendous insight, describes her experience with full-time parenting and homemaking as invalidating. "I've been caught up in what happens to an awful lot of gals that are at home, and that is you tend to lose your self-esteem because you've got no one from the outside. You've got a lot of personal relationships, but there is nothing that you do that is really outwardly recognized."

"After Mark was born and we were living in Jamestown [Rhode Island], that was the pits," recalled Molly, a mother of two. "I couldn't do anything; I felt really trapped. It was like day-to-day survival." Beatrice, 25, said that staying home with her children full time completely undermined her self-confidence, which she once viewed as unshakable. "My confidence is gone, I guess because I've been around little kids so long," she admitted. "I can remember when my husband was in college—I was pregnant; I worked and my house was perfect; my kid was perfect and I taught and did all this stuff. I just don't think I'm capable of that any more." Susan, 29, from New York, was accustomed to living in a university environment and had moved to a city apartment after giving birth to her first child. She found the isolation debilitating. Her comments during her interview were disjointed and obscure.

> I didn't know anybody and the few people I talked ... the only thing that was good was that I felt good that what I was doing was right for my child.... Yet here I was, a bizarre adult enclosed and somehow supposed to ... I would walk and pretend to shop ... other people were shopping and I didn't know what the hell they bought.... I would walk around like I was going to buy something.... I bought a vacuum cleaner. It wasn't like I could get a lot of help from David either ... there was none ... and a lot of giving to boot ... so I felt very drained.

Betty Friedan observed similar behavior in the women she interviewed back in 1963 and recognized it as the conduct of a person experiencing a deterioration of identity and who is groping for something real to hold on to. She noted,

> If a woman's need for identity, for self-esteem, for achievement, and finally for expression of her unique human individuality are not recognized by herself or others in our culture, she is forced to seek identity and self-esteem in the only channels open to her: the pursuit of sexual fulfillment, motherhood, and the possession of material things. And, chained to these pursuits, she is stunted at a lower level of living, blocked from the realization of her higher human needs.[18]

Psychologist A. H. Maslow puts it another way: "Capacities clamor to be used, and cease their clamor only when they are well used. That is, capacities are also needs. Not only is it fun to use our capacities, but it is also necessary. The unused capacity or organ can become a disease center or else atrophy, thus diminishing the person."[19]

Delores, 27, while caring for her three young children, worked hard to keep a stiff upper lip amid conflicting internal messages, lest she be consumed by self-doubt.

> I think I have inner resources that keep telling me that I'm
> really a fairly decent person. I do read a lot and that helps my
> self-esteem. Yet, emotionally, the message that [I'm not OK]
> keeps knocking at the door and defensively I'm telling myself
> I'm a pretty together person. But I feel like I have to remind
> myself about 100 times a day.

Many of the 1978 women fought to retain a sense of themselves as individuals. But since they waged battle alone, they
usually lost, turning instead to their children for personal satisfaction. Writer Juliet Mitchell describes such a gamble as highly
problematic. "When the mother renounces her autonomy through
reproduction, anything the child does is a threat to her," she
writes, "... and there are few more precarious ventures on which
to base a life."[19]

Explained Becky, a 29-year-old mother of six and a former
nurse,

> The problem is that there's nobody ever there saying you are
> doing a good job. In the old days there were rewards, because
> they [mothers] had grandparents there, they had people that
> saw what kind of job they were doing as a mother. There's
> nobody that sees the kind of job I'm doing as a mother, and I
> find myself reaching for [feedback] all the time, like asking,
> 'What do you think of the kids, Bill?' I even reach for [feed-
> back] from the kids. We really need any kind of good pat on
> the back that we can get.

Janet, a mother of two from Texas, saw both her self-esteem
and range of abilities plummet soon after her immersion into
motherhood. "I went from being very ambitious and very confident to today, when I would put my self-esteem at the very
bottom," she admitted. "I had always gotten everything I ever
wanted through my own efforts. Now, I can't even make a decision about what I want to do. I can't believe that I can't make a
decision. It really is tough."

Although a clear majority of the 1970s moms reported that
they were guilt-ridden (83 percent) and in some phase of The
Mother Crisis (92 percent), most of them also claimed that they
were happy in the role of mother, as well as with their decision to

stay home. The incongruity of their responses is indicative of a form of collective denial among the women or an amazing ability to live with the ambiguity of the role. All of them were totally willing to give up their lives and to deny their own feelings in the belief that doing so would be best for their children. To consciously acknowledge that they were unhappy would have created the need for some sort of action on their part. Most of the women were either unwilling or unable to accept that much personal responsibility. A few made halfhearted attempts to find part-time work or to pursue a hobby, then found some reason or excuse that prevented them from following through with the initiative. The atmosphere in which these women found themselves, one in which there was little or no physical and emotional support, and in which it was either difficult or impossible to get their needs met, led to the next-to-the-last stop on the downhill spiral that is The Mother Crisis—Loss of Choice. In our view, it is virtually impossible to descend that far into the abyss without continuing on to the pit of the Crisis—Loss of Self.

The fact that so many of the women interviewed in 1978— women who were sacrificing themselves completely for their children—were still not absolved from mother guilt demonstrates the tyranny of "good mother" idealism. Left to their own devices in a virtual social vacuum, these women punished themselves relentlessly for not measuring up to the ideal. Sometimes they punished each other.

"My feeling is, 'Why do people have kids if they can't deal with them,' " condemned Maggie, 30, a mother of five. But most of the time, they castigated themselves. "I feel guilty about working; we don't need my work to live," explained Flora, a Wisconsin mom and a former secretary who sought outside employment for relief.

> In fact, my salary is practically traded in for a baby-sitter, so I feel like I'm taking things away from the family to take care of my own private fun. I also feel trapped in the generation gap. I was brought up to believe that the role of the mother is in the home—my father thought it was just horrible for [his daugh-

ters] to go to high school. But at the same time, I was growing
up when women were beginning to go out and do things.

Lori criticized herself severely for having a common reaction to
the stress of tending to a newborn. "While I was pregnant I
thought the ideal mother would bring up a psychologically sound
child. Then I go into motherhood and can't stand waking up in the
middle of the night and can't stand this child that I have to feed. I
feel very guilty about that." A common belief among the women
was that any time spent on themselves meant that they were
robbing their children of something of critical importance. "I feel
like I'm depriving them a little bit, like when I want to read,"
admitted Hanna, who worked as a teacher before having children.

Since so many of the women either refused to acknowledge
their discontent or blamed themselves for having any, the vast
majority stayed stuck in their dilemma, making only shallow
attempts to seek a way out. Another reason their efforts were so
meager is that many of them feared that when they did ask for
help, they wouldn't receive it, and if they did look for support or
understanding, they wouldn't find any. This "Why bother?" attitude, coupled with the fact that there really was very little help
available, contributed to feelings of entrapment and defeat.

"When we first moved here 3 years ago, I didn't know what to
do with myself," recalled Nancy, from Rhode Island.

> Joanne was only 3, so I had to be home, but I was just bored
> out of my mind, and Jeff kept saying, "Play bridge, decorate
> the house, why can't you be happy?" And I said, "No, that's
> not it." Finally, I was going to go back to work at a modeling
> agency but found I had to spend too much money on baby-
> sitters and traveling, and it just wasn't in the cards for me.
> Besides, my husband wasn't behind me and, at that point, I
> felt like I had to have him behind me, like I needed his
> permission.

Despite the fact that the women we interviewed had ample
opportunity to discuss their family support systems, the majority
of them said little or nothing about them. Nancy was one of a scant
few who did. It was an obvious omission. The role of the father in
the parenting process wasn't even discussed. Most of the women

talked about raising their children strictly in the context of the home environment, a place where husbands didn't fit, since they were relegated to the role of breadwinner. Extended family members weren't talked about either. The fact that the women didn't expect family support implies that they accepted the traditional role definitions of the time, in which the husband is responsible for the financial support of the family and the wife is responsible for the children. The 1970s moms might have accepted these provisions, but they clearly weren't comfortable with them. Perhaps that's because, as Dally maintains, such a belief system is highly suspect. "Bringing up children alone, as do so many modern women, without much active assistance from the father, as has always been the tradition, is, despite the joys and rewards, a tremendous burden, and anyone who denies this is indulging in idealization," she argues.[20]

Just where have fathers been, anyway? The answer is, they've been hiding out for the past 200 years, notes Scarr.

> Prior to that, the family was an economic unit that worked together. Then father withdrew from the household when work and home were separated by the Industrial Revolution. The same economic and social forces that kept women out of the work force excluded father from child rearing.... Just as mothers were captives in the home, fathers were hostages in the workplace.[21]

Scarr poignantly observes what the 1970s women testify to, which is, "Fathers ... were shadowy figures, lurking on the periphery of the family campfire.[22]

On a broader scope, the 1970s moms also submitted to society's insistence that they parent on the home front alone. The way Western society is physically structured contributes to this idea of centralized child rearing. As our society has become increasingly complex, children have no part in it. They have to be segregated away from much social life and from most of the world of work. Consequently, women are left alone for the greater part of the day to find a way to meet the needs of their children, themselves, and each other. The tremendous difficulty that women face in getting their needs met illustrates society's tendency to minimize or dismiss those needs. One of our culture's most egregious deficiencies in it support of mothers and children is in the area of health care. Providers and medical facilities in the 1970s were then, as they are to an even greater extent now, ill-equipped to deal with the physical, mental, and emotional complexities inherent in the process of becoming a mother. Although hundreds of thousands of women suffer from some form of mild to moderate postpartum depression every year,[23] there is no medical specialty that addresses the problem. The medical community is only now seriously beginning to tackle the issue, and it is nurses who are doing most of the work. Home-care agencies are springing up across the country, many headed up by RNs or other professionals who were once employed as labor and delivery or obstetrical nurses. In addition to the tremendous upheaval in their hormones that women experience after childbirth, many also have emotional difficulties, problems that, in an atmosphere of support, might resolve themselves instead of mushrooming into full-fledged symptoms of depression. The very image of a depressed mother, however, flies in the face of every societal myth defining how a mother should be. How does society protect itself against the destruction of its myths? It denies that new mothers have real problems, or decides that those who do aren't normal. This collective form of denial robs women of the resources they might otherwise have to relieve their distress.

"Mothers have emotional problems? The very idea is anathema to our way of thinking," notes author and mother Carol Dix in *The New Mother Syndrome: Coping with Postpartum Stress*.

> Most mothers-to-be won't even consider the possibility.... Content with that "joy of motherhood" image ... she does not want to conceive of such a negative picture. Mothers cannot be depressed by motherhood, we think. They must have been prone to depression, or vulnerable to psychological disorders before the birth.[24]

Since depression in motherhood is not supposed to exist, concludes Dix, women either deny its presence or suffer alone in shame and guilt. Although our research material didn't provide us with the medical histories of the 1970s moms, the women who did report feeling depressed did not reveal troubled backgrounds. It's surprising to me that they mentioned their despair at all. Like those of a severe postpartum depression, the most dramatic symptoms of The Mother Crisis are total despair and thoughts of suicide. These symptoms appear at the final stage, which is the core of The Mother Crisis—Loss of Self. A handful of the 1970s women progressed to that bottommost, dangerous stage.

"After I had Judy, I lost 25 pounds, which was marvelous—but it was strictly because I was exhausted," noted Beth, a mother of three from Texas. "My relationship with Eric was in the pits and it was just awful. I didn't think so much about taking my own life, but more hers [the baby's]. I just couldn't handle it." Dr. Dyanne Affonso, Dean of the School of Nursing at Emory University in Atlanta, claims that there is really no postpartum care in the United States to speak of. "In other cultures, new mothers are aided in their healing and recovery process by being relieved of all responsibilities except caring for the baby," she explains. "In the United States, we see childbearing as a product. Once the baby is done, it is done," she says. "With ten to twelve-hour hospital stays, society is saying to women, 'You will do your healing on your own.'"[25] Affonso contends that the country's health-care delivery system needs a complete overhaul. "If we can't deliver care at the hospital, we have to deliver it at home,"[26] she declares.

For most of the century, giving birth was considered a major event from which it took months to recover. Members of the extended family tended to the new mom for weeks after the birth, often taking charge of cooking, cleaning, and caring for other children. Through the 1940s, most women stayed in the hospital a week, and those who could afford it often hired private nurses to stay with them another week or two at home. In the 1960s and '70s, a routine birth was still a 3- to 4-day hospitalization and a C-section was a week. Pushing women out of the hospital in 24 hours for a routine birth or 48 hours for a C-section is the latest blow to an already frail postpartum system. Yet the stress of labor and the needs of women who go through it are unchanged. If a woman

with postpartum depression doesn't get help early, and the cor-
relative emotional and psychological factors aren't addressed,
maintain the experts, the condition often persists.

Louise, a 35-year-old nurse from Virginia, experienced an
extended depression that lasted through the births of several children. Her suicidal thoughts persisted, she thinks, because of a
deep-seated desire for perfection.

> I had these [suicidal] feelings mostly when I felt that I was a
> terrible mother—that I wasn't meeting the needs of my kids
> at all—that they would be better off without me and that
> dying would be the easy way out, because then they wouldn't
> have to worry about a mother that just ran off and left them.
> Those times are fewer and farther between now, but I still
> have them. With me it wasn't fatigue. Rather it was more
> inbred expectations of perfection from myself that caused me
> to feel that way. I have a very perfectionist mother. I never
> thought about killing myself; I just hoped I would have a
> heart attack and die.

It's important to remember that all of the women who participated in Jane's primary (1978) study were esteemed, capable,
educated, motivated individuals who had access to the highest
level of support available. Yet most of them still suffered The
Mother Crisis at some time or another in the evolutionary process
that is motherhood. What happens then, we wonder, to the
women who not only lack emotional strength and abilities but
who also attempt to mother in a vacuum of support? How do they
manage? My suspicion is that perhaps they don't. Take the 1995
Susan Smith murder case, for example. Here's a mother with a
documented history of family trauma, childhood sexual abuse,
and a medical background that included two suicide attempts and
chronic depression. Given her single-parent status and the financial difficulties that she was having at the time of the murders, the
fact that Smith sought some type of relief from her pain and escape
from her responsibilities is not at all surprising. In her confession,
Smith wrote, "I felt I couldn't be a good mom anymore, but I
didn't want them [the children] to grow up without a mom. I was

never so lonely or sad in my whole life."[27] The sheriff who investigated the murder case observed that, on the surface, she appeared well put together. But it was his job to unearth the hidden truth. "In every regard she seemed to be a normal person except when you got to her emotions,"[28] he said.

Our research has clearly demonstrated that women work harder at parenting because they are expected to; that they assume primary responsibility for child rearing because the buck usually lands squarely in their laps. If they don't have parenting skills or a support system to tap into for help, very often they just can't cope.

Samantha, 29, from Virginia, recalled how the stress of caring for her first child, with no help from her husband, practically did her in.

> I've been very very desperate, especially when Eric was little and he was getting me up every blessed night and it seems like it must have been two years, literally, in the middle of the night to nurse him and he was just growing so fast that he was hungry all the time, and Bob just doesn't believe in letting kids cry all night. I tried letting him cry a couple of nights when Bob wasn't home and got desperately worn out and I said to myself, "You got yourself into this so you've got to cope with it; this is the way your life is laid out for you so you better get on the stick."

Samantha's was not a far cry from the typical proclamation of the 1950s-era mom, whose popular admonishment to any woman who complained was, "You made your bed, now you've got to lie in it."

In a 1986 study published by *Developmental Psychology* magazine, a group of university professors studied the effect of marital support on a new mother's sense of well-being and satisfaction with life. One of their main premises was that spousal support is an important ingredient in intact families. Results indicated, in fact, that the marital relationship is the primary source of support and that there is a strong relationship between spousal support and maternal well-being. For mothers of firstborn infants in particular, it was only the amount of support provided by the husband and the mother's satisfaction with the husband that correlated positively with life satisfaction. For mothers of later-born infants, satisfaction with their own mothers was also related to well-being, perhaps because the mother is in need of more help from the grandmother when she has more than one small child to attend to.[29]

Brenda, a former English teacher from Rhode Island, exemplifies how a lack of such support contributes to a dissatisfaction with life. "It was after Christmas and I said to Bill, 'I hate the kids; they haven't really done anything awful, it's just that I feel like they don't appreciate anything I do for them. The more you do, the more they expect.' I guess I wanted recognition." In the same breath, Brenda added,

> I don't know what's wrong; nothing should be wrong. I wanted to move and we moved; we had the house I wanted; I had a car to go wherever I wanted; I had money; if the washing machine broke we could have it fixed; I could buy the kids anything they needed. I didn't know what was wrong, except that I did nothing well, and I figured that if I did die, it wouldn't matter to anyone at all.

Judith, a mother of three, shared similar feelings after being at home full-time for a number of years. "I had almost hoped someone told me I had a terminal disease," she admitted. "I just didn't have the guts to go out and kill myself." Karen, a mother of three from Wisconsin, tried at first to rationalize her feelings of despair, then when that didn't work, dismissed them altogether.

> I've thought on several occasions that death would be a way out of my problems, but then I would leave three children, and that wouldn't be convenient for various reasons. Yet my kids are the ones that were causing these feelings, and if I had no kids, then I wouldn't be having this feeling that I want to get out of this whole experience. It was always such a paradox when I think back on those times when I was terrifically depressed for one reason or another and I thought, "Gosh, what would happen if I just drove [the car] off the road or ..." I always snapped out of those experiences, or having those feelings, because I realized I couldn't leave my children, yet they were the ones causing me all this pain and terrible anguish, and it was sort of silly.

Judith recalled taking action to alleviate her despondency. "I can always tell when I'm feeling bad, because I go to the paper and cut out want ads," she said.

> Then I'll call the person to inquire, and sometimes I'll even send out a resume. I'll really get worked up, but at least that's constructive, because it kind of helps me through the period. But I can remember thinking at one time that I almost wished someone would tell me I had something terminal. I wouldn't do anything different; I'd just sit back and let it happen.

According to Scarr, the worst adjusted and unhappiest women are mothers who wish they could be employed. "They feel trapped and lonely, lack self-confidence and appear disorganized,"[30] she says. Furthermore, asserts Scarr, depressed mothers spawn depressed children. "Children of depressed mothers avoid them and shun attention from other adults. The children seem to develop an avoidance of emotional involvements with others when their mothers are depressed."[31] Scarr concludes that there is great cause for concern over role adjustment among mothers and thus the impact of mothers' adjustment on the children who are around them full time.

Studies show that depression often erupts out of a perceived loss of choice, as evidenced by so many of the 1970s moms who were in a full-blown Mother Crisis. But that's not to say that all the mothers who experienced a Crisis wound up severely depressed. A woman can enter The Mother Crisis cycle, which is continuous, at any point and still feel its blow. The sense of entrapment and complete loss of choice that women feel when they are overwhelmed by the Crisis has actually been present all along—they just weren't aware of it until forced to look it squarely in the eye. The Mother Crisis is, first and foremost, a crisis of awareness. For how much choice did the women actually have to begin with? The standard definition of motherhood as outlined by cultural myths certainly doesn't allow women to comfortably choose what type of mothers they will be. And once they're stuck inside the parameters of this narrowly defined role, women are offered few opportunities to escape. The most serious stage of The Mother Crisis— Loss of Self—is actually an exaggerated form of the catalyst that propels women into a crisis in the first place—a lack of choice due to the presence of motherhood myths.

While a mother's feeling of entrapment might begin with cultural myths, it is perpetuated by our society's refusal to provide appropriate resources for her and for her children. Nearly everything a mother did with her children in 1970s America was a struggle. Although none of the 1970s women we interviewed were aware of it, their communities were simply not child-friendly. Apartment complexes and condominiums frequently discouraged, or would not rent to, families with children. Community facilities, both public and private, were rarely designed with mothers and children in mind, often lacking the most basic child-care equipment, such as changing tables, nursing rooms, and walkways that are wide enough for a baby carriage or stroller. These were some of the obvious shortcomings of our culture. It is the subtler ones, however, that have done the most damage. Nonetheless, all send the same message—that mothers and children are not valued enough to seriously consider.

Take our country's public child-care policy for example. There's never been one. Government officials, as well as their constituents, have traditionally taken the view that children are the sole responsibility of their parents, not society's. The perspective is much different from that of countries that place a high value on families, that consider their well-being paramount to the good of society, and therefore take a public-minded approach to their care. "Parents [in America] do not get the policies they need because parenting, per se does not command sufficient social status to merit them,"[32] asserts British psychologist Penelope Leach, in her book, *Children First*. Leach points out that other roles that parents perform do command respect and are therefore granted equivalents to the flexibility parents need. The academic world is a case in point, she argues. "Almost every Western country still gives some financial support to graduate students who qualify for postgraduate work. Nobody gets rich on what is usually available but because a graduate student is an honorable, even admirable, thing to be, the recipients feel the struggle is worthwhile. Is a Ph.D. really of more value to society than a well-launched child?" asks Leach. "If a parent was regarded as an especially important thing to be, and parenting a job so important to society that the individuals doing it merited all possible social support, similar justifications and arrangements could apply to people producing children."[33]

In stark contrast to the West is Denmark, which, for many years, has provided almost universal publicly funded day care and a genuine equality of opportunity for mothers and fathers in the workplace. This approach confirms a philosophy that recognizes the individual needs of all family members, encouraging freedom of choice through opportunity rather than a denial of choice via penalization and the withholding of support. In the United States and other capitalist countries, the opposite is true. Details about Denmark's child care policies and those of other European countries are presented in Chapters 8 and 9.

"Many mothers, especially in North America and the United Kingdom, see only one parenting choice: between staying home and being broke in a boring backwater or finding daycare and joining the rich regatta of mainstream work before it leaves them 'out of it' forever,"[34] declares Leach. Parents who leave jobs and careers for several years to care for children full time typically lose a great deal of status in the workplace and a tremendous amount of earning power. Mothers who return to work soon after giving birth to either salvage or protect their careers face incredible pressure to go back home and metamorphose into the "Good Mother" persona. "The proposition that women who are mothers should place themselves in a permanent professional slow lane relative to all men (including their partners) and all non-mothering women is clearly discriminatory,"[35] observes Leach. Women are damned if they do and damned if they don't in this country. It's a social climate that pushes the stress levels of mothers precariously high.

Some experts have tried to clarify why the United States balks at enacting public child care policies. In 1984, Scarr concluded that its hesitation was then, as I feel it is today, primarily fear-based. "One reason why child care in the United States is extremely inadequate is that day care policy is tied to welfare policy. For the past decade antiwelfare sentiments in this country have approached hysteria," she maintained.

> Newspaper headlines about "welfare cheats" are popular diversions on slow news days. Mothers who are said to have more babies to get more from welfare are believable characters in the current social climate. The fact that day care arose for the poor (middle-class mothers didn't work until recently) and the fact that legislation is being formulated for low-income families makes day care guilty by association with welfare and poverty, two very unfashionable topics today.[36]

If at-home mothers found support anywhere in 1978, they found it among themselves. They certainly didn't get it from childless women or from feminists. In *The Second Stage*, author Betty Friedan admitted that the women's movement, despite its many inroads to success, has never championed the role of motherhood in the context of choice. This omission, she maintains, is every bit as invalidating as those made by the government, by businesses, by our culture, or by men. "I think we must begin to discuss, in new terms, the choice to have children," she wrote.

> What worries me today is "choices" women have supposedly won, which are not real. How can a woman freely "choose" to have a child when her paycheck is needed for the rent or mortgage, when her job isn't geared to taking care of a child, when there is no rational policy for parental leave, and no assurance that her job will be waiting for her if she takes off to have a child?[37] The second stage, challenged Friedan, involves coming to new terms with the family—"new terms with love and with work."

I am fully convinced that until such new terms are drawn up—and I still don't think they have been—women from all walks of life will continue to experience The Mother Crisis. For it's my belief that no individual can live in contentment without having the freedom to develop fully as an individual and to choose how she is going to live. Mothers in the 1970s clearly lacked these options. Beginning with a faulty definition of motherhood, women springboarded into the whirlpool of The Mother Crisis, spinning around and around, mired in perfectionism and guilt, sucked into the dark void of support, eventually drowning in a complete loss of self. This is the soul sickness that permeates the lives of women in The Mother Crisis. Until such changes as sketched by Friedan occur, it will be every mother's challenge to save herself.

# *Grieving the Loss of Self* ౭ *Women Who Sacrifice Themselves for Their Children Lose Their Sense of Self*

*G*iven the brouhaha that erupted over women's long-standing fight for equal rights, it's amazing that the problems of mothers have never emerged. For nearly a century, American women have fought for justice in every area of their lives except that of motherhood. Perhaps that's why there's been virtually no debate at all on the rights and needs of mothers. But this is an issue that should not be addressed on an intellectual level. It's purely, and unequivocally, emotional. Mothers have needs that women without children do not. If a mother's needs go unmet for

long, she experiences a tremendous loss—the loss of herself— which affects the children she nurtures and the community she serves. It affects the very fabric of our society and its future. Society loses because the talents and skills of countless numbers of women are left untapped. Our children lose because the most influential person in their lives have no self-esteem. Although it's vitally important for all human beings to enter adulthood as esteemed individuals, women can't pass something on to their children that they haven't got.

Despite the fact that society didn't acknowledge their loss, mothers in Jane's 1978 study felt a part of themselves die, and they were grieving. Before a woman in The Mother Crisis can even begin to think about justice, she must first begin to heal. Society has a great role in helping its mothers begin that process, and (we hope) rediscover themselves. It's my hope that the information presented in this book will generate serious discussion about the societal myths that undermine the esteem of women who are becoming, or will eventually become, mothers. Popular definitions of what and how a mother should behave force women to ignore or deny many parts of themselves in pursuit of the "Good Mother" ideal. This doesn't have to be so. I don't believe that it's necessary for women to subjugate themselves and abandon personal development in their desire to have children. In fact, as our research has indicated, for them to do so is downright destructive. Motherhood and individual fulfillment are not mutually exclusive conditions, as current myths about motherhood suggest. It is only when women put all their energy into trying to realize an ideal that they deplete themselves of energy that might otherwise be spent in self-realization and fulfillment. The widespread notion that having children is an either–or proposition—that a woman either has children and adopts the "Good Mother" persona or continues on as a person in her own right—is a product of a society that, for economic reasons and others, needed to create such a split.

Soon after the turn of the century, when modern society became industrialized and men's lives changed dramatically, society needed to view women as innocent and pure to stave off the many changes that industrial change brought. Notes author Sandra Scarr,

> It seems natural to believe that mothers are important to their children's development, but the notion that mothers have special and irreplaceable roles in children's lives is rather new. The image of woman-as-mother, rather than as household manager who also has children, is an invention of the

nineteenth century. Children, who from the Renaissance to the mid-nineteenth century had largely been ignored, suddenly had psyches that required special care.[1]

According to Scarr, the notion that babies and young children require specific kinds of stimulation to ensure outcomes that parents desire, for example, is extremely damaging to families. "It preys on parents' insecurities and focuses their attention on mechanical doo-dads rather than on their children as real people,"[2] she asserts. In reality, babies get all the stimulation they need by being included in normal household activities.

The concept of woman-as-mother has received a great deal of reinforcement throughout the twentieth century: reinforcement from a government that has failed to designate money for child care, from religious leaders who argue that women should stay home for moral reasons, and from men who are afraid that women seeking fulfillment in the form of work will rob them of their jobs. "Make the role attractive, make it right, and women will stay home and do it, and they did,"[3] noted Ann Dally, author of *Inventing Motherhood*. One of the 1970s moms interviewed, who had moved to the United States from Canada, said that she had to conform to cultural expectations of women so that she could stay in the country. "I had to promise that I only wanted to be a nice housewife and be home and raise my children," recalled Frankie, from Ontario. "I had to appear to not be a threat to anyone, and to [make them believe] that I wouldn't take away anyone's job. I was told downtown to just say, 'Yes, I'm going to stay home,' just so that I could get a permanent visa."

## WOMEN ARE ENCOURAGED TO CHOOSE ROLES RATHER THAN INTEGRATE THEM

According to Judith Schwartz, author of *The Mother Puzzle: A New Generation Reckons with Motherhood*, women themselves have discouraged one another from having complete identities. By bolstering the status of the mother role and thus intensifying their own oppression within that role, they perpetuate motherhood ideals, she claims.[4] Feminists, too, have supported the idea that women must make a choice between individual fulfillment and motherhood. To many women's rights activists, to acknowledge that women have a need to integrate the role of motherhood into their identities is to admit that women need help and are therefore weak. Women who have strived for years to be viewed as capable, unemotional, and strong simply aren't willing to risk their hard-won images long enough to embrace the human truth that all people have needs and that asking for help is not a sign of weakness but of strength. Many of them, and rightly so, view neediness as the pathway to oppression. For it is when women were stereotyped as helpless—in other words, needy to the extreme—that they were most suppressed. When Betty Friedan, in *The Second Stage*, voiced concerns of the feminists who were having babies and accused earlier women's rights proponents of going too far in rejecting family life, many critics labeled her a traitor.

And so the women in Jane's 1978 study were forced to make a choice—to remain whole and miss out on the demands, joys, and rewards of motherhood, or to lop off pieces of themselves in order to fit into the mother mold. I suspect that if society did not force women to choose, and that if women rejected motherhood myths instead of internalizing them, there would be no Mother Crisis. Women in America would have the freedom to become mothers without abandoning themselves. In *The Second Stage*, Friedan addressed the motherhood dilemma in the context of women's rights. "When a woman is denied access to satisfaction of those needs in society as a person in her own right, she makes home and the family into a vehicle for her power, control, status and self-realization,"[5] she contended. Try as they might, the women interviewed in 1978 were simply not able to accomplish such a feat in the confines of the home. It just wasn't possible for them to develop individually in such an isolated environment. I agree whole-heartedly with Friedan's premise, however, that the right to choose one's life path is crucial to the personhood of everyone, including women: "The right to choose has to mean not only the right to choose not to bring a child into the world against one's will, but also the right to have a child, joyously, responsibly, without paying a terrible price of isolation from the world and its rewarded occupations, its decisions and actions."[6] The experiences of the women in our study dramatically bear out Friedan's assertion that the price of motherhood is far too high for most women.

Danielle, 36, from Nebraska, remembered how she eventually came to realize that living as half a person was destroying her: "I wouldn't admit that there was anything really wrong, but I'd go out and jog for five miles and ride my bike—I'd do things just to get away from [the sadness]. But you can't; you have to face it. It really took me a long time to come to grips with myself." Once she did, however, Danielle, unlike most of the 1970s moms, took action, one step at a time. "I'd sit and say, 'OK, this morning I'll turn the "Dinah Shore Show" off and think about what I want to do. I'm going to be 36, and I have to decide what to do with myself because I know I'm not going to be able to sit there waiting for the school bus.'" Several months later, Danielle made a decision. "I intend to get a job," she declared. "I don't know what it's going to be, but it doesn't frighten me anymore. I'm getting confidence in my ability to do things, and I'm not afraid any more. I spent a good year being afraid of everything and being afraid that I was going to lose my mind, but I didn't."

Janet, 34, also from Nebraska, felt a deep sense of loss after several years as a full-time mom. She reported that the change in her job status decimated both her relationship and her sense of self. "My husband and I were married five years before we had kids, and we were, like, really together," she explained.

> Now we fight more. But it's not the fighting ... I just feel like I'm in a different world entirely; when I'm talking to him, he doesn't even know what I'm talking about, and when he talks about his world and stuff, I can't understand it. I went to Barnard College and John went to Columbia University, and it really doesn't do much for my self-esteem, because I see myself actually descending in my [own] eyes and in his eyes and in society's eyes and I don't like it.

With many of the 1970s moms, grief hovered just below their level of consciousness, yet talking about their experiences brought it to the surface. "I feel like I am smart enough to be doing other things, and I feel like sometimes I'm not challenging myself," noted Louise, a mother of two. "During the times when I don't feel challenged, I know that I'm probably wasting something in myself."

Becky, 31, a mother with an extremely isolated home life, seemed guilty and uncomfortable while talking about her psychologically splintered existence. "We go out to a cocktail party and I'm saying to myself, 'Gee, I'm talking to people my own age; I'm not talking about who has to go to the bathroom.' I think that's the part that has always bothered me, [about at-home mothering] possibly, about being restricted because of my children. I don't resent being oriented toward my children," she added, cautiously, "but I feel that there are times when I need to be working at a higher level of intellect."

On the flip side of the mother issue, and no less important, are the women who are forced to deny part of themselves to pursue individual goals. Again, notes Friedan, "To deny the part of one's being as a woman that has, through the ages, been expressed in motherhood—nurturing, loving softness and tiger strength—is to deny part of one's personhood as a woman." On the other hand, for those women who choose to stay home, "the stunting of abilities and earning power is a real fear because professions and careers are still structured in terms of the lives of men whose wives took care of the parenting and other details of life," she observed. "The point is, the movement to equality and the personhood of women isn't finished until motherhood is a fully free choice."[7]

At her clinic in Washington, D.C., Dr. Eleanor Morin Davis, counsels women mired in conflict due to an inability to integrate the part of themselves culturally identified as motherlike—nurturing, patient, gentle, and so on—and the part that is defined by society as self-motivated or career-based—creative, assertive, and ambitious. According to Morin Davis, the split exists because there is no bridge between the parts. The main goal of counseling sessions is to build such a bridge. How does she help women do that? "I just keep talking and letting them know that what makes a full person is a full range of human emotion and the capacity to develop all aspects of themselves." Morin Davis claims that women in America still feel as if they have to choose between developing as a mother and developing as a person. Most of the women she counsels are working mothers who report feeling "fragmented" or "torn to shreds."

"The women who come to me have this conflict because they're not able to be comfortable with both these sets of feelings," she explains.

> They're also having big trouble because they're not getting their needs met in the workplace or as a mother. They're doing what they need to do to survive, and sometimes that involves cutting off very important parts of themselves and denying things in themselves. They, therefore, become rigified into certain physical states and feelings about themselves, stuck in one role and very fearful of the other, or taking on only one role, even though they have yearnings in both directions.

According to Morin Davis, the range of a woman's needs broadens after she becomes a mother. "These are needs that grow partially out of the whole psychobiological matrix of pregnancy, birth, and infant care, needs which are very specific and intensified." But having such needs does not, as motherhood myths lead us to believe, negate a woman's need to be independent and develop personally and creatively, she adds. Society's insistence that women who seek both are merely looking for a way to "have their cake and eat it too" is yet another example of how our culture discourages women from trying to live as whole human beings. The mores prescribed for women today aren't much different from those that governed our culture in 1935, when anthropologist Margaret Mead observed that women had two choices—either to conform to cultural norms that dictated how a woman should behave and therefore to be "less of an achieving individual, or to be an achieving individual and therefore less of a woman."[8]

Our society's tendency to encourage women to divide themselves is linked to its economic and power structure. Stay-at-home mothers are notoriously steadfast consumers, have virtually no influence in corporate America (few women are at the helms of the nation's Fortune 500 companies), and, too busy to make a fuss, rarely threaten the status quo at any level of government. But are the powers that be actually benefiting in the long run, I wonder? I think not. Despite all outward appearances, no culture can flourish with more than half its population living at near-survival level, either emotionally or physically. Although a cause-and-effect relationship has yet to be established, I believe that underdeveloped women who are underutilized in the workforce and communities are one of the reasons our culture is in trouble. Studies show that our children, the people who will shape our nation's future, suffer dramatically when their mothers are anything less than whole. According to a study of 1,300 families by sociologists at Ohio State University, stay-at-home mothers who are bored and/or frustrated may be holding up their children's early development. In contrast, the study found that verbal and behavioral testing of 3- to 6-year-old children whose parents were happy in their jobs showed good progress, even though they spent less time with Mom and Dad.[9]

A 1994 University of Iowa study concluded that employment is positively related to emotional well-being for women, given certain conditions. The study found that mothers who earn enough to improve family income, who are employed because of couple preference, and who receive help with housework and child care show less depression and anxiety than women who are homemakers.[10] In 1963, Friedan went so far as to liken the plight of the modern suburban housewife to that of concentration camp sufferers.

> The guns of the SS were not powerful enough to keep all those prisoners subdued. They imprisoned themselves by making the concentration camp the whole world, by blinding themselves to the larger world of the past, their responsibility for the present, and their possibilities for the future. The ones who survived, who neither died nor were exterminated, were the ones who retained in some essential degree the adult values and interests which had been the essence of their past identity.[11]

*VENERATED MOTHERHOOD IMAGES CREATE A PRISON FOR WOMEN*

The women in Jane's 1978 study who experienced some degree of The Mother Crisis were strikingly similar to Friedan's suburban housewives who were buried alive by the "problem that has no name." But the mothers were locked in a prison of a different kind. The prison created by The Mother Crisis is actually a prison within a prison. The at-home moms in the 1970s were not only subdued by societal norms regarding women but also by their isolated environments and the myths about motherhood that motivated them from within. It was their own externally imposed and internally held convictions about how a good mother should be that kept them shackled. Whereas the suburban housewife might be imprisoned by a passionless existence, women in The Mother Crisis are bound tightly by their own unrealistically high expectations of themselves and mother guilt. As their comments illustrated in Chapter 3, they beat themselves up for failing to live up to impossible-to-achieve motherhood ideals. They didn't ask for help with child-rearing duties, even when they desperately needed it. They also gave up a lot of the things that were important to them, because they felt it was in the best interests of their family or their children to do so. Out of the 71 women interviewed in 1978, more than half reported that they stayed at home full time out of a sense of duty and because they thought it was best for their children (42 percent), or because they weren't satisfied with their careers (9 percent). Although 47 percent stated that they chose the lifestyle to please themselves, most of them still experienced some degree of The Mother Crisis.

As Chapter 3 illustrated, many of them felt driven to perform their roles perfectly and experienced a tremendous sense of guilt when they couldn't. Because they lacked the support they needed to live balanced lives, many of them couldn't get their needs met. Even when they weren't aware of their entrapment, it was obvious that these mothers were tormented. They lived a life of quiet desperation, as described by Penelope Leach in *Children First*:

> For most people in postindustrial societies, being at home full-time when almost all other adults are in workplaces full-time soon means isolation, loneliness and that uncomfortable combination of overwork and boredom that comes from being constantly confronted with unremittingly repetitive, trivial chores.[12]

If these conditions don't change, predicts Leach, more and more women will reenter the workforce while their children are still quite young. "It is the impoverishment of life at home, as much as the enrichment of paid work, that has so dramatically reduced the ages at which many infants enter daycare, and the numbers of care-givers available in domestic settings,"[13] she declares. Fortunately, for those of us seeking alternatives to the existing social order, this is a cultural, not a universal phenomenon.

Many times throughout the nineteenth and twentieth centuries, visionary or progressive groups have espoused the idea that children need not belong exclusively to, or be reared exclusively by, their parents. Such groups believed that children brought up communally by loving care-givers who were not their parents would grow up to be better adjusted adults than children reared primarily by their parents. Parents, too, were thought to benefit from sharing child-rearing chores with the community. A good example of success in communal living is the *kibbutz*, established in Palestine in the early part of this century, and the *Bruderhof* in the eastern United States in the mid-1950s. One of the main ways such communities put their ideals into practice is by diluting the rights and responsibilities of individual parents for their children. Sharing child-rearing responsibilities is meant to free women from the bonds of conventional families. Women are to be economically independent of their husbands and free of continuous child care. Children are also to be freed from the emotional bonds of the nuclear family by sharing in the love of the larger community.[14]

*Kibbutzim*, which began in Palestine in 1910 and flourished, strive to embody the ideals of economic collectivism and social equality of men and women. Men and women therefore rotate jobs, including those traditionally assigned exclusively to men or to women in Europe and the United States. To free women from exclusive responsibility for rearing children, the *kibbutzim* established children's houses with professional caregivers. Fathers are expected to participate as parents to the same extent as mothers. Unlike European and American families, families in the *kibbutz* are not economic units and they do not have exclusive responsibility for the socialization and control of their children. This is due to a fundamental principle of *kibbutz* life: the liberation of women and children from the subjugation of the traditional family, which the founders viewed with profound distaste.[15] This is chiefly because *kibbutzim* founders focused on dismantling the traditional bourgeois family, with its close mother–child ties, which they perceived as promoting selfishness and individualism. Communal child rearing was seen, since the earliest days of the *kibbutzim* movement, as a major task for the whole community. Another child-rearing principle of the *kibbutz* was that experts in child rearing could socialize the children better and more objectively than the parents. This ideology led to relegating the parents to second place as socializing agents. The major socializing agents became the nurses, the teachers, and the peer group. Since the parents were no longer the sole representatives of authority, children's attitudes toward them were expected to become more positive. As the system evolved, there emerged a major trend toward closer parent–child contacts and more individual caretaking. In the late 1970s, *kibbutz* life had changed to include strong nuclear families. Because the typical *kibbutz* family may include more than two generations, it has developed into an extended family, with several generations and several separate household units.[16]

According to psychologists Albert I. Rabin and Benjamin Beit-Hallahmi in the book *Twenty Years Later, Kibbutz Children Grown Up*, the Israeli *kibbutz* has made the most successful attempt at building a utopian commune. The *kibbutzim* movement nurtured the ideals of returning to nature and rearing a new type of human being. The high point of the movement was in the 1930s and '40s, with the population of the *kibbutzim* reaching 7.5 percent of the Jewish population in Palestine in 1957. Since 1948, when the State of Israel was founded, the *kibbutzim* have been declining in political and social power but have gained economic power and success. In 1980, there were 253 *kibbutz* communities, with a total population of 110,000, making up 3.3 percent of the Jewish population of Israel. They hold 33 percent of all cultivated land in Israel and produce 40 percent of the food supplies. They are responsible for 7 percent of the gross national product.[17]

Communal sharing in the *Bruderhof* is more than an economic arrangement, as in the *kibbutzim*. Members work together, eat together, meet almost every night, and raise their children together. Communal child rearing is only one, but an essential, part of the entire shared life of the *Bruderhof*. The *Bruderhof* supports itself through a communal industry—the manufacture and sale of high-quality and expensive wooden toys. The community celebrated its fiftieth birthday in 1970. It was founded in Germany in 1920, and has since undergone migrations to England, Paraguay, and finally, in 1954, to the United States.[18]

According to Dr. Sandra Scarr, author of *Mother Care/Other Care*, there are many similarities in the rearing of children in what author and sociologist Benjamin Zablocki calls "intentional communities."[19] They share child care, and they value their children.

> The care they provide is probably no better or worse in the abstract than care in nuclear families where mother provides the majority of child care. Communities such as the Kibbutzim and the Bruderhof do a good job with their children, just as many nuclear families do. That gives us options for child-rearing, once we figure out how sharing responsibilities for child-rearing can fit into late twentieth century American life.[20]

Although the *Bruderhof* consists of a collection of families, everything is done within the community to strengthen family life. Each family lives together in its own apartment. According to Zablocki in his book *The Joyful Community*, "Special times are set aside just for families to be together. Large families are considered natural and wholesome and each new baby is welcomed by the whole community with joy."[21] There is no opportunity for economic enslavement in *Bruderhof* marriages, since neither partner is dependent on the other for money. But in the spiritual sense, *Bruderhof* marriages are not egalitarian. The community distinguishes fundamental differences between men and women. Individual marriages are made with the spiritual good of the community in mind. Individualism and the ego are thought to be qualities that should and must be repressed.

On the islands of Hawaii, there exists a family structure, the *hanai*, that is similar to the extended families of eighteenth-century mainland America. Children of native Hawaiian parents are frequently given to brothers, sisters, cousins, aunts, or grandparents to raise as their own in a system that resembles, without the paperwork, open adoption. The children know who their biological parents are but recognize their *hanai* relative as their true mother or father. Children therefore receive nurturing and guidance from many adult family members and enjoy strong bonds between *hanai* brothers and sisters, as well as biological siblings.

For the past 40 years in America, it has been widely and passionately believed that a child's "sense of security" can only come from a warm, continuous relationship with one person and one person only.[22] This belief was first popularized in 1951 by Dr. John Bowlby in a monograph commissioned by the World Health Organization in its quest to confirm what is best for the world's children. He wrote:

> What is believed to be essential for mental health is that the infant and young child should experience a warm, intimate and continuous relationship with his mother (or mother-substitute) in which both find satisfaction and enjoyment.... A state of affairs in which the child does not have this relationship is termed "maternal deprivation."[23]

It is clear that Bowlby feels that this constant attention is more important than how a mother feels about it, and whether it suits her personality and ultimately her child. In America, where Freudian theory is heavily touted, it is believed that the so-called "maternal deprivation" of communally reared children results in more mental illness, more immature emotional development, poorer identification with parents, and too great a reliance on peers.[24] However, a 1954 study of children in several *kibbutzim*, conducted by social scientist G. Caplan, revealed that there were no more personality disturbances among older *kibbutz* children than in comparable American samples, and that young adults were remarkably nonneurotic.[25]

Although markedly different in their social constructs than the intentional communities, Scandinavian countries—Denmark, Norway, and Sweden—also present a working model for families and child rearing that frees women from the job of exclusive and continuous child care. In these countries, the mothers of young children have a higher employment rate than the mothers of other Western European countries. A characteristic feature of these social democratic welfare states is the importance attributed to the principles of universalism and equality. The Scandinavian societies in the 1970s underwent remarkable social change. Boundaries between the public and the private were redrawn, and the division of labor within families and households were renegotiated. Mothers of preschool children became one of the fastest growing groups in the labor market. Scandinavian policies in the 1970s introduced legislation that either established or expanded entitlements concerning maternity, paternity, and parental leave, as well as increasing state support for child care. Denmark, Norway, and Sweden, which commonly regard day care for children as a public responsibility, offer employed parents wage compensation and some opportunity to care for young children while retaining job security. Of the three countries, Sweden has the most comprehensive system of leave of absence in connection with parenthood, which is discussed further in Chapter 8. In the 1970s, government-appointed commissions in all three countries prepared the ground for increased public investment in the education and care of preschool children. "Good" day care was regarded not only as good for children but also good for the economy, which needed mothers' labor.[26]

The fact that so many cultures succeed in assigning the responsibility of child care to both parents and the community suggests that the United States could adopt similar practices. Like policymakers in Scandinavia, I believe that such an approach benefits children and the economy. I also believe that it benefits parents. The American assumption that only women possess the wherewithal to parent a child full time is ludicrous to more than a few experts and clinicians. "Of course a man can take full daily care of his child," declares Leach. "Any suggestion that he cannot is as insultingly absurd as the suggestion that his partner cannot run a corporation."[27] I don't believe that American society must be turned upside down in the process of recognizing the needs of mothers and children. A revolution on the scale of the civil rights or women's movement is simply not necessary. Instead, I suggest that American society reorganize so that mothers and children receive the attention they deserve from the community at large. Like Scarr, I believe that for a smooth transition into a community-centered approach to parenting, "child care must fit the pattern of work and family life approved by the parents and by the larger social group to which they belong."[28]

According to Scarr, it is America's "commitment to the two-parent nuclear family that has led us to discount the possible strengths of other types. Children with more contact with parents and other adults fare better than children with fewer adult contacts, even if they have a lot of contact with one parent."[29] Scarr contends, as I do, that America resists social change where family matters are concerned, not so much because there's evidence that such change would damage children, but because adults fear it. Notes Scarr, "Changes in family forms can be a social problem, but not always because they are bad for children. Sometimes they are just upsetting to adults. Alternative family forms are a greater threat to entrenched values than to children."[30] They are a threat, for example, to the conservative right wing, which perceives the nuclear, stay-at-home-mom family model as the only family worth preserving. They are a threat to women who fear any kind of influence on their children other than their own.

The 1978 women who suffered The Mother Crisis to the severest extent—complete loss of self—were trapped by the misconception that to rediscover themselves would mean abandoning their children. It was easy for the women to stay entrenched in the idea, given their isolated environments, lack of unbiased information about the developmental needs of children, and virtual obsession with personally meeting their children's every need. "Parents suffer when their babies protest separation," notes Scarr.

"The combination of guilt about working and guilt about the baby's unhappiness at your leaving can be devastating unless you understand the temporary developmental nature of his protest."[31] One wonders whether these mothers would have been nearly as guilt-ridden over leaving their children to pursue other interests if they had had access to fact-based, rather than myth-based, information about child development, such as that presented by Scarr: "No permanent harm will come from temporary separations, no matter how loudly he cries," she proclaims. "There is just nothing you can do but keep your friendly calm and wait until he gets a better brain that can remember you are coming back in the afternoon."[32]

The majority of the mothers interviewed in 1978 could not cut the ties that bound them relentlessly to their children. Smothered by motherhood myths and self-perpetuated feelings of self-doubt, most retreated into a life devoid of opportunity for personal growth and development. Although many were unaware of their predicament and had only a vague understanding of the source of their discontent, a few of the women knew exactly why they felt bad and resented their position.

"When you go off to college and they promise you the world ... and then all of a sudden you have children and you are not doing anything ... you really feel like you've been had," said Connie, 34, a former educator and mother of three. "I mean, subconsciously, I guess I believed that I was always supposed to have children, and I guess that I was supposed to take care of my own children—that was the hidden agenda—but, on the other hand, I am educated and I'm just like a man. But what are you supposed to do with that?" Maggie, 33, from Rhode Island, minced few words in describing her dilemma: "I'm not fulfilled as a mother; I don't find motherhood as great as it's supposed to be or the image I had of motherhood before," she stated matter-of-factly. Lindy, 27, who worked as a secretary before having children, reported having no aspirations beyond the mother role, and wasn't aware of any personal loss. "I don't know what I'll do when the kids are up and gone," she admitted. "Maybe [my daughter] Cindy will bring me home some grandchildren." Joan, a former nurse, blamed herself for the isolated environment in which she found herself after giving birth to twins. "I felt very frustrated with myself for allowing myself to get into that position," she said, "although I suppose, looking at it realistically, I didn't have that much to do with determining my situation. When you quit your job to have a baby, you're starting a whole new way of life, and being on call 24 hours a day for feeding is depressing."

According to Ann Dally, author of *Inventing Motherhood, The Consequences of an Ideal*, people turn to depression when they have lost something that is psychologically vital to them or feel unable to escape from an impossible conflict.[33] The 1978 mothers felt the impact of both impasses. Depression, explains Dally, substitutes for a solution, and the sufferer is trapped and gives up. Whatever the causes, the fact is that many mothers have become depressed during at least some period of their active mothering years, and this depression, if severe or prolonged, can have a profound influence on their mothering capacities and on their children. "This is particularly true when they are the chief or virtually the sole influence on their children's lives," she maintains. "The disturbed mother whose influence actively prevents her children from making close contact with other adults is usually more damaging than the one who lets her children go free or neglects them."[34]

Women in The Mother Crisis who sink into depression do so because they are unable to acknowledge the grief they feel over the losses they experience or to cry out for help or respite. If only the women knew how to take better care of themselves without feeling guilty. Perhaps they could have been spared a portion of their grief. But, just as our society discourages mothers from perceiving themselves as whole, it also discourages them from viewing their own needs as equally important as the needs of their spouses or their children. Many of the women mentioned that they felt "guilty" and "selfish" when spending "household" money on clothes, college classes, or anything else that was for their own personal use or enjoyment. Despite their misgivings, the 1978 mothers were very much the opposite. They were, in reality, almost completely selfless, in other words, "devoted to others' welfare or interest and not one's own." For these women, moving beyond the boundaries of that definition was almost sacrilegious, the supreme violation of the "Good Mother" ideal. Mothers must learn how to balance their needs with those of the children and adults who depend on them, and to understand that taking care of themselves is not the same as being selfish. "There's nothing wrong with being selfish if selfishness means being concerned about your own needs," declares Morin Davis.

> You need to be selfish; it helps you empathize with the baby. If you recognize what your needs are, you use that as a base to understand the baby. Some women say they're too "self-ish," to justify a decision not to have children, but even there, selfishness is not usually the issue, selfishness is a label put on those who try to have their needs met. It's traditionally been used in rhetoric attacking women.

Jane, a 34-year-old mother of two who was on the brink of awareness about her own sense of loss, said, "I cannot make a decision that has to do with my own inner satisfaction; I'm very surprised by this."

No matter how many times I witness it, it is very sad for me to watch a woman in The Mother Crisis come into awareness about herself. Yet, at the same time, I know that I am observing a turning point, an event pregnant with potential for change. My hope for all women in The Mother Crisis is that they can find some means of pulling themselves out. But one thing is certain; they cannot do it alone. The only real solution is a social and cultural one. Or, in the timeless words of Margaret Mead, "What we need most ... are new and diverse ways in which men and women can share equally in the responsibility for the children they want to have and the life they lead together."[35] I'd like to take Mead's proposal even one step further by suggesting that mothers' work should be everyone's work. To succeed, parenthood must be shared. Locking women into a job where there's little chance for success is nothing short of barbaric. Parenting is simply too demanding and too important a task to delegate to any one person without providing proper support or the means by which one can live a full life.

# PART II

# Motherhood Today ❧

# *A Sacrificing of Identity* ∝ *Women Who Give up Their Identities Set Themselves up for The Mother Crisis*

*O*ne of the most prevalent issues of the 1990s has
been what media
mavens have dubbed "a re-
turn to family values." Jour-
nalists, talk show hosts, politicians, and religious leaders
alike have gotten tremen-
dous mileage out of blaming
societal ills on America's
abandonment of the 1950s-
era family. The cure, they argue, is a return to the principles that eschew the so-called
"rampant materialism" of the
1980s and embrace a more
fundamental way of life. The
problem with this view lies
in its narrow definition of
family. The soothsayers up-
hold one type—the two-

parent, mother-at-home, father-at-work variety—as the medicine
that will cure what ails America. In his acceptance speech at the
1996 Republican National Convention, presidential candidate Robert Dole proclaimed, "It doesn't take a village to raise a child, it
takes a family." The statement, which countered Hillary Rodham

Clinton's view of family- and community-based child rearing, defined the GOP's platform regarding motherhood and child care.

Such ideology is the water in which the women in our 1995 study were baptized as they came of age. Like their 1978 counterparts, participants of our important follow-up exercise adopted full-time careers as at-home mothers in the belief that it was best for their children. Although they stayed home for the same reasons as the 1978 moms, they were motivated by an entirely different set of ideals.

## MANY WOMEN WHO GREW UP IN THE FEMINIST SEVENTIES STILL CHOSE TO STAY HOME WITH THEIR CHILDREN

The 1978 women made a passive choice to stay home because they identified strongly with an image of woman-as-mother that was deeply imbedded in their psyches. In contrast, the women we interviewed in 1995 actively chose the at-home mothering role as a form of maternal altruism. Unlike the women of the 1970s, the majority had well-developed identities that included a sense of themselves as individuals in the world, with talents and abilities that they actively applied to a variety of personal and professional pursuits. In response to the survey question that asked them to describe themselves prechildren, a full 86 percent of the women used mostly positive terms, adjectives such as "confident," "resourceful," "independent," "sexy," "interesting," "happy," "spontaneous," "ambitious," "reliable," "creative," "motivated," "successful," "determined," and "bold." Of the 109 mothers surveyed in 1995, 106 were employed outside the home before having children. Unlike the 1978 moms, the majority of the 1995 participants were not employed in traditionally female occupations, representing instead the broad range of professions that have opened up to women over the past two decades. Fifteen were former teachers; only 8 had worked as secretaries and 6 as nurses. Eleven were employed in the health and beauty industry, but the remainder (66) worked in professions that included sales, management, business, journalism, travel, engineering, law, and design. A full 95 percent reported that they considered their work worthwhile (compared to 87 percent in 1978), and half reported that they had aspired to a higher position, more than double the number who sought to advance in 1978. Yet, when faced with the decision on how to best care for their children, each of them cast aside whatever personal goals they had and replaced them with an array of motherhood ambitions. They readily relinquished their goals to meet our culture's—and their own—expectations of what a "good" mother should be. They pursued accomplishments in at-home mothering with the same amount of zeal that they put into their premotherhood vocations. Some of them possessed a Martha Stewart–like determination to transform the combined roles of wife and mother into something resembling an industry, demonstrating clearly this generation's inclination toward goal-oriented behavior. But Stewart, despite all her televised glory, is actually a throwback to the Victorian era. The specialty of this modern mogul is domestic science—cooking, sewing, decorating, redoing, painting—total control of the home front. Domesticity has paid well for Stewart. She is reputed to own a $1.7 million home in East Hampton, New York, complete with personal staff and entourage that attend to her daily needs. Intentional or not, Stewart has set a standard for American homemakers that is impossible to reach.[1]

These mothers-to-be came of age in the 1970s, when the status of women rose higher than it ever had ever been in this country, but also when age-old myths about women were dying a slow death. Although women were encouraged to develop fully as individuals, to pursue personal goals, to work, to go to school, to examine all of life's options rather than to blindly embark on one, single predetermined path, they didn't always get support from community, family, or friends.

"I always wanted to be something great, but my mother always came up with reasons why I shouldn't try," recalled Sally from New Jersey. "I have a Turkish friend with gorgeous jewelry that her mother gave her 'just in case something happened to her husband.'"

Still, women all over the world were challenging the existing social order and often winning. For the aspiring female, there was certainly no shortage of role models. In 1970, tennis pros Billie Jean King, Rosie Casals, Esme Emanuel, Ceci Martinez, and others boycotted the Italian Open because they found the $600 first-place prize for women insulting. The famous tennis match rewarded male players who placed first with $7,500 in prize money. They refused to play the Pacific Southwest Open in Los Angeles as well, where the ratio between prizes was a whopping ten to one. Gladys Heldman provided the alternative through Virginia Slims, with a tournament in Houston, where the money was about five times as good. The following year, King, then 27, became the first woman athlete to earn more than $100,000 in a year (more than any male tennis player that year).[2]

In 1971, young women were appointed as Senate pages for the first time in U.S. history and the Women's Action Alliance, the first national center on women's issues and programs, was founded in New York City by Gloria Steinem and Brenda Feigen Fasteau. In 1972, the ranks of women delegates to the Democratic National Convention swelled to 40 percent (compared to 13 percent in 1968); women comprised 35 percent of the delegates to the Republican forum. In 1974, the U.S. Passport Office first allowed the use of a woman's "maiden" name, the National Association of Women Business Owners was formed, and Lorene Rogers, the first president of a major university, was appointed to head the University of Texas in Austin. The 1970s were actually chock-full of women emerging as stars on a virtually all-male playing field, a phenomenon that encouraged many women of the time to pursue personal goals of their own.

In 1975, Carla Hills was appointed Secretary of Housing and Urban Development, the third woman ever to serve in the U.S. cabinet. The following year, Barbara Walters signed a multimillion dollar contract with ABC and Dixy Lee Ray, former head of the Atomic Energy Commission, was elected governor of Washington State. The so-called "Decade of Women" also illustrated how solidarity could threaten the status quo or make gains for women in areas where the patriarchy had failed them. Women in Iceland orchestrated a day-long strike in 1976 to show their importance to the economy, virtually shutting down the country. Like women reformers in the nineteenth century, feminists created institutions in response to women's unmet needs and their desire to be free from dependence on male-dominated institutions. Such gains gave women a sense of unity and hope for the future. In 1976, seven Philadelphia women's groups formed a fund-raising coalition, Women's Way, to parallel the United Way, which funded few women's programs at the time.[3] The Girl Scouts devised a new curriculum to acquaint young women with a broad range of life choices. The American Association of University Women, the YWCA, and the League of Women Voters took up feminists issues regarding female identity, rights, and autonomy with vigor.[4]

The images presented by women at the forefront of the women's movement were anything but demure. Those who led were vocal, assertive, and ambitious, rarely hesitating to exert either their power or their will. On March 18, 1970, 200 women occupied the offices of the *Ladies Home Journal* and stayed for eleven hours of sharp debate and negotiation. A journal for women, they argued, should provide day care for its own employees, pay a minimum of $125 a week, hire more minorities, and replace its male editor with an entirely female senior staff.[5] According to author Sara M. Evans, the power of the women's movement lay in its capacity to stimulate deep thinking about, and to pose as a problem, concepts such as femininity and motherhood. In effect, consciousness raising defined the personal issues of daily life, she wrote: "Housework, child rearing, sexuality, etiquette, even language—as political issues susceptible to collective action and solution. Nothing was beyond discussion."[6]

New definitions on acceptable behavior, and acceptable roles, for women flew about during this challenging decade like so much flack, causing much confusion among women about how they should behave. Still, thousands of women got hit by the pieces that commanded individuality and choice. Author Judith Schwartz discusses women who came of age during and after this time: "For many of us in our twenties and thirties today, our personal values mandate having a career. Even if jobs alone don't define us, work is at least an important part of the definition." The career-based identity works well for many women until they become mothers. That's when the real conflict arises. "Our predicament is that what we want for ourselves is by definition, contradictory," writes Schwartz. "We want to devote time both to a career and to our children when we have them."[7]

These truly were confusing times, and the responses of the women in our 1995 study reflect that. "It seems that I have always worked," noted Sarah, a counselor and mother of four from Oshkosh, Wisconsin.

> I started working in high school. It was assumed in my family and my social structure that we would work; that we'd have careers. When I was very young—teens and early twenties— I assumed that my employment wouldn't be very important; that I'd marry someone who would make a lot of money and I wouldn't have to worry about it. But then I realized in my mid-twenties that this was not the case. When I was originally in school, I got a speech degree and that didn't take me anywhere, so I went back to school. I realized I needed to do something that I would enjoy, that would fulfill me, because I needed to.

### ENDURING MOTHERHOOD MYTHS INFLUENCED WOMEN'S CHOICES

Despite modern societal messages that women can and should fulfill themselves through education and careers, long-held images of womanhood persisted in our culture in the 1970s and '80s, influencing how many of the women surveyed viewed themselves and their livelihoods. Women growing up during this time were bombarded by a variety of mixed messages about how they might best live out their lives. One such message was that a woman isn't truly a woman unless she fulfills her potential both as a female and as an individual. The underlying theme of this message—one that was thrown about by religious and political leaders and "experts,"—is that a woman is a female first and must accept all of society's conditions for that status before she can recognize herself as an individual. In other words, society granted conditional approval for women to succeed outside the home as long as they fulfilled their "feminine" obligations first.

I agree with Maxine Harris, author of *Down from the Pedestal*, who believes that America's patriarchy continues to define women on its own terms to preserve their subservient status. It does this by propping them up on an ideological pedestal and presenting a glorified image of woman as man's true superior. But this image, however celebrated, only serves to limit women's options, narrow their self-perceptions, and squeeze the parameters of society's canons of acceptable behavior. As transparent as it might seem today, it's a ruse that's clever enough to have worked for hundreds of years. The fallout is a country filled with women caught in a hollow search for a true identity.

"When one is trapped by an image, overly identified with its prescribed pattern of behavior, one relinquishes choice and self-determination in living one's life,"[8] notes Harris. "Image leaves little room for individual differences. One size fits all often translates into one size fits none."[9] I also concur with, and our study reflects, a conviction held by Dr. Christine Northrup, a physician and author of *Women's Bodies—Women's Wisdom*, that "the patriarchal organization of our society demands that women, its second-class citizens, ignore or turn away from their hopes and dreams in deference to men and the demands of their families."[10] According to Carol Tarvis, who wrote *Every Woman's Emotional Well-Being*, the power of this patriarchy is evident in its continued ability to define women. "What is power?" she asks. "Power is merely the ability to get others to do what you want. The dominant group defines the roles of the less powerful ... activities that the dominant group does not choose to do, like housework."[11]

Despite the strength of the patriarchy, thousands of young women in the 1970s awakened to the call of the women's movement and flocked to colleges and universities in search of identity and direction. Ample opportunities existed for them to find both. Great numbers of them seized it. By 1979, 23 percent of the medical school graduates and 28.5 percent of law graduates were women, compared to 8.4 percent and 5.4 percent, respectively, in 1970. A large number of institutions initiated women's studies programs in response to student demand. According to Sara M. Evans, author of *Born for Liberty: A History of Women in America*, 30,000 courses about women were listed by colleges and universities by 1980.[12] Women, both single and married, were getting and keeping jobs outside the home as well. By 1980, 51.1 percent of all adult women held jobs outside the home, including more than 60 percent of women with children between the ages of 6 and 17, and 45 percent of women with children under age 6. By 1985, 53.4 percent of women with preschool-age children were in the labor force.[13] Yet at the same time that women were beginning to realize their beyond-the-home potential, antifeminists such as Phyllis Schlafly were castigating them for abandoning their feminine natures. It was Schlafly's misguided belief that the social and political advancement of women would lead to the dismantling of family values. Schlafly, and others like her, believed that feminists rejected womanhood—the God-given roles of wife and mother. Paula J. Kaplan, author of *Between Women: Lowering the Barriers*, says that women like Schlafly were threatened not so much by the rhetoric of the feminists as by their insistence on self-examination and awareness, in addition to the fact that they presented women with choices. Kaplan explains,

> We see what is perhaps the fear of choice itself. If [a woman] no longer has privilege and pedestal, then what? The fear of choice is in part the fear of the unknown, which haunts us all. Few of us actually like the people who bring us face to face with our fears. No wonder they fight against feminists.[14]

The comments of Kerry, another Oshkosh mom and the mother of a toddler and a newborn, illustrated how America's cultural battle over women's roles created a certain amount of identity confusion. "When I was working and got out of college, I didn't know what I was going to do. I actually thought I was going to get married, because to me that was just the thing you did. That was part of becoming a mature woman—supporting yourself and being grown up." Such confusion clearly demonstrates how our society's tendency to define the role of women, rather than to allow women to define themselves, puts unnecessary stress on a woman who might otherwise spend her early years doing what a young man would naturally do—try on different roles until he finds one that fits. Instead, the women who grew up in the 1970s were fed a steady diet of choices that weren't actually choices at all. They were simply another set of standards by which they were expected to measure themselves. They were our culture's way of appeasing feminists who sought opportunity above all else.[15]

To their own detriment, modern feminists settled for increased opportunity and achieved precious little else. Focused on achieving equality outside the home, they failed to recognize that equality inside the home must come first. It's a serious omission. Women must address their home-based needs first before they can make great strides in the outside world. Because most women still bear most of the burden of domestic duties, they are forced either to assume too many roles for one person to handle or to choose one over the other, whether they want to or not. The situation as such causes women to adopt an "I'll do the best I can" attitude in an atmosphere that offers them no real assistance or support. In effect, society has granted women permission to be whole as long as they remember that femininity in the traditional sense— becoming a wife and mother, and embracing all that these roles entail—supersedes all else. In her book, *Man's World/Woman's Place*, author Elizabeth Janeway says that society, frightened by woman militants, perpetuated a "self-defeating promotion campaign for Happy-Wife and Motherdom.... The Freudian mythos was invoked to justify a repeated affirmation of the enormous importance of woman's natural role as mother," she writes. "No social activity, women have been told ever since, can be more vital than this nurturing work; and as usual with mythic statements, this applies to all women."[16]

The decision of Kitty, a former dental hygienist and mother of two from Applegate, California, illustrates how this premise influences women's lives:

> I wanted to go to work because I had gotten an offer to work in a dental office. It was not necessarily a filler of time—I just enjoyed working and learning a lot about dental hygiene. But when I had kids, I decided to stay home with them because ... I wasn't torn between my work and my family.

Although Kitty obviously enjoyed working, once she became a mother her "opportunity" to continue in that capacity vanished. A failure to relinquish that part of herself meant that her children would suffer, she concluded. It's a choice that men in our culture are not required to make. By assigning parenting responsibilities primarily to women, society gives men both the permission and the opportunity to have careers and be fathers, too. Consequently, young men are able to envision with ease how they will carve out a place for themselves in the world. This social condition allows them to plan their futures without having to deny or ignore the fact that they might someday become husbands and fathers, or to anticipate that their fathering years will hinder their personal and professional growth.

Weeser, a 30-year-old mother of two from Applegate, grew up among a group of peers that pressured her to develop as a person, but nonetheless acknowledged that marriage would undoubtedly suspend that growth: "There was a circle of people that I grew up around who thought it was not acceptable to get married until you had gotten a degree, had your career, traveled here and there and then done something with your life, and then you could get married," she recalled. "So when I married at 19, I sort of shattered the morals; everyone thought I was crazy." Thirty-eight-year-old Dawn, a mother of four from Downingtown, Pennsylvania, was one of only a few women whose parents coached her to make individual growth a priority, yet the message was still there that a woman would likely have to choose between marriage and career. "I guess it was expected of me … to get married eventually, but never to have only that one choice. My parents expected me to go to college more than they expected me to get married," she said. "So the expectation to get married wasn't there, but it was there to get an education. Get through college; you did that first. Then you figured out what you wanted to do."

Connie, another Downingtown mom and a 34-year-old dietician, was conflicted right from the start, yet heeded her parents advice to get an education as everyone in her family had done. "I knew what was expected," she declared. "My grandparents, parents, everyone was going to college. I'm a fourth generation [graduate] of Penn State. So I was expected to go to college. I more or less assumed I'd marry right after I graduated, but that didn't happen. So I worked, because what else was I going to do?"

It's baffling to me that Connie, with the advantage of her education, would ask such a thing during a time in American history when women were fighting diligently for the right to answer that question themselves, when they were busy straining for recognition, choice, empowerment, and support. "What else was I going to do?" "Why, just about anything you want to do," might well have been the stock answer of the day. Yet, following through with such a sentiment was, as many women found, too difficult a feat to perform.

Kathy, 34, from Charleston, South Carolina, and the mother of a toddler and an infant, recalled her original life plan with some derision. "I worked before I had children to support myself and to use the education that I got in college and practice what I had spent four years learning. I wanted to leave home and be very independent and set up my own apartment and get busy on my own life. I also thought I would continue in a career after I had children and be a mother at the same time," she admitted. "I didn't think I would give up my career."

Judith Schwartz, author of *The Mother Puzzle*, interviewed one woman who sheepishly confessed, "There's a part of me that thinks being a housewife isn't enough, even though, intellectually, I think that should be okay."[17] Barbara, a mother of two from Kailua, Hawaii, rebelled against traditional females roles, even though she felt most comfortable when she embraced them. "I did not have good grades; I was always the social butterfly," she admitted. "My parents wanted me to take a typing class and be a good secretary and marry the boss, because I would be a great wife. I rebelled against that so hard and blew both my parents minds with the career [in broadcasting] that I had. Now that I'm a wife and mother, I feel like I'm in my perfect niche." Although such role confusion causes obvious problems when a woman is developing an identity, it causes even more trouble once she embarks on the path of motherhood—an issue that will be covered at length in Chapter 7.

## *THE BACKLASH AGAINST THE WOMEN'S MOVEMENT GAVE WOMEN MORE REASON TO STAY HOME*

The 1980s became the decade for a cultural counterattack against the women's movement, a phenomenon that author Susan Faludi has glibly dubbed a "backlash." This barrage against emerging new ideals about women served not only to discourage America from embracing modern female images but also to perpetuate old myths about women's rightful place. Powerful messages were again heaved at women, urging them to succumb to the influence of extreme cultural traditionalism. Feminist Andrea Dworkin contends that many women envision their lives in the context of storybook fantasy, where images of women are anything but real. "Women live in and through fairy tales," she maintains. "Our fairy tales tell us about the Wicked Witch, the Beautiful Princess and the Fragile Mother, and indirectly they give us lessons in how we should live our lives."[18] According to author Paula Kaplan, the Cinderella story may be the most familiar example of how society presents us with womanly ideals.

> Cinderella's goodness is highlighted by contrasting her unhappiness, suffering, deprivation and toiling for others with her stepsisters' laziness, self-indulgence and vanity. Cinderella is even pretty in rags, but the implication is that her selflessness and suffering earn her the right to a fairy godmother and to captivating beauty.[19]

The goal of those leading the backlash was to strengthen the influence of myths about womanhood while at the same time discounting, distorting, or destroying new concepts that deemed women either powerful or whole. "The image of the powerful career woman is one that has received a great deal of public scorn, ridicule and fear in recent years," notes Harris. "The career woman, powerful in her own right, often seems demonic."[20]

In her landmark book, *Backlash: The Undeclared War against American Women*, Faludi observes that the 1980s served as a bulletin board for messages that blamed feminism for the problems of women and society—everything from burnout and hair loss, to alcoholism, heart attacks, and infertility. Faludi argues that backlash proponents provide answers to their own rhetorical questions, one of which is "How can American women be in so much trouble at the same time that they are supposed to be so blessed?"[21] The prevailing wisdom of the 1980s supported one primary answer to the riddle, asserted the author, and that is: "It must be all that equality that's causing all that pain. Women are unhappy precisely because they are free. Women are enslaved by their own liberation.... They have pursued their own professional dreams—and lost out on the greatest female adventure."[22] As a staunch observer of social phenomena, Faludi chronicles numerous articles in her presentation of evidence proving the existence of the backlash. She points to an article by law student Mona Charen in the *National Review* entitled "The Feminist Mistake," which stated:

> In dispensing its spoils, women's liberation has given my generation high incomes, our own cigarette, the option of single parenthood, rape crisis centers, personal lines of credit, free love and female gynecologists. In return it has effectively robbed us of one thing upon which the happiness of most women rests—men.[23]

She also highlights a *Los Angeles Times* piece, which stated that baby-boomers have been duped by feminism, and a *Newsweek* article by Kay Ebeling, which labels feminism as "The Great Experiment That Failed," and asserts that "women in my generation, its perpetrators, are the casualties."[24]

In her scrutiny of modern periodicals, Faludi observed that publications from the *New York Times* to *Vanity Fair* have issued a steady stream of indictments against the women's movement. "They hold the campaign for women's equality responsible for nearly every woe besetting women, from mental depression to meager savings accounts, from teenage suicides to eating disorders, to bad complexions,"[25] she declares. Faludi notes that popular psychology hawks the same diagnosis for contemporary female distress. "The authors of the era's self-help classic *Smart Women/Foolish Choices* proclaim that women's distress was an unfortunate consequence of feminism, because 'it created a myth among women that the apex of self-realization could be achieved only through autonomy, independence and career.' "[26]

The propaganda spouted by proponents of the backlash countermovement resonates with the same kind of self-righteousness and bias as late-eighteenth-century medical theorists who argued that development of a woman's brain would atrophy her uterus, and offers just as little evidence to support its outlandish conclusions. Furthermore, it wrongly assumes that feminists, like the early women's rights reformers, wanted to abandon the traditional female pursuits of marriage and motherhood. Nothing could be further from the truth. The majority of women taking part in both movements were married; most had several children. It was simply not to their political, social, or economic advantage to call attention to this fact. According to Faludi, backlash supports have even resorted to victim blaming in the passion to strip women of their beyond-the-home options and rewards:

> The U.S. Attorney General's Commission on Pornography even proposed that women's professional advancement might be responsible for rising rape rates. With more women in college and at work now, the commission members reasoned in their report, women just have more opportunities to be raped.[27]

In her effort to understand why middle-class America is so threatened by feminist accomplishments, the author takes note of the true status of women as illustrated by a variety of studies conducted during and after the 1980s. In *Backlash*, she reports that in a 1990 national poll of chief executives of Fortune 1000 companies, more than 80 percent acknowledged that discrimination impedes the progress of female employees—yet less than 1 percent of these same companies said that remedying sex discrimination was a goal that their personnel department should pursue.[28] Other heavily weighted issues have also faded from the limelight. The availability of many kinds of contraception has declined and new laws restricting abortion—and even information about abortion—for young and poor women have been passed. Women's struggle for equal education is far from over, too, she maintains. In colleges, undergraduate women receive only 70 percent of the aid undergraduate men get in grants and work–study jobs—and women's sports programs receive a "pittance" compared with men's, she says. Women also still shoulder 70 percent of the household duties, according to Faludi, who cites a national poll in which the number of women reporting that their husbands share equally in child care shrank from 40 percent in 1984 to 31 percent in 1987. If women are so free, equal, and advantaged, she asks, then why are the gains that they've made in greater jeopardy today than they were a decade ago? Seen against the backdrop of these statistics, the claims that feminism is responsible for making women miserable is absurd, Faludi concludes. I have to agree. And like Faludi, I believe that the antifeminist backlash has been set off not by women's achievement of full equality but by patriarchy's fear that, given the chance, they just might win it. Just when support for feminism and the Equal Rights Amendment reached a record high in 1981, the amendment was defeated the following year. Just when women were on the brink of achieving protection against sexual assault, federally funded programs were halted. Just when women pulled together their largest number of supporters for the right to abortion, the U.S. Supreme Court opted to reconsider it.[29]

## *THE CHRISTIAN RIGHT WING SENDS MOM HOME*

Despite the fact that the nation's evangelical right wing has habitually been one of the most vocal antifeminist sects, the rhetoric of its chief players has become increasingly subtle—so subtle, in fact, that many well-educated, modern women have begun to consume it with vigor. Early guilt-inducing tactics employed by some religious crusaders—many of whom portrayed feminists as demonic—are no longer used by more socially sensitive religious leaders. To their credit, most of them are genuinely concerned with what they refer to as the "preservation of the family." Yet at the same time, they fail to recognize that the messages they aim at women, and which are meant to be supportive, are as nocuous as ever. As the head of Focus on the Family, a 20-year-old nonprofit organization dedicated to strengthening the home, psychologist and author Dr. James C. Dobson counsels both men and women on a variety of family issues. In the November 1995 issue of that institution's magazine of the same name, Dobson answers questions posed by three women confused over choosing a mothering style. One woman wanted to know if it was "right" for a woman to make it her exclusive career goal to be a wife and mother; another admitted that she wanted both a career and a family and children, and couldn't figure out how to accomplish both. Still another wondered if getting an education was a worthwhile venture at all for a woman who is planning to eventually get married and have children. Dobson, in a clear attempt to provide encouragement, validation, and support on both an emotional and spiritual level, furnished guidance that smacked of single-minded traditionalism and long-standing cultural myths.

"You bet it's all right!" proclaimed Dobson to the first woman.

> Motherhood is an honorable profession that didn't have to be defended for thousands of years. But in the last few decades, young women have been made to feel foolish if they even dared to mention homemaking as a goal.... There is no more important job in the universe than to raise a child to love God, live productively and serve humanity. How ridiculous that a woman should have to apologize for wanting to fulfill that historical role!

Dobson's response to the second woman's dilemma was to encourage her to get her degree, but in the next breath he advised, "If by that time you are married and want to become a full-time mother, you can put your career on hold for a few years or leave it altogether. Remember, you can always return to it after the children are grown," he matter-of-factly declared. To the third woman he admonished, "The purpose for getting a college education is to broaden your world and enrich your intellectual life. Whether or not it leads to a career is not the point."[30]

Although it might appear that the psychologist is taking a modern approach to women's problems concerning motherhood, his responses are reminiscent of the messages aimed at women more than a century ago. His rejoinder that motherhood is a lofty profession worthy of great respect rings with the same resonance as Roosevelt's speech when it was delivered in the early 1900s. The problem is that, today, some 90 years after our nation's twenty-sixth president deified the role, mothers still get less true recognition, validation, and support in our society than any other special interest group. Dobson doesn't acknowledge this fact or recognize its relevance in a woman's decision. Instead, in typical patriarchal, Christian fashion, his counsel strips the women of choice. In essence, he advocates one parenting style—full-time, at-home mothering—not through guilt, but rather by granting women the permission to stay home, along with God's blessing. It's a subtle message indeed. But in terms of providing women support in the truest sense, Dobson is actually a wolf in sheep's clothing—he simply fails to do it. Whereas on the one hand he advises women to complete their education, on the other, he counsels them either to set them aside or forsake them once the children are born. No other parenting options or alternatives are examined. His third admonition—that obtaining a career through education is not the point—is nothing more than a blatant assumption. Is not the point for whom? I wonder how many men the good doctor would offer this same, prejudicial point of view? Although I honor Dobson's intentions to bolster America's families, I challenge his assumption that they can be strengthened only by women's return to the home. That's one way of doing it, but certainly not the only way. Presenting it as a panacea for American families only serves to foster idealism and the notion that there is one perfect way to parent. Many of the 1990s women bought into this notion, nonetheless, and seemed to have a great need to defend it. Some 25 women in our study were members of the national mothers' support group, FEMALE, which, when it was first initiated, stood for "Formerly Employed Mothers at Loose Ends." Interestingly, the group, whose members are all stay-at-home moms, recently changed its name to reflect what one member said was a desired change in image. Today, the acronym stands for "Formerly Employed Mothers at the Leading Edge." To me, the new title indicates that the group had a need to separate from what this same member said was the image of "a bunch of scattered housewives," thus elevating their status to the level of pioneer.

Although the various factions of society touted one type of lifestyle or another for women in the 1980s, many women attempted to combine roles and have it all. The concept of super-woman was spawned out of their brave attempts. It's an image that caused tremendous stress, dissatisfaction, and conflict. Failing to live up to societal standards for either role, many women gave up and finally chose one over the other. I believe that many mothers in our 1995 study made their lifestyle choices by observing these women and by analyzing other directives issued by society about women's right and proper place. I also believe that for many who teetered on the fence, it was the backlash that pushed them to one side—that of career motherhood.

Carrie, 26, a mother of three from Arlington, Texas, and a former fashion merchandising professional, decided to stay at home full time after becoming disillusioned by visits to several day care centers that sported environments that, according to her, were less than ideal.

> I just got really bad feelings ... and I went home and said, "I'm not going to do that—I don't care how lonely and bored and sad and isolated I am—I'm not doing it if I can help it. I mean something might happen. I might have to go to work. I may not be able to be there for five years for each of my children like I would like. But if I can, I will."

A great number of the women interviewed in 1995 reported that they chose to stay home full time so that they could instill their values in their children. All of those who chose career mothering for this reason operated under the assumptions that working women could not live up to this task and that day care providers, however competent, would only undermine their own, more positive, influence. "Even if you have a good caregiver, the bond between child and parent is not there," declared 29-year-old Michele from Palm Beach, Florida. "I feel a need to nurture my children, to share my values and morals with them," echoed Ellen, a former sales executive from Westport, Connecticut. Thirty-five-year-old Kathy from Carol Stream, Illinois, was straightforward about her fears regarding any form of outside help. "I don't want someone else teaching [my kids] values of their own," she admitted. Although our study doesn't reveal its origin, this is a theme that seems to permeate the thinking of these women. More light will be shed on this issue in future discussions about motherhood myths.

One Nebraska mom, Janet, 29, a former elementary school teacher, said that she relinquished her career to stay home every day "because my husband and I feel that raising one's own children is the most important job there is." Therein lies the assumption that if a mother is not with her child every moment, then she is failing at her job. Of course child rearing is an important job. We certainly don't dispute this notion. But to insist on a single approach to any given duty, however significant, is a tenuous undertaking indeed. With most serious endeavors, people typically do just the opposite; they examine all the options. What makes motherhood different?

These are just a few of the issues faced by women who became mothers in the 1990s. They are the ones that speak to the development of identity and the creation of a full, meaningful life. Women in the 1990s who opted to stay home full time with their kids frequently sacrificed both. Many denied this distressing state of affairs in an effort to justify their decision. But they couldn't deny their feelings. Like the women who responded to Jane's provocative 1978 survey, these modern moms embraced many cultural ideals about women. And in order to hold on to them, they had to turn their back on themselves.

# Motherhood Myths Narrow Women's Choices ∽ Old Myths about Motherhood Endure in Modern Society, Influencing the Lives of "Liberated" Women

*M*otherhood myths are so enduring that they have survived throughout the centuries virtually unscathed, intact enough to continue to bear the label of myth but employed by enough people in society, and with enough of an updated twist, to also be considered modern. Like their 1978 counterparts, the women in our 1995 study embraced a great many ideal images about mothers and motherhood that have withstood countless attempts by women throughout the centuries to either dismantle or depose them. The most prevalent of the mother myths is

the Good Mother and all the images that she represents: Perfect Mother, All-Powerful Mother, Natural Mother, and Martyr Mom. Myths about the motherhood role include the following seemingly eternal presumptions: Anything less than a full-time mother will somehow damage the children; all feelings about motherhood must be good; motherhood is instinctive; motherhood is nirvana;

and a "good" mother must sacrifice her life in order to be loved by her children; a mother who has needs outside the mother role is selfish and therefore does not fit into the "Good Mother" persona.

## THE "SUPERMOM" MYTH MAKES MOTHER'S JOB HARDER

The only motherhood myth that emerged somewhere between the 1970s and the 1990s was one reflecting our society's obvious attempt to reconcile the dual roles of working mother while maintaining the patriarchal status quo: Supermom. In the past two decades, women have embraced it with as much fervor as any of the other long-standing ideals. However, most women did so to preserve their status, their livelihood, or their access to choice. The definition of Supermom implies that to have it all, a woman must do it all—work for pay, keep the house, raise the kids, nurture the marriage. Many women—like many men—do want it all. They simply lack the resources and/or the support to hold onto to it once they get it. The Supermom myth suggests, however, that women who fail to meet its standard are somehow deficient. As with most myths, this assumption is a falsehood.

In her own observations, author Judith Schwartz noticed that many working mothers in the 1990s were asking the same question that home-based moms asked a generation before: "Is this all?" "Some decided that enough was enough; the job wasn't worth it. When this happened, it usually reflected the business world's inability to accommodate mothers rather than an individual woman's inability to accommodate a job,"[1] she concluded. Unfortunately, it's the nature of the patriarchy, or any hierarchy, for that matter, to blame its underlings for their inability to succeed. According to Susan Faludi, leaders of the backlash movement embarked on a crusade to do just that. Women who castigate themselves for failing at the Supermom role are simply more evidence of the power of the modern backlash against women. The backlash not only perpetuates old myths, but it also designs and supports new ones and encourages women to contort themselves to fit into the molds. In effect, notes Faludi, "It pursues a divide and conquer strategy: single versus married women, working women versus homemakers, middle versus working class. It manipulates a system of rewards and punishments, elevating women who follow its rules, isolating those who don't."[2] The backlash is most powerful when it goes private, she explains. "When it lodges inside a woman's mind and turns her vision inward, until she imagines the pressure is all in her head, until she begins to enforce the backlash, too—on herself."[3]

The women in our 1995 study, all of whom are stay-at-home moms, rejected the notion of Supermom with one hand and embraced it with the other. They rejected the concept when its definition portrayed a mother as working outside the home. They embraced it when it identified Supermom as a woman who embodied all the attributes of the Good Mother ideal—perfectionism, selfless altruism, sacrifice, martyrdom and the like, with the added dimension of industry *à la* Martha Stewart. As one Charleston mother stated when reflecting on why she continued to feel guilty despite her full-time devotion to her family, "For some reason I believe that I should be outside building tents with [the kids] or something. I don't know where [this image] comes from. It comes from everywhere, from society. You read about it in parenting magazines. You see it on TV." Denise, from Texas, feels the burden of the Supermom ideal as well: "There's this myth that your children have to be able to recite the alphabet by the time they're two, and they have to be able to read by the time they're 4," she said. "They have to have a working knowledge of physics and chemistry by the time they're 6, you know. You do sort of feel that kind of pressure to give your children everything they can possibly absorb." The image that these women endorse is the same one that's kept America sweetheart Martha Stewart, amid all her domestic bliss, on the front covers of the nation's most popular magazines and in our living rooms and kitchens at breakfast time for the past decade or so—the image of the modern-era Supermom.

Hollywood has also done its part at buttressing the modern Supermom myth. In the 1987 movie *Baby Boom*, Diane Keaton plays an overachieving, highly educated advertising executive who inherits the parental rights to a baby girl. Overcome by maternal instincts, and heeding the call of her loudly ticking biological clock, she kisses her six-figure income good-bye and moves to rural Vermont. A few months later, when her itch for the fast lane returns, she simply launches a line of homemade baby foods which, of course, becomes an overnight success. In the meantime, she's found the perfect partner—a sensitive, kind, intelligent, sexy country gentleman—played by Sam Shepard, and falls madly in love. She manages to juggle all her roles, pulling all of them off without a hitch. The message of the movie is clear—if a woman is clever enough, resourceful enough, and puts her priorities in the right order, none of the real conflicts of motherhood will affect her. The theme of this film implies that women don't need support from the corporate world to succeed as working mothers, because they can, if they work hard enough at it, transcend them. The experience of real-life women is that this notion is pure baloney. According to Dr. Maisa Hamilton-Bennett, founder and CEO of the Hamilton Life Institute, role overload is the primary burden of working mothers today.

> Most of the working moms I know juggle too many responsibilities. Despite women's lib, the household is still primarily a woman's domain. Even with nice sweet husbands who help out, women who come to me for therapy are depressed, overwhelmed, anxious and can't keep up. They feel like failures because it's impossible to successfully discharge all the responsibilities in one day.

The psychologist claims that one of the reasons women have so much trouble coping is that the image of Supermom prevents them from setting priorities. She's not certain whom these women are trying to impress, themselves or someone else. "I'm not sure who is setting the standards but I think [the pressure] is more internal than external." Like Schwartz, the therapist has observed a mass exodus of working mothers from the workforce. "Lots of them are saying, 'We don't want it all,' or 'It's not worth it,'" For the woman who truly thrives in her profession, the loss can be devastating.

Mary Hantske, RN, BSN, IBCLC, and cofounder of Family Affairs Inc. (a maternity home-care agency), believes that corporate America has a long way to go in its support of working mothers. Because she witnesses firsthand the problems that working mothers face, Hantske knows where the real deficiencies in our system lie. "Even though companies have family-friendly policies in place, the attitudes of the colleagues and principals speak louder," she says. "The policies are there but I don't think the support is there. Women who come back to work and want a flexible schedule, or who want to readjust, are expected to have the same schedule and to produce results the same as before. It's sad; we don't support our working moms." Although the Family and Medical Leave Act, which was signed into law by President Clinton in 1993, guarantees women in companies of fifty or more employees an unpaid pregnancy or adoption leave of up to twelve weeks, and holds their jobs for their return, many working mothers report underlying tensions at the office. According to a 1991 survey by the Families and Work Institute, only 16 percent said their supervisor was supportive when they needed to take care of family matters, and only 7 percent said their co-workers were supportive. More than half felt they had to choose between advancing their careers and devoting attention to their families.[4] Some experts contend that there are built-in biases about mothers or mothers-to-be who work. Jane Halpert, Ph.D., director of the industrial psychology program at DePaul University in Chicago, set out to prove the theory. Halpert videotaped a woman performing certain job functions when she was nine months' pregnant, then doing the same tasks the same way five months after giving birth. The psychologist asked viewers to evaluate her performance in both cases. The pregnant worker rated more negative comments from male and female viewers. According to Halpert, disapproving viewers felt the pregnant woman was too emotional, distracted, or just didn't belong in an office.[5]

Keeping a job is harder for working moms, too. Today's slower economy has provided legal cover to some employers, who can terminate pregnant workers without breaking the law. That's because the Pregnancy Discrimination Act of 1978 has a gaping loophole—if a company is reorganizing, pregnant women or new mothers can be legally dropped from the payroll.[6] In their

1993 book, *Women and the Work/Family Dilemma: How Today's Professional Women Are Finding Solutions*, authors Debra Swiss, Ed.D., and Judith P. Walker report on their survey of 902 female, Harvard-educated doctors and MBAs.[7] Instead of success strategies, they heard angry stories about a hostile and inflexible work environment. In a nutshell, America's corporate and social culture glorifies the Supermom ideal, while simultaneously sabotaging the efforts of the women who try to attain it. Employers would be much better off, maintains Swiss, if they abandoned mother myths and faced economic reality: Accommodating working mothers is more efficient and cost-effective than constantly searching for and training new talent.[8]

Whether you're a mother who works outside the home or strictly within it, the Supermom myth can strangle you in its grip. Judy, from Arlington, Texas, felt guilty about relaxing with a magazine because, in her view, today's modern Supermom myth doesn't grant her permission to do so. "A lot of people impose that on you, saying, 'Your kids have to be doing this, this, and that, and you are the mom so you have to be doing this, this, and that.' Nobody says, 'Sit down and watch your favorite TV show once a week or make sure you read that whole book.'" This same mother admitted that she often feels just as much pressure to perform from her friends.

> I think they're just trying to help, but they don't really know my work load or anything. They say, "You should sign him up for soccer, he should be doing this." Or, "You mean you don't have him in swimming lessons already?" And those type of things. And then, if you watch any TV shows, like "Oprah," they make you feel like you should be doing more for your kids.

## ARCHAIC MOTHERHOOD MYTHS PROMPT WOMEN TO SACRIFICE

Although Supermom is, indeed, a new and powerful myth, the one mothering myth that has dominated all others in our country from the 1950s until now is that good mothers stay home full time with their children. Despite the fact that this supposition has never been scientifically proved or disproved, countless numbers of women and men still subscribe to it,whether they apply it to their own lives or not. As our study, and many others, clearly indicate, women who work outside the home often feel guilty about not fulfilling their role according to this ideal, whereas women who stay at home sacrifice a great deal to embody it. The results of our 1995 study indicate that husbands are playing more of a role than ever in the decision over whether mom will stay home with the kids. In 1978, 28 percent of the respondents reported that the decision was a shared one; 71 percent said the decision to stay home was theirs alone. In 1995, only 48 percent of the mothers reported that they made the choice unilaterally; 38 percent indicated that they had their husbands' input. *The chief similarity between the two studies, and the most relevant finding in relation to The Mother Crisis, was that only 22 percent of the mothers in 1978, and 19 percent in 1995, decided to stay home because they wanted to.* The majority of women in both studies said that they made the choice either out of principle or because they thought it was best for the children (see Appendix). The main difference between the two reports is that more of the 1990s moms stayed home out of fear. Many of them stated that they didn't want "someone else" raising their kids. When we examined the responses to this question in detail, it quickly became clear that mothers of the 1990s espoused the "Good mothers stay home," convention with the same amount of certitude as their 1978 predecessors. Interestingly, the women of the 1990s were no more likely than the 1970s moms to consider delegating the role of full-time parent to their husbands.

Michelle, a mother of five and a former teacher from West Palm Beach, Florida, said that she's staying home with her kids because "Nothing can replace the nurturance of a mother. Even if you have a good, competent caregiver, the bond between child and parent is not there." Another West Palm Beach mom, Tina, declared, "My husband and I agree that children do better emotionally and mentally when they grow up with the security and commitment of a full-time parent." Tina, a 37-year-old mother of two, didn't mention whether she and her husband ever considered him as an applicant for the job.

Julie, a 36-year-old mother of three, also from Arlington, Texas, said that she and her husband "both feel very strongly that it's a responsibility and privilege that goes along with having children." But Julie didn't say whether her husband felt an equal responsibility for putting in his time as a full-time parent, or whether he felt like less of parent because he would not be home full time. It seems that, even today, "good fathers" can be away from home as much as they need or want to be. Simi Valley resident Vanna, 36, who majored in child development in college, had an emotional response to the question, stating, "My mother always worked full time; she was never there. I always felt that children should come first, and to me that means staying home with them." And Debbie, from La Brea, California, and a 37-year-old mother of three, was adamant in her conviction that the children were her sole responsibility. "Since 'I' decided to have children," she wrote, "then 'I' should be the one raising them. I feel very strongly about always being there for them." The responses are a clear indication that these women expected the bulk of the parenting responsibilities to land, and in their opinion, rightly so, in the mother's domain.

Although many theorists argue that the idea of continuous and exclusive mothering arose from a Freudian mentality, there is historical evidence that indicates it actually had a much earlier start. According to French author Elisabeth Badinter in *Mother Love: Myth and Reality*, there was a turnaround in the maternal role in the eighteenth century from that of subordinate parent to that of chief maternal and domestic engineer. Mother emerged as the emotional and spiritual anchor of the family, thus assuming an elevated status. The development of a universal maternal persona that occurred in France, and that cut across class lines, was later confirmed by Freudian theory, resulting in mixed consequences for women, she maintains. On the one hand, it allowed women a certain level of respect and enabled them to find fulfillment and pleasure in their role as mothers. On the other hand, so strong was the pressure to be a certain kind of woman that those who didn't fit the mold were made to feel there was something wrong with them.[9] This shift in the definition of a mother's role had a major effect on the family, she says. "The considerable growth of the mother's responsibilities during the nineteenth century gradually obscured the image of the father," she writes. "His importance and his authority, so great in the seventeenth century, entered a period of decline, for, by taking the leading role in the home, the mother had greatly encroached on his functions."[10] Not that men seemed to mind. Badinter is astute in her observation that men seemed to have no objections over women's usurping of power on domestic terrain. "In all fairness it must be admitted that the man was stripped of his fatherhood," she acknowledge. "All the evidence would indicate, however, that this privation in a society run by men was greeted with more than a little complacency on their part; they seem to have been willing victims."[11]

Despite two centuries of myth building, leading up to a solidified cultural ideal, the jury is still out over whether motherhood is really the first and instinctive concern of women. History has shown us that when women are freed from economic constraints and have personal ambitions, they do not always choose to give up their interests, even for several years, for the good of the child.[12] Plus, our own research has shown us that when women reject their personal interests to pursue the Good Mother ideal, they frequently suffer a great deal. Given these real-life observations, it's astonishing that so many of the motherhood myths manage to survive at all. But survive they do. Society provides ample reinforcement for them, particularly the one that demands that a good mother must stay home. Women, for a variety of reasons, perpetuate it among themselves. Women who responded to the survey in the 1970s embraced the "Good mothers stay home" myth but didn't seem inclined to justify their decision. Many of them simply said, "I stay home because it's my job," and that was that. But the 1990s moms gave clear-cut reasons for their actions, indicating that there was a lot more speculation about the choice and, consequently, a much greater need to defend it.

*MOTHERHOOD MYTHS PROVOKE WOMEN TO COMPETE WITH EACH OTHER AND THEMSELVES*

According to author and women's rights activist Elizabeth Janeway, cultural myths actually serve society quite well, regardless of their deficiencies. She declares,

> It is the nature of myth to be both true and false. False, in fact, but true to human yearnings and human fears and, thus, at all times, a powerful shaping force. Myth is born out of psychological drives. What we do not have, that is what we need; and that is what we present to ourselves as desirable and, finally, as "right."[13]

It seems probable to me, given the responses we received from mothers from coast to coast, that what Janeway says is true. "Myth has its own furious, inherent reason to be because it's tied to desire. Prove it false a hundred times and it will still endure because it is true as an expression of feeling."[14]

In interview after interview with groups of women from Florida to Hawaii and beyond, Jane and I marveled at the tenacity of motherhood myths and the dynamics that sustained them, and noticed, as Janeway did, that

> myths endure because they offer hope, because they justify resentments, but perhaps, most of all, because they provide a bond of common feeling.... They gain strength from the connection that they supply to their believers, the shared desires, the joint wishful thinking that backs up one person's fantasies with another's, with those of a like-minded group.[15]

The author's theory might explain precisely why stay-at-home moms in the 1990s responded so defensively to questions regarding their choice of lifestyle and why they regard women who don't embrace the same myths as they with a salient amount of suspicion and distrust. This phenomenon is explored further in the Chapter 8 discussion about the current discord between working and at-home mothers.

A hint of what lies ahead in this discussion can be heard in a statement made by Colleen, a 33-year-old former teacher and mother of two from Kearney, Nebraska, about the children of a two-working-parent household: "I saw firsthand some of the consequences of noninvolved parents," she proclaimed. "I will always have time to pursue my personal dreams. I will not always have the chance to actively parent." Monument, Colorado, mom Karen, chimed in, adding, "Children need someone at home for a sounding board, and they need a schedule," as if working parents can't provide either. It was fascinating to me to learn that the majority of the mothers in our 1995 study believed that stay-at-home parenting is the only way to instill values in their children and that any form of day care undermines this important undertaking. Many were fearful that day care would somehow damage their children, scarring them for life, either emotionally or psychologically. They believed that mothers who worked were somehow less invested in their children's welfare or overall well-being.

"I do not want my children in a day care, raised by strangers," declared 31-year-old Lori, from Florida. "I did not have children to let someone else raise them. A child needs to develop family security."

"We feel that we want our children raised by us, not by other people. That way they will learn our morals," echoed Julie, a 36-year-old former elementary school teacher from Nebraska. Thirty-three-year-old South Carolina mom Christi matter-of-factly stated, "I want to give them a secure home life," as did Illinois mom, Kathy, who said, "I feel it's important to give them a feeling of security and a firm foundation in life; I don't want someone else teaching [them] values of their own." Thirty-five-year-old Margaret, a former journalist from Minnesota, voiced the same sentiment: "It's important to guide children in their earliest formative years—to instill values and so forth." And so did Ellen, from Westport, Connecticut, who said, "I feel a need to nurture my children, to share my values and morals with them. By being here, I am also able to identify their strengths and weaknesses and channel their talents." The not-so-hidden assumption in these women's responses indicates that they consider a household comprised of two working parents as unsuitable for child rearing, that it, somehow, can't offer as much stability, nurturing, guidance, or love.

"We believe that it's important for children to have a stable and loving home. This includes a mom that stays home," said Lorraine, a 29-year-old mother of two with a master's degree in finance from West Palm Beach, Florida. Kitty, 32, from Isle of Palms, South Carolina, hinted at the same presumption: "My husband and I feel we should be our children's primary caregivers so that we can mold their morals and give them stability." Tina, from West Palm Beach, Florida, broadened the assumption even further in her statement: "Children do better emotionally and mentally when they grow up with the security and commitment of a full-time parent." However common, these are remarkable assumptions, given the lack of available supporting evidence. Still, such convictions provide wonderful fodder for our country's media mill. In 1980, researcher Clair Etaugh documented a predominantly disapproving attitude toward working mothers in the popular press, the main themes being neglect of the children, neglect of the husband, and neglect of homemaking. "Unless a mother has to work to keep the family from starvation, many people are suspicious of her motives,"[16] she said. Such convictions provide the building blocks for a wide range of auxiliary myths about what is and what is not "good" mothering.

If she could have her way, Ann Weinstein, director of the Parents Place, a San Francisco–based resource center for parents, would abolish the image of the Good Mother completely. "We need to get rid of the whole concept of 'good' because the opposite is 'bad,' " she declares.

> Motherhood is one of many roles women have in a lifetime. Their task is actually the job of helping their children develop from a totally dependent infant to an independent adult. They do this by providing a loving, caring environment with age-appropriate challenges and rewards, realizing that they are but one—a very powerful one—of the influences that will shape their child.

According to Weinstein, responsible mothering is concerned not only with the child but also with the world that child will grow up in. In her service to parents, the director has discovered, as have we, that the myth of the Good Mother leads to other extremely powerful subsidiary ideals—two of which are "All-Powerful Mom," and "Perfect Mom." Mothers who subscribe to the belief that they are solely responsible for their child's outcome set themselves up for a lifetime of conflict and stress, she maintains. "When a parent thinks she is totally and completely responsible for a child, she can't hear the good things about that child," Weinstein explains. "The only thing that pops out, in an evaluation, for example, is the negative. If a person is totally focused on perfection, she doesn't hear the good things. She then becomes the critical parent. The sad part about this type of thinking," adds the director, "is that the person fails to appreciate the many stages of childhood. She sees each stage only as preparation for the next one." The images of Perfect Mom and All-Powerful Mom had just as much impact on the lives of the mothers in our 1995 study as they did on the lives of the 1978 participants and, in some ways— due to the added dimension of the Supermom myth—more. Twenty-seven-year-old Ann, a mother of three, admitted that she always feels as if someone is watching her, keeping score. "You know, you always have to have everything," she explains.

> If you don't have baby wipes, the other moms say, "I'll loan you one." But they look at you funny, like, "You can't even remember to get baby wipes?" I mean, I feel like I have to do everything right all the time, that someone is watching—or the kids are watching. So I can't cry if I'm having a bad day, because I don't want to set a bad example for my children. So it is a little frustrating.

Carrie, from Wisconsin, says the Supermom myth puts additional pressure on at-home moms because of heightened expectations. "If you're staying home and you're not perfect, people think, 'What's wrong with you?'" Because they juggle a variety of roles, women who work have an out, she contends:

> You're working and you're doing PTA and into everything that you can possibly get your hands into, then everyone's going to respect you so much more because you're Supermom and you're doing it all. They say, "So what if she's not doing such a great job in this area; look at everything else she's doing." Whereas, if you're a stay-at-home mom and

you're not doing the perfect job they say, "What's wrong with
you; that's all you have to do."

Although Delores, from Dallas, Texas, doesn't subscribe to
this ideal, her husband does, and she feels the pressure of his
demands. "If I took the kids to their friends to play or we did
something, in my mind that was a successful day. But I will never
convince my husband that this is the success of the day. His idea of
success is that he comes home to a clean house and supper ready
on the table, and nobody is fighting and everything is calm."

The problem, says director Weinstein, is that "there's too
much emphasis on the idea that there's only one acceptable model
of child and one acceptable model of mom when, in fact, there are
99 million. There's lots of fantasy involved. We live in a society of
advertising," she explains. "We live in a society where there are
bites of knowledge, where you only get the first line—the sexy
one. Everybody thinks they're going to get the Gerber Baby. The
pictures are unrealistic, partially because there are no more extended families, no real models of moms raising kids." Judy, a
mother of three from Nebraska, experienced tremendous anxiety
over her efforts to execute the "proper" parenting techniques.
"I'm sad my big one is going to kindergarten, yet I'm glad he's
going because I'll have time with my second one to try to correct
or change the way I'm dealing with him," she explained. "I can
take the time and spend the time to do it the right way." Debra,
also from Nebraska, felt the wrath of the Perfect/All-Powerful
Mother myth all wrapped up in the same bailiwick. And she was
irate about it. She declared,

> I didn't ask for this responsibility. I'm a human being, you
> know. Why should it be my responsibility to be ... whatever it
> is, because this kid is going to watch me and imitate me. It
> really makes me angry, because I feel like I can't be who I
> want to be at times. I have to be somebody else, because I
> have this huge responsibility to this child.

The myth of All-Powerful Mom not only demands perfection
from a woman but implies that mother is ostensibly omnipotent.
An incredible number of educated women buy into this theory,

despite what might logically appear to be an obvious lack of credibility. In a discussion about the guilt mothers feel while raising their children, Brenda, mother of two boys from Charleston, South Carolina, declared, "You're molding these people; you're trying to form this person. And you have the power to make or break them." Tanya, from Colorado Springs, blames herself for any form of undesirable behavior exhibited by her preschool-age son.

> I was telling my friend that my son has grown horns and sprouted a forked tail. I'll say something and he'll say, "No, it's not!" He's just arguing with me; so it's a weird stage. But we were talking about it and she said, "What do you think it is?" And I said, "Well, I think it's because I don't spend enough quality time with him. You know, I'm not reading books as much as I should be." I feel like, I'm home so, my God, I'd better be the best mommy in the world.... I feel like if we have a lousy day, it's my fault. It's really hard for me because I feel like I have to be everything to them and wonderful for them.

Candy, a mother of two, feels the same. "I am responsible for my child's every movement, at least in my mind. So when he does something wrong it is my fault." Deadra, from Maryland, reported that she always feels inadequate:

> around the dentist, the doctor, the school system, the church. I mean, I just sucked it all up, that somehow they knew more. If I wasn't, say, having my child floss his teeth, then I was failing, because the dentist says that your kids should floss their teeth. If I wasn't doing that religiously or making sure they did it, I wasn't good enough. I bought into everybody's rules and expectations.

Badinter explains Candy and Deadra's responses: "From responsibility to guilt there is only one step, quickly passed over when the child has the slightest problem. Henceforth, it would be the mother who would be called to account for any and all deviations from the ideal."[17] Or as writer Schwartz so eloquently states, "The monolithic ideal of the perfect mother wrongs all mothers in that it denies their lack of power and resources in society and leaves them feeling guilty about their mother behavior.... Women [have] become bound to their children by the enormity of their capacity to ruin them."[18]

Although the need to perform perfectly in the mother role might be one outcrop of the image of All-Powerful Mom, so is the illusion of control. Women who feel obligated or destined to mold perfect people out of their kids—and who sincerely believe that their influence will make the most difference in their children's lives—oftentimes expect specific results for their efforts. Noted Stacy, 32, from California, "I thought I was going to have nothing but girls. Well, okay, this is my opportunity to change a man and to raise him to be somebody who's going to respect women and to be a good person." California mom, Robin, who is a mother of two, feels responsible for her children's afterlife as well as their earthbound existence:

> I feel like I will have done my job if, somehow, I can know my children love God and eventually go to heaven. I think that is the reason I have children and God has blessed me with children. That's what I owe these children—the chance to grow up to be good people. Kind of like a confirmation thing that people talk about in groups with people who have children seriously sick. You've done your job; you've gotten them to heaven.

Were Robin to bump into the likes of author Sandra Scarr, she might have to seriously reevaluate her role.

"Specifically, I see children as biologically sturdy individuals whose development is guided by the interplay of biology and experience and who can thrive in a wide variety of life situations," avows Scarr. "Therefore, parents play a crucial, but not exclusive role in their children's development."[19] Scarr believes, as I do, that the myth that mandates exclusive and continuous care from mom springs from modern psychological findings, the majority of which are inconclusive. "Closely linked to the politics of what women ought to be is the psychology of what children are supposed to need,"[20] she explains. "Babies thrive with good day care, just as they do at home with an attentive mother. In fact, children are usually better off with a satisfied substitute caretaker and a happy part-time mother than with an angry, frustrated full-time mother."[21]

Peel away the layers of the Good Mother ideal and at its core you'll find the hidden message that real motherhood means sacrifice. Most of the women in Jane's 1978 study accepted this theory without question when deciding to become full-time mothers. But they slipped into The Mother Crisis when they couldn't find happiness amid the day-to-day shortcomings of the job. In 1995, women were more introspective and intellectual about choosing parenting as a career. Most made a conscious decision to sacrifice a livelihood with the expectation that, because their children would benefit, so, vicariously, would they. In other words, they believed that, since a Good Mother receives all her fulfillment through her children, any sacrifice endured would be worth it in the end. It's my contention that the women in the 1995 study who experienced some conflict and denied it, did so mainly because they felt the need to defend such a seemingly well-thought-out decision. To identify it as a mistake was simply too humbling an experience.

## NO INDIVIDUALITY FOR THE "GOOD MOTHER"

Many of the previously discussed myths about motherhood are about what a mother should do for her children. A variety of other images supporting the Good Mother ideal are about what a woman should be for her children. Because they speak to the very essence of who a woman is, these concepts cause much discontent for women bordering on The Mother Crisis. Such images allegedly define the ingredients of a Good Mother's character. The most tyrannical of them are passive mother, selfless mother, and "feminine" or nonassertive mother. Some people like to refer to this image as Martyr Mom. A woman who, on some level, believes that she must demonstrate these traits to be successful, and then cannot, will face a crisis of identity somewhere along the line. Notes author Schwartz, "The common depiction of motherhood that we recognize as the ideal is grounded in three basic myths— the idea of maternal self-sacrifice, the belief in an innate, unvarying maternal instinct, and the notion of maternal fulfillment."[22] According to Schwartz, such an ideology about motherhood has established a polarity in which having or not having children reveals certain qualities in a woman: nurturance as opposed to self-interest, maturity as opposed to immaturity, fulfillment as opposed to unfulfillment.[23] Upholding the standard definition of *mother*, she says, is society's way of absolving the culture from having to take any measures to enhance women's lives. One of the more subversive ways our culture perpetuates its mother myths is through its continued promotion of fairy tales in which women are rewarded for passive, subservient behavior. According to author Paula J. Kaplan, the story of Snow White and the Seven Dwarfs is about this role.

> To become ripe and ready for marriage, Snow White must take care of seven little men. The fact that they are both little and male prepares her to nurture both children and husband. She does this, like most Western housewives, alone and isolated. Not only is she encouraged to perform these nurturing housekeeping services in return for a roof over her head but, indeed, it is her major activity in the story.[24]

Kaplan also points out that Snow White doesn't have to do anything but lie passively and look beautiful in order to eventually snare a man, her prince. Women who repeatedly try to live up to the Martyr Mother image find out quickly how elusive it is. Yet, they keep up the chase, because they are convinced that it is not only attainable but necessary. "My kids didn't ask to be born," said Maryland resident Helen, who was born and reared in England. "We really, really wanted kids and [sacrifice] is what you do for your kids. You know, your kids come first in all situations, at least while they're at this age. And I don't think there's any way to negotiate that. I mean, my children, their safety and their well-being, and their needs come first always." Carrie, a musician and mother of three, also from Maryland, steadfastly agreed. "If you're going to have children, then you have to commit to making their lives good, giving them a good life. And some of that ultimately means you have to sacrifice your own wants. I don't think you sacrifice your needs," she said, "because you are going to get what you need no matter what."

Tina, a 36-year-old mother of two from Pennsylvania, never

wanted to have children, but once she finally did, she was so consumed by motherhood that it wasn't long before only a shadow of her former self remained. And she insisted that the transformation was by choice. "I never wanted to have kids, and when I got married I still didn't know if I wanted to," she admitted.

> But my kids have opened up emotions in me that I never knew were possible; they have slowed down my life happily. I stayed home with my kids, I think, because I thought so much about it before having them—about that aspect of myself, about what I was going to have to give up and do. The part I wasn't ready for was how consuming it would be emotionally. You do die to yourself; I don't care what anyone says. You are not first anymore. I hate to say it, but that's how it should be.

Marcy's beliefs about what a mother should be caused her to feel guilty about working. "It was a real pull when I was working part-time," noted this 40-year-old Nebraska mother of three. "I wanted to be home more and I couldn't, and I was only working three days a week, with two full days home, but still I wanted to be home. I felt that was the mother's role, that is where my children needed me." Despite her own yearning to represent the ideal, Jennifer, a mother of two from South Carolina, was paralyzed by the requirement that good mothers must sacrifice either their wants or their needs. "I want so badly for my kids to turn out [*sic*], and I want so badly to be there for them and do all the right things—that's what keeps me from going out of the house sometimes, because I want to be there for them all the time," she said. "I want to teach them and train them, and I want them to succeed so badly that I feel like I have to give them everything I have to help them along. And that keeps me home more than I should be."

Some women like to think they've abandoned the notion of sacrificial mother but put the myth into action in their own lives nonetheless. "I don't think any woman should think that anytime they say 'yes' to themselves that they're saying 'no' to being a mother," declared Jennifer.

> But I know that I act that way a lot, even though I don't believe it. This past year, I've sometimes felt trapped. But the

past few months I've been trying to do things just for me.... It seems like such big thing to get a baby-sitter—it makes it seem like I'm saying "no" to being a mother. It seems selfish to me that I want to turn my kids over to someone else while I do something, even though I know in my head that I need that.

Judy, from Kearney, Nebraska, had never planned to stay home with her kids. Consequently, when she embarked on the job full time, she imagined herself neatly ensconced in the myth of motherhood as nirvana from which she would derive total fulfillment and perform unerringly in her tasks. "It was a big problem for me," she admitted, with a wry grin. "Since I had never planned to stay home, my fantasy was very 1950s TV. I really thought I was going to start wearing shirtwaist dresses and aprons and that I was going to be able to manage everything very well. I had no concept of what it was like to be home with the kids." Florida mom Kami said that TV influenced how she rated her performance as a mother. "On TV the message is really happy or off the wall," she said. "It seems like the Cosbys never screamed at each other, never threw things, never slammed doors. And the Brady Bunch—it's not like real life, but it makes me feel guilty."

Marian, 36, a former legal secretary from Pennsylvania, chose career motherhood because she had been raised by a mother who worked. "My mother wasn't there to do things with me, to do what I do with my children anyway.... I had a grandmother who really was not interested in playing, so I was on my own," she explained. "A good and perfect mother is someone who stays at home and has no life outside of her children and does everything for the children and everything for the benefit of the child," she said. "I think that society views it as selfish if you take care of yourself and put your needs in front of your children. For example, you're viewed as selfish if you get a sitter to go have your nails done once a week or [people will] ask how long are you going to be at the beauty shop for a perm and a cut, this type of thing. I think [this image] is pretty real." Arlington Texas mom Darla believes that at-home mothering is a role prescribed by God. "I feel like God wants me to have my children. I feel like God wants us to do that, that's the job He set before us when we had children. And, I mean, there are certain things that, you know, He expects out of you as a mother." Another Texas mom, Jan, 37, felt the wrath of the Perfect Mother myth when she had two cesarean sections and couldn't nurse one of her babies. The disappointment over not experiencing the picture-perfect birth and delivery was never resolved; consequently, she loosed the full fury over those feelings onto herself. "Oh, it was horrible when I couldn't nurse her," she exclaimed. "It was terrible; I just didn't understand it. Not having a vaginal delivery hurt my self-esteem. I still to this day feel like I haven't really had a baby." Jan's experience bears out Janeway's assertion: "Myth exists in a state of tension. It is not really describing a situation, but trying by means of this description to bring about what it declares to exist."[25]

The idea that all women contain the same innate maternal instinct that moves them to think, feel, and act in certain predetermined ways—I call this image Natural Mother—erodes the self-esteem of more women than perhaps any other myth. A great many women internalize this ideal. Notes Marcy, 32, a former teacher from Maryland, "When I'm feeling guilty, I'm comparing myself with other people and feeling inadequate. I have these expectations of myself that I'm always going to be a calm, loving mother that knows all the answers, and I fall short of my expectations and feel guilty. I feel inside that I'm not as good a mother as I could be. I thought that I could be more loving and all these other things."

"It was a very difficult thing for me to accept that I could scream at this wonderful little child," acknowledged Callie, a mother of two from Colorado. "I thought I would be more in control to handle it. It's hard to admit that you don't have complete control of yourself all the time to be this perfect mother with a quiet little voice."

Marcy feels guilty anytime she outwardly shows her anger toward her children and purports that her husband's attitude only aggravates the feeling.

"Why do you even want to be home with them; you're always angry," he'll ask me. But, really, I don't think I give
myself enough credit for all those times I am calm and answer
right with them. But then there are those times when they
annoy you and they annoy you, and it gets to a volcano and
suddenly it bursts, and that seems to always be when he's
home, and so he thinks that I'm always angry.

Another Texas mom, Beverly, admitted feeling disappointed with
herself, too. "I didn't have as much patience as I thought I would
have," she said. "When, suddenly, I had my dream and I could be
home full time, I was going to be this wonderful loving mother,
and I think I felt like ... but I was so lonely, and so I was sharper
with my kids."

According to Janeway, such feelings of disappointment experienced by women and their spouses are not surprising at all,
considering the incredible potency of the Natural Mother myth.

New mothers are expected to act by instinct; this expectation
in itself sets them apart from the rest of society, where people
assume that they will be taught the basic rules of the jobs they
have to do. The expectation that they will be able to act by
instinct sets women apart, also by suggesting that they operate on a more primitive level than is normal for the rest of the
world.[26]

The idea that motherhood is a sacred calling and, therefore, totally
fulfilling, is founded in the Natural Mother myth. Debra, from
Wisconsin, revealed that her Catholic upbringing taught her that
motherhood was the best thing that any woman could strive for. "I
grew up thinking that being a mother was the highest calling I
could have. I can't really think of anything that I could do that
would be more important to the world. So I really think that doing
for my children is doing for the world, too."

After months of exhaustive examination of our 1978 data, and
as our interviews with the 1990's women came to a close, Jane and
I came to realize from a personal standpoint what other authors
have only been able to surmise—that many women cling to idealized images out of fear, and that women who subscribe to society's
belief system become empowered. Notes writer Maxine Harris in

her book *Down from the Pedestal*: "As a mother, a woman can feel powerful in two ways—first she can feel a sense of accomplishment in having raised her children … she may even feel a sense of awe over having helped to 'create' another individual."[27] The attainment of power through role assumption—and the validation and recognition that comes with it—is nonetheless a tenuous undertaking, as many women who experience The Mother Crisis have come to understand. "Why do women find themselves trapped by images?," poses Harris. "A desire to be loved, connected and approved; a fear of what lies ahead and of one's ability to craft creative solutions. A desire for power and responsibility."[28] As theorists of The Mother Crisis, we venture to ask, "At what cost?" We'll let the mothers themselves provide the answers to this essential question.

## CHAPTER 7

# The Mother Crisis Revisited ∝ Mothers of
## the Nineties Drown in Waves of Anger and Denial

*T*oday's mothers are angry. It's a phenomenon that hasn't yet made the talk show circuit or even the "Lifestyle" pages of your daily newspaper. Yet this multidimensional social problem is so widespread that I am tempted to dub it universal. I'm not talking about your garden-variety anger, the kind that noisily erupts over a bad-hair day, a glass of spilled juice, or coming home to find out that someone ate the last Dove Bar and didn't bother telling anybody. I'm talking about the kind that simmers and seethes but rarely boils over; the kind that makes itself known in subtle ways, through the sidelong glance, the clenched jaw, and the sarcastic remark; the kind that turns debutantes into dragons, seductresses into shrews.

"I feel like there's been a double-speak in our culture about putting motherhood on such a pedestal but yet at the same time not valuing it at all," complained Kath, a 30-year-old mother of four.

> Both seem to be going on at the same time, like maybe we can get mothers to do all this work if we pretend that we really do care while we really treat them like shit. The problem is that we're not working for money and we have a market economy. How does motherhood and raising children tangibly stimulate the economy? Sure, we shop at Target. We probably ... account for most of the sales tax in this city, but until someone figures that out, the government isn't going to be spending money for mothers and kids

A mother of two from Palm Beach, Florida, Anne shared Kath's belief that our culture treats its mothers rather shabbily. "I get frustrated and angry. We only get that one day out of the year—Mother's Day. It's the only time people want to acknowledge that we've done something." Marcy from Kearney, Nebraska, chimed in with a similar point of view: "I think society now feels like it's not enough or that it's kind of like 'You stay at home because you can't do anything [else].' That if you were really capable you would be out working and that you must not be capable of doing anything if you are just staying at home."

*Anger* is actually too mild a term for what mothers are experiencing in our country. *Rage* is a more appropriate adjective. Today's mothers have fury as their bed partner. "So what if mothers are angry?" one might respond to our thesis. Haven't mothers always been angry over something or other? Perhaps so. But we feel that it is important to find out why. This, and many other things, is what Jane's 1978—and the subsequent 1995—study on at-home mothers attempted to uncover. Why are mothers angry? Behind the rage of the more than 95 women that we interviewed in 1995 is a cacophony of other emotions. As Kath pointed out, modern-day stay-at-home mothers are invalidated by American society. Mothers today, whether they work in the home or outside it, are exhausted, stressed-out, burned-out, isolated, misunderstood, lonely, and downright depressed. Stay-at-home moms perform life's toughest job in a virtual vacuum of assistance and support. Because they receive little, if any, recognition, approval, or feedback, they're hungry for all three. Most of all, they want a break; a few hours away from their kids, a few minutes away from their own guilt. Paradoxically, we found that many mothers won't accept help even when it's offered. They simply refuse to give themselves permission to take it. In the pages ahead we'll explore why—why there is so little help for mothers, and why there are so few at-home mothers who will accept it.

### CHASING THE MYTHS INTO THE MOTHER CRISIS

I believe that it is society's deprecating view of motherhood, coupled with the prevalence of motherhood myths, that prevents American society from extending a helping hand to its mothers and also keeps many mothers from believing that they deserve it. As discussed in the preceding chapter, the myth of Good Mother has a monumental influence on women today. All the myths, such as Supermom, which fall under her imposing shadow, together represent the first step in the downward spiral that we've identified as The Mother Crisis. The Good Mother speaks to every woman from the time her children are born, sometimes before. She directs her thoughts, her feelings, and her actions. Most women remain unaware of her presence until they begin to challenge her authority. As with the women who participated in our study, that generally doesn't occur until a mother first becomes aware of her own pain.

"The Good Mother's voice is the one we have listened to about how to be a mother, how to feel as a mother, how to behave as a mother," says family therapist and author Melissa Gayle West in her book *If Only I Were a Better Mother*.[1] "Her demands are the ones to which we yield. She is always Right. We are always Wrong."[2] West attempts to help women heal their pain by spotlighting her own. Her story is an extraordinary representation of The Mother Crisis, told with sensitivity and wit. In excerpts from a journal that she kept during her first years as a mother, the author tells how her confusion over her feelings affected her day-to-day interaction with her child.

> I got bored around Eloise. At times everything I did with her seemed grey, stupid, lifeless. I found myself counting the minutes until her next nap, until Rodg got home, until it was time to take her to day care. I felt drowsy, stuporous around her. I couldn't stop yawning. All I wanted to do was curl up on the couch and sleep for a long time.... I felt resentful of her, but not too resentful: Good Mothers don't resent their children.[3]

Although many of the women we interviewed experienced feelings similar to those of West, few were aware that The Good Mother's oppressiveness was the cause. As a therapist, West was tuned in to her emotions and to her own psyche. She used her discomfort to develop further insight and to grow. She understood women's need to repress their feelings, not because she is a therapist, but because she did it herself. "I took Eloise to the mall, took her to the drugstore, the grocery store, took her shopping to distract myself from my own pain and from my child," she wrote. "I ate too much and too much of the wrong things.... I was a master at being present physically and absent in every other way.... Some part of us, listening to the Good Mother, would rather die, emotionally and spiritually, than feel such pain."[4]

Unlike many of the women who participated in our study, West understood that numbing her emotions wouldn't make them go away. She discovered that the feelings would leak out anyway, in a myriad of different, and uncontrolled, ways. West admitted that she became more irritable and critical of others. She learned that as long as she listened to the relentless nagging of the Good Mother within her, she could not be true to herself. "As long as I listened ... I could not be me, Melissa," she journaled. "Likewise, Eloise did not have me, Melissa, for a mother; she had some numbed, whitewashed, sanitized version."[5]

The Good Mother doesn't take into account that mothers are real women with individual needs, perceptions, and emotions; that feelings don't rise up from some common well of motherhood sensitivities. "Mother love is a human feeling. And, like any human feeling, it is uncertain, fragile and imperfect,"[6] notes Elisabeth Badinter, author of *Mother Love: Myth and Reality*. "Contrary to many assumptions, it is not a deeply rooted given in women's natures. When we observe the historical changes in maternal behavior, we notice that interest in and devotion to the child are sometimes in evidence, sometimes not."[7] The idea that all women are endowed with a maternal instinct that includes only the narrowest range of human emotions is the soil that nurtures the Good Mother and its adjoining motherhood myths. It is perhaps the basest of gender biases, perpetuating a social structure in which women's choices are limited by the fact that they, to the exclusion of men, are active participants in the miracle of birth. Elizabeth Janeway, author of *Man's World/Women's Place*, steadfastly agrees:

> Man's world, women's place, remain, and our society continues to ascribe different psychological attributes to each sex, and to assign different duties and ways of living to men and women because it is assumed that they have differing capabilities, moral, social and intellectual as well as physical.[8]

Because of such assumptions, when a woman becomes a mother, her freedom to choose evaporates. As long as she grants the Good Mother safe haven in her psyche, choices over lifestyle, behavior, even identity, will be vastly diminished. As long as she listens to Good Mother's rantings and cajoling, she will be destined to pursue the realization of her image. She will flounder about in an endless search for perfection, planning and executing maneuvers designed to accomplish an impossible ideal. She will fail, of course, and slip into guilt, a guilt that's perpetuated by the cultural conviction that Good Mother perfection is attainable. Unless she challenges the status quo at this point, she will tumble into the lonely world of self-doubt and criticism, until eventually, in despair, she will experience a complete loss of self (see page 1). It's a sad picture indeed, but one that we found in living rooms across the country. Not all women descended into the pit of The Mother Crisis, of course, but many were well on their way. Women in all stages of The Mother Crisis poured out their hearts to us in little bits and pieces.

Kami, from southern Florida, bore perfectionism as her Nemesis. For more than 5 years, she doggedly chased the Supermom image.

> In the beginning, when I was working, I was also taking care of the baby. I was dusting, I was pumping breast milk while I was at work, I was doing all this crazy stuff, and I was tired. I mean, I fell into bed and passed out. And then got up with the alarm clock, drinking coffee, trying to go for the next day. And I was wrecked after that. And I just figured out, there is no way; that it's impossible to do. You can't do everything that everybody expects; you just can't do it all.

Still, the energetic mother of two didn't stop trying until after she'd quit her job to stay at home and decided to baby-sit her sister's child while taking care of her own. "That was the straw that broke the camel's back," she admitted. "My kid screamed and screamed. I had an image of what a perfect mother was, and a perfect mother had children that were perfectly in order all the time and were perfectly clean, and when you went out somewhere, they didn't run around and scream; you know what I mean? A mother that was in control—that was the perfect mother. So that year broke me," she said. "I went nuts, you know; I hit the wall. I said, 'This is not working. Something has to change here, because this is not working.' "

Like their 1978 counterparts, the women we spoke to in 1995 felt guilty about failing to live up to the Good Mother ideal. "My guilt is about getting angry with [my children]," noted Marcy, a mother of three from the Midwest.

> I never wanted to be that kind of a mom who would yell or get angry with the kids, and I don't remember my mom doing that. I feel guilty over getting so angry at them. Sometimes I feel guilty because I'm not as good a mom as I think somebody else is, or [because] I never learned the techniques that they learned or how to use those teachable moments. I feel guilty because I don't know how to use them or how to make it a teachable moment.

Nancy, a social worker from Silver Spring, Maryland, recalls feeling tremendously guilty the last time she left the house. "I was apologizing as I was leaving," she said. "I was apologizing for Robby's temper tantrums; I was apologizing for the way the house looked. I realize that that is what I do—I apologize. I apologize to my husband for my anger."

Despite the many similarities between the women Jane interviewed in the 1970s and those we spoke to in the 1990s—their collective frustration, overwhelming guilt, sense of abandonment, and the like—there was one glaring difference between the two groups. The 1970s women knew that there was something grossly amiss in their obscure, stay-at-home world; the 1990s mothers, in general, denied that there could be. Sure, they stated plenty of facts about how things were bad on the outside and how they could be better. But few freely discussed how they actually felt on the inside, about how the reality of the job fell short of their expectations, about how bad they felt about themselves and their lifestyles. We suspect that the 1990s women were significantly more defensive because, unlike the majority of the 1970s women, their decision to stay home was an active one. In her book, *Secret Paths: Women in the New Midlife,* author Terri Apter concurs:

> Today's women do not become homemakers as women of previous generations have done—by having little choice or awareness of other options. Awareness of expanding options, however, often makes traditional women feel defensive, and in their defense they often suppress their dissatisfaction.[9]

Although hidden beneath a smoke screen of intellectualization and rationalization, the components of The Mother Crisis were visible among the 1990s women nonetheless. Tracy, a mother of two from Eagan, Minnesota, reeled from the stress of parenting virtually alone, although she refused to elaborate about the true nature of her distress.

> I remember there were [times] during that first year that my husband—he's a physician—would get home very late. I'd get the baby down to bed and I'd turn to look at him and just … let go. I would burst into tears or something just because it had been a stressful day and I had no outlet, and he would, you know, he never … I mean, he had a long day, too. Twelve hours is a normal day for him, so he wouldn't understand what I was going through. I would just need to bawl and I would, like, take everything out on him because there's no one else to take it out on.

Moms who responded to our 1995 study put a great deal of thought into their decision to stay home full time with their kids.

The reasons that they gave for doing so were broader in scope than those of the 1978 respondents. A full 17 percent reported that they didn't "want someone else raising their kids." Twenty-six percent stayed home because "It's my job." Twenty-five percent did so because "It's important to [the children]." Ten percent chose the path of career motherhood by default, responding, "I can't get the job I want." When answering how they felt after a few years of stay-at-home mothering, fewer 1990s women (26 percent) than 1970s respondents (42 percent) reported that they were unhappy, although a full 89 percent of the 1990s moms believed that they were in The Mother Crisis.

Although 80 percent of the 1995 respondents said that they were pleased with their decision to stay home, 33 percent said they'd rather work, if given the opportunity. Such statistical discrepancies reflect the contradictory nature of the 1995 responses. When asked why they continued to stay home full time with their kids, the percentage of women answering "It's important to [the children]" shot up to 58 percent, suggesting that obligation replaced desire as their primary motivation.

"Good Mother" idealism puts tremendous pressure on at-home moms to stay right where they are. And there's little evidence to suggest that the image is getting any less influential. In an early-1990 survey of 400 students at a New England and a Midwestern college reported in *Redbook* magazine, students were asked who they thought more admirable and "committed" to being a mother. Stay-at-home moms were at the top of the list, followed by those who worked only because they had to; mothers who worked because they wanted to were in last place. According to writer Lynn Darling, the reaction to motherless children is so visceral that it colors all our perceptions about the mothering role.

> If you want to make an audience feel sorry for a child, you take away the mother. So why should society do anything to help a mother leave home? Why should we come up with flexible jobs and good day care when all they do is take the mother away? We feel sorry for the child, and it affects all our thinking on these issues.[10]

## *HOW MUCH DO WE REALLY VALUE MOM?*

The fact that at-home mothers are outwardly revered doesn't achieve for them a corresponding level of economic or social status. Few homemakers in our second study felt empowered financially. In fact, most said they were disempowered because they didn't bring home a paycheck. Many reported that friends and acquaintances outwardly discount their work at home. Mothers who stay home are angry about this. In a 1992 article that appeared in *Good Housekeeping* magazine, one stay-at-home mother was quoted as saying, "People give lip service to mothers and apple pie, but when I'm walking down the street with three little kids, I get a lot of reactions—either they think I'm a saint or I'm an ignorant person who doesn't know how to use birth control."[11] According to author Darcie Sanders, women are forced to reconcile the differences between two extreme mother images—

> the cliche of the idle, lazy housewife sitting at home watching TV soaps [and] the idealized Victorian image of the always nurturing compassionate, even-tempered and wise full-time mother. Women who choose full-time mothering are likely to spend a great deal of their emotional energy walking a cultural tightrope between these two equally ridiculous stereotypes.[12]

Sanders found, as have we, that at-home mothers are an incredibly diverse group, especially today. "Many mothers at home are liberals or feminists who happen to believe in raising their own children," she said, "Not necessarily arch-conservatives who believe that a woman's place is in the kitchen."[13]

Like Sanders, I believe that all mothers interested in having their work valued and honored can be viewed as feminists, whatever their political orientation. The goal that Jane and I share—and I'll talk more about it in the chapters to come—is to find ways that society can work—sans lip service—toward genuinely elevating the status of America's moms, stay-at home or otherwise.

The most relevant finding in our two sister studies was that the experiences of mothers today aren't much different than those of mothers in the 1970s. Despite a time span of 17 years—an entire generation—the women in both studies encountered the same frustrations and problems in the full-time-mother role. The chief complaints of both groups of women were "constant demands on time," "lack of time for self," "coming last after everyone else," "not getting own needs met," "lack of acknowledgment over a good job," and "feelings of inadequacy." It was both surprising and distressing to us to find that women have made so few gains in the last 20 years in a role that our culture supposedly regards as momentous.

Discussions with hundreds of mothers revealed that society continues to impugn the worth of the women who raise its young in countless numbers of ways. Such deprecating treatment impacts women far more than platitudes about their so-called "place of honor" in a distinguished, celebrated role. "When women don't feel valid and valued, they begin to feel powerless," contends Ann Weinstein, director of the San Francisco–based Parent's Place. "When you feel powerless, it's hard to identify your needs and you feel guilty about wanting and needing things. Being a mom becomes everything. I think it's epidemic," she declares. "Stay-at-home moms lose some perspective." In her role at the resource center, the director is on the front line of modern parenthood conflict. She knows what parents today need the most and how deficient our society is at helping them meet those needs. She, too, condemns our culture's hypocrisy.

"We keep talking about how we honor families and it's such a crock because we continually make it difficult to be a parent whether it's health care, day care or having companies honor your parenthood. There's a lot of talk but very little concrete stuff." Weinstein has observed firsthand how the cultural demeaning of at-home moms has a negative impact, not only on the mother, but on the children as well. She noticed, as did we, that modern stay-at-home moms feel a great need to defend their choice of lifestyle. "The women feel in some ways that they must justify their decision. Consequently, there's a great concentration on their children to achieve. There are families in which there's an awful lot of pressure on the child to achieve to make it okay to have made the choice [to stay home]." It's like the child has to achieve to allow Mom to feel that her decision was alright. "There's also a tendency to do everything perfect," notes the director. "Every parent wants her child to have the best life but there's too much emphasis on criteria, as if someone has the magic answer. Parents are so intense now. But there's no magic formula for at-home [mothering]."

Hamilton-Bennett explains how our culture's expectations of mothers, with all the adjoining hypocrisies, hurt both the woman and the child. Despite society's idolization of the role, "the value of the work has always been downgraded," she contends.

> Therefore it's hard for women to find a significant identity when they are at home. Part of someone's identity is in the work that they do. Also, society does not value children, or there wouldn't be such high rates of abuse and neglect. So to be at home with children who aren't valued, then to be a woman and to be working around the house doing work that's not valued, a woman starts wondering, 'Is what I'm doing worthwhile?' Husband's come home and don't appreciate that you spent two hours with a Brillo pad getting the burned spot off the stove. The person who's going to notice that stuff are the kids, and they take it for granted that that's what mother do. It's a big letdown. So there are two issues— worth and identity.

She maintains, "It's our challenge to make the role one that feels good so that a woman can transfer that pride to her children."

It's a sad commentary, indeed, on a calling that's been aggrandized and immortalized throughout the ages as sacred. Women in our culture are grossly misled, slam-dunked into motherhood via the promise of societal exaltation. So the majority go willingly, like lambs to the slaughter, expecting glory and power as their gainful rewards. When the rewards don't come, at first they are puzzled, but then the vast majority begin to doubt themselves as worthy. I view this process as criminal. Jane and I watched women of all kinds abase themselves first before challenging the myths that promise one thing and deliver another. The corollary of such self-debasement is the cycle we've identified as The Mother Crisis. Why women degrade themselves rather than object to the status quo could be the topic of another book. Our focus, instead, is on what happens to women, to children, and, ultimately, to society when they do.

Kim Miller, co-founder of Family Affairs Inc., a maternity home-care agency, sees first-hand how women struggle with the performance pressure wielded by society's paradoxical treatment of the Good Mother myth. "We get a lot of calls from mothers who are desperately looking for support," she reveals. "Some people are looking hard; others feel like there is something wrong with them [for needing it]. Mothers experience a loss of self-esteem, of identity and mobility," she maintains. "There's a lack of value about being an at-home mom that, although society is getting better at it, is still prevalent. People think that if you're a stay-at-home mom you're on vacation, so moms have a guilt feeling for admitting outright that they have needs." Miller eloquently states what any at-home mom already knows. "It's very easy to get caught up in taking care of the kids and the house. The self becomes secondary or worse. There's an intensity in interacting with kids; the majority of your time is spent with kids, so you lose touch with yourself."

According to Miller, most medical services provided to mothers are notoriously inadequate. And, because of our nation's tight economy, many are getting deplorably worse. "Society is short-changing its moms," she declares.

> Moms and babies are being sent out of the hospital too soon. Society is sending the message that women are superhuman. That's why there is such a need for *doula* [a woman who assists another woman through pregnancy, childbirth and postpartum] service. They're sent home 24 hours after giving birth and many have other children. And they're expected to make a meal for the family and pick up. Now that's barbaric!

In response, women such as Miller and her partner, Mary Hantske, an obstetric nurse, are picking up where our nation's profit-driven provider system has left off. But since most private insurance carriers refuse to cover the cost, many women can't afford it. The picture in homes from Maryland to Hawaii is of hard-working women, isolated, without help from extended family, and without a great deal of spousal support. Community-based, church-sponsored and government-funded programs typically require women to leave their homes and seek out child care, another roadblock to connectedness. As Margaret Mead so astutely observes: "I think American women are increasingly overworked. The idea of all-purpose wife is perhaps the most difficult that society has set for women. Educated women have never been asked to pay so high a price for the right to be wives and mothers."[14]

## *HOW WOMEN KEEP THEMSELVES STUCK IN THE MOTHER CRISIS*

The issue is that American mothers are devalued and, consequently, underserviced. But that's still only one layer of The Mother Crisis. The other, and most significant layer perhaps, is comprised of the internal mechanisms that drive a woman to undervalue, and therefore underserve herself. When a woman embraces myths that tell her that anything short of perfection is failure, that getting angry at her children will damage them for life, or that taking care of herself means that she's neglecting her kids, she's bound to wind up in The Mother Crisis or, perhaps, in a therapist's office. If mired in The Mother Crisis, a deep sense of guilt will move her to refuse help or to disregard her own needs. I'm speaking of basic needs, such as companionship, intellectual stimulation, creativity, and the like, the loss of which is exacerbated by the myth-based, and oft-believed premise that only a Bad Mother would resent the sacrifice, no matter how agonizing. When pressed for the truth, many of the women we interviewed admitted that they missed the things that once gave them personal fulfillment, yet they rationalized why it was impossible for them to spend time away from their children to seek pleasure. Many of their excuses for not doing so were, on the surface, easily justifiable—lack of child care, money, or time. But when one woman would suggest a solution to the problem, another would come up with a handful of reasons why it simply wouldn't work. While reaching out with one hand for help, these sensible, thoughtful, educated, 1990s moms pushed it away with the other.

I believe it was fear of failure that held them back. Each seemed to suffer tremendous foreboding whenever moving too far astray from the Good Mother archetype that they so tenaciously, albeit unconsciously, held on to. Even when outwardly spurning her image, they refused to evict the Good Mother from their psyches. While claiming to believe that it's okay for a mother to address her own needs, they found it necessary to justify such behavior by ensuring that it's never at the expense of their kids. This is yet another example of Good Mother idealism run riot. For we've found no evidence to suggest that children will be irreparably damaged if they don't have mom all to themselves all the time. Quite the contrary. To be able to watch mom go out and have fun—even when they'd rather have her home—is a good thing for children to experience. Some of the women we interviewed believed it to be a good thing, too. They just had a great deal of difficulty putting their convictions into action. Nebraska mom Brenda, a 34-year-old mother of four, is an illuminating case in point.

"I think we need to take some time for ourselves just to be better mothers. If we take ten minutes for ourselves every day, we'll probably just feel better about ourselves and do a better job." Brenda is one of many mothers, however, who somehow can't manage to follow through with her intent. Julie, also from Nebraska, was on the brink of understanding that her needs mattered as much as those of her kids. "I am finding I am more selfish than I want to be," she said. "Oh, like I want to go to bed when I want to go to bed. I don't want to lay with my daughter until she goes to sleep. I think that's being selfish, yet I realize I have to watch myself because you can't always do what other people want you to do. I want to work on that." Such confusion is a natural consequence of Good Mother imperialism coupled with society's tendency to discourage any kind of separation between a mother and her child. One of the many dangers of taking the myth to the extreme is that a woman can become so engrossed in her child that emotional boundaries virtually disappear. Then both the child and the mother will have difficulty either developing or retaining a strong sense of self. This process sets up daughters for a future Mother Crisis of their own, one reason why The Mother Crisis was just as prevalent in 1995 as it was a generation before.

Jeanne, 34, a mother of two from Minnesota, admitted that she doesn't even take time to trim her fingernails, because she's constantly responding to the demands of her children. Intellectually, Jeanne knows that neglecting herself isn't healthy, but, under the spell of the Good Mother fantasy, she continues to do so nonetheless. "It's stupid," she acknowledged. "If you don't have any down time, any 'me' time, you're not going to be a 'good wife,' you're not going to be a 'good mother.' " Kathleen, 33, from Woodlawn, California, also takes her role to the extreme by neglecting her own basic, physical needs. But unlike Anne, she fails to see that there's anything wrong with the practice. "I think the job of motherhood has a certain amount of sacrifice involved—like you never sit down to have a meal," she declared. "I do have a fantasy that someday I'm going to sit down and eat a whole meal, and there's not going to be some little pint-size drill sergeant saying 'Want tea, want juice, want this, want that,' and we're going to eat calmly and quietly." Instead of demonstrating to her children that a mom has rights, too, Kathleen waits until her daughter is down for her nap and eats her own lunch in the middle of the afternoon.

Anne, 31, from Palm Beach, Florida, admitted that she, too, is her own worst enemy. "I think I judge myself; like I can't go do something for myself until I do something for everybody," she explained. "I can't go to dinner unless I feed the children first. Heaven forbid that a baby-sitter heats up macaroni and cheese." But Anne herself acknowledged that such martyrdom eventually takes its toll. "Every once in awhile it gets too hard and I snap," she said. "I go nuts because it's too hard. It [the Good Mother ideal] is just too hard a goal. You just can't live on the leftovers of your life. You have to take off the top once in awhile. But I don't, because I make it too hard on myself to do that."

Women who embrace the Good Mother myth resolutely often have trouble letting go of control—control of the children, control of the children's care, control of the household. We observed this phenomenon in both studies, demonstrated primarily through the women's reluctance to allow their spouses to parent in their own unique way or to chip in with domestic chores. Many of the women admitted that they frequently criticized their husbands which, in effect, actually discouraged the very help that they wanted and needed. Yet, according to many experts, this tendency is a natural outcropping of diminished status or experience. "Indeed, the less control which a woman exercises over other areas of her life, the greater will be the satisfaction she derives from managing the lives of her children,"[15] notes author Elizabeth Janeway. "A mother whose authority is limited to the nursery will attach much more emotional weight to what happens there than will another who works outside the home." Janeway points out that, traditionally, bearing a child raised a woman's social status. "Beyond that, the weight of her authority increases because she now speaks for, and acts for, and can make demands for, more than one person. Of course this is most important in a small community. But what else is a family than a small community?"[16]

## *FAMILY SYSTEMS AND SOCIETY PERPETUATE THE MOTHER CRISIS*

Women become mothers expecting heightened status and power. Instead, they encounter tremendous disappointment when our system fails to tangibly acknowledge their import. For many women, it's a shocking experience and a blow to their self-esteem. For the women we interviewed in 1995, a full rebound was impossible. Most were rightfully proud of their choices and accomplishments, but elbows-deep in child care duties and domestic chores, most didn't have the time or the wherewithal to pull themselves up by their bootstraps. The majority landed in some stage of The Mother Crisis, inwardly doubting themselves, while outwardly defending their worth with all the passion of the damned. Once they realized that, even as career women, we appreciated their choice to stay home, many of the women we spoke to cast aside their shields and began to freely speak their minds. Tina, a mother of two from Pennsylvania, illustrated, among other things, how her husband's mythical view of motherhood influenced her choice of lifestyle.

"When I quit my job and started having children, I felt really comfortable with it because David was backing me—he really felt like this was the thing we should be doing in our lives; that our jobs are inconsequential, that children are the important thing," Tina recalled.

> So I was sort of put on a pedestal by him. Then I discovered how hard the job was. I felt kind of isolated and my self-esteem went down ... after about a year and a half of it, because every time I went to a party or something like that, someone would say, "Where are you working now, Tina?" And I would say "In the home," and they would say, "Oh," and leave it at that. I felt like I needed to stand up and say "Look, don't you people understand that this is a difficult job?"

Tina revealed that, since joining her local mothers' club, her self-esteem has shot up significantly. "Because there are so many people here to support the way I feel," she explained.

According to Marcy, a former legal secretary and mother of three from Nebraska, her husband sometimes intimates that her work at home lacks value. "The comment has come up a couple of times when he said, 'And you spent my money?'" she revealed.

> It bothers me because I feel like it's *our* money. I can see where he's feeling like he's out there getting a paycheck, but in my mind, my work is equal in value to his work and that it's our pot [of money]. That's the only time I feel like [what I do] is not valuable, when he refers to what we have as his money rather than ours.

Betsy, a former journalist and 28-year-old mother of two from Minnesota, interprets her husband's obvious lack of feedback as a message that she is not doing a good job, and that the duties she performs at home are not important enough to be noticed.

> When I first stayed at home I was thinking, "Okay, what am I supposed to do here?" I'm new at this job—not only taking care of our kids and seeing that they have some activities to do, but I felt like I had to get the house into tip-top shape and sparkling order. So I would scrub the bathroom and scrub the kitchen, and really do a lot of hard cleaning work that I didn't usually do when I was working, and I expected my husband

to notice that when he came home. When he didn't, 1 felt outraged, and I felt worthless and I thought, well, "What am I doing? Every other time I've done a good job at something, it's been acknowledged, not only by myself, but by someone else." That external acknowledgment is helpful to keep you going. I just felt worthless.

Betsy's experience is an excellent example of how lack of recognition can discourage even the most dedicated performer. All the women we interviewed willingly chose the job of full-time, at-home parent, yet after months and years of having their hard work go unacknowledged, many began to wonder, "What's the point?" Society's refusal to value the work that mothers do actually discourages women from remaining in the very place—the home—that our culture prefers them to be. This outrageous contradiction is multi-generational in its effect. The following vignette is a case in point.

Suzanne, 27, from southern California, feels bad about the fact that she, a career mom, is her daughter's chief role model. "A few months ago, I was asking my daughter, 'What do you want to be when you grow up?' And she said, 'A mom,' And I didn't feel good about that," she admitted. "I feel guilty that I haven't done my job. On the other hand, I thought, 'Maybe it's okay to be a mom.' But there are so many [confusing] messages out there."

Barbara, a mother of three from Colorado, left her teaching job to stay home with her daughter, thinking that it was the best thing for her child. Within a matter of days her level of satisfaction was at an all-time low. "There were probably four to six months when I didn't feel really good about my choice," she admitted. "My self-esteem as a mother or as a contributing member of society wasn't there. I felt that [being] a mother wasn't enough."

To Anne from southern Florida, going out with her kids is the scariest part of mothering. She becomes anxious and embarrassed when either she or her children fail to behave just right. "I feel like I'm an annoyance to the bank when I show up and I've got one kid crying and the other kid under my arm, and I'm trying to fill out the slip and I can't quite sign my name right," she said. "I feel like an annoyance to society with my kids because they look at you like, 'Can't you stop that kid from screaming?' So that's the hardest part, I've faced emotionally. I just feel like I'm annoying people all the time."

According to William Mattox, Vice President of Policy for the Washington, D.C.–based Family Research Council, at-home mothers today don't get the respect they deserve. "Many mothers today who devote themselves primarily or exclusively to the rearing of children find themselves in a position where they must seek to explain why they're doing this thing in this day and age," he explains. Their second major challenge is in enlisting the support of a culture that's no longer family-friendly. "Life today is more hairy for everyone," he says.

> The changes in the last three to four decades mean that people are more likely to be living apart from extended family networks and are more likely to be living in neighborhoods that have fewer mothers at home. The lifestyle patterns of 1990s America do not lend themselves to the type of backdoor friendships that might have occurred more naturally in previous generations.

In effect, maintains Mattox, our country has failed miserably at designing communities that meet the daily needs of those who use them the most—women and children. Several years ago, the executive moved his own family from Washington, D.C., to a Maryland suburb, expecting "stereotypical suburban bliss and a rich neighborhood network," he recalled. Instead, he found a world where: "instead of interacting with your neighbors, you pass them in your car." Another missing element in suburbia, notes Mattox, is the presence of a multigenerational influence. "It's all middle-age families with kids," he says. "There are no grandmothers or singles. In many respects, it's very important [for parents and children] to have this diversity and the opportunity to interact with nonparents and the elderly.... the essence of communities today puts a lot of young mothers at a disadvantage," he contends.

According to Janeway, the notion that suburbia as a lifestyle by design is superior to other forms is incredibly misleading.

> If we look at suburbia with the Moynihan report in our heads, we can see that middle-class "normative" families, fleeing the

city and its threats, have converted themselves unwittingly into the same sort of family-with-an-absent-father that was reckoned as highly disruptive of social structure when it occurred in the slums. No doubt the women who made the move to the suburbs concurred in it, or most of them did; but in fact it was more a move based on a view of woman's role as being pretty well nonexistent outside the family.

The Moynihan Report, written in 1967, concluded that the Negro family was in chaos due to the absence of the black father from the family. It did not take all the social pressures into consideration, so ended up blaming the males for the problems.[17]

Sally Dewald, an RN and former owner of the now-defunct Newborn Home Care of Hawaii, reminded us that invalidating stay-at-home moms is not the exclusive practice of government, institutions, or men. Women, many of whom are mothers themselves, do it too. "The first thing a working mom will think if she knows you're at home all the time is "I can just pawn this or that off on her,' especially when it comes to school-age kids," she says. According to Dewald, this can translate into an identity problem for a woman, because her role is not recognized as a job. "Everything is shuffled onto her, from neighbors, friends, community. They expect her to be there. Stay-at-home moms don't get any rewards like the rest of the world," she says.

> They need acceptance ... and respite. They don't get special benefits like retirement, either. I think it's very, very important that Social Security honor them all for the work they've done, that they don't just draw on their husbands' [benefits]. But we seem to be stuck in a time zone that is magical. I don't know whether it's "Leave It To Beaver" or whose time zone it is, but [today's] mothers cannot get their needs met.

Dewald, who is a mother of six children and a grandmother as well, understands that before women can expect respect from society, they must first learn how to respect themselves. "The women who stay home with each other don't support one another," she contends. "I have found in my own experience that you can't trust all women. Therefore, women can't be truly women. I have learned to relate to other women; and friends as confidants, but in my generation, women did not bond. You had a husband and you were supposed to bond with him. You didn't dare have outside women friends."

This phenomenon doesn't exist to the extreme that it once did, we found, but a glimmer of mistrust among women was apparent during our interview sessions. There was also a certain degree of competition. Women still don't seem to be comfortable with their differences, so powerful are the images that cloud their perceptions of themselves and each other. This discomfort with individuality often makes it impossible for one woman to support another who has chosen different ways to nurture herself or her child. Such a mind-set emotionally isolates women who are already physically isolated by their environments. Brenda, a mother of two preschool-aged boys and a former merchant marine, admits that the members of her Charleston based FEMALE group don't always support the individual. "FEMALE attracts overachievers. They have to be highly motivated, high-energy people to commit to a group that meets as often as FEMALE does," she said.

> Heaven forbid that you act frazzled. You are supposed to entertain beautifully, keep the yard, the house, and not even break a sweat. I don't always believe women are supportive of each other. I think women can be very catty, and if they see another woman's area of shortcoming, they pat themselves on the back because they don't have that problem. I think it's a well-known thing that women can be each other's worst enemy.

Kitty, also a member of the Charleston group, agrees. "I've actually heard some women describe another woman who had a new baby [by saying] she couldn't handle it because she is a 'low stress,' person. They're not hateful women; they're nice. But they have set a standard for themselves and believe that everyone should try to reach it."

Another way that mothers sabotage themselves, says Dewald, is by buying into the idea that they're supposed to be able to raise their kids alone. "I don't know where this came from but I call it the frontier mentality," she says. "The idea that 'I have to do it all myself.'" The home-care provider asserts that mothers should connect in their communities like people do after a catastrophe. "When you have hurricane, everyone pulls together and shares their food." Something akin to that is happening now in our country through the formation of mothers' clubs. In my view, The Mother Crisis is the emotional equivalent of a natural disaster. The strain of flying solo at home year after year has moved many women to seek out new friends for survival. But, all too often, it's not enough. The gut-level bonding necessary for close friendships doesn't often occur. Many of the women in our study admitted that despite knowing one another for years, they had never discussed the issues and concerns about mothering that were closest to their hearts. Many were either too embarrassed or ashamed. Anthropologist Margaret Mead describes the experience as such: "Living so close to others who are busy with exactly the same preoccupying details of homemaking, harried by exactly the same difficulties, often encourages a narrow and uncomfortable competitiveness rather than friendly cooperation. But the alternative—exclusion from one's neighbors' interest—would be an unbearable solitude."[18] Several of the mothers' groups we called on existed in such an atmosphere; the members were content—until our visit—with a type of coffee-klatch camaraderie. Many times during our discussion groups, we saw the walls fall. One woman's detachment from another would temporarily disappear. This process would be much easier if America's mothers weren't pushed so hard to perform.

"If our so-called experts stopped expecting women to do all the child-rearing and acknowledged that much of the rage and helplessness that mothers feel is natural rather than one more female failing, women would not have to blame each other or themselves for being imperfect mothers," notes author Paula J. Kaplan.[19] "They could stop hiding the desperate feelings that the responsibilities of motherhood bring and, knowing they are natural, could share them with each other and exchange information and support."[20] Kaplan believes as I do, that mothers are afraid to complain about their lot, afraid that if they do, they'll lose the respect of others. I urge them to cause a stir anyway, for the respect is only an illusion.

"Each isolated woman is scared to complain about how impossible it is to remain serene and superhuman at handling all household crises because she believes that in doing so she reveals herself to be a failure, a bitch, or some unnatural creature,"[21] says Kaplan. "Having to keep their secrets to themselves keeps women separate from each other, daughters separate from their mothers."[22] Margie, 34, a former marketing professional and a mother of four, had the courage to speak up and tell her story.

> I feel guilty because I wish I could sit there and be logical with [the children] and not yell when my first instinct is to yell and get up and do it myself. I'd rather sit down and be this Mother Theresa, you know, and be so calm. Sometimes I feel like my husband tries to make me feel guilty, like, if the house isn't perfect. He doesn't actually come home and say, "Ah, look at the house," but he might give me a look and I'll jump, feeling guilty and defensive.

Crystal, 28, a mother of two from Florida, was quite forthright in her admissions as well. "I get tired of my kids sometimes, you know, because it's a 24-hour-a-day, seven day-a-week job. Mom doesn't get sick days. Mom doesn't get vacation time. Mom doesn't get days off. And I get real defensive when people say, 'Well, you chose to stay at home with your kids.' Well, you know, my husband chose to be a chef but he still has bad days."

Thirty-four-year-old Ramona, from Connecticut, admits that she takes out her frustrations on her husband, demanding that he alone meet her needs, needs that go unmet every day. "He's on his feet all day; he doesn't sit down. So he comes home, plops down in a recliner, wants to have a beer and watch TV, and I'm like, 'Oh no, you're not, you are going to play with these kids. We are going out to dinner and you are going to talk to me!'"

Many of the 1990s moms, in fact, looked exclusively to their husbands to meet their emotional needs and frequently resented them when they weren't able to do so. "I was expecting him [my husband] to fulfill all my needs because I was not able to fulfill my own; I didn't feel like I was worthy," declared Carrie, from Dallas, a 26-year-old mother of three. "So I expected everything, every bit of my self-worth to come from him, since I didn't have family or anyone else telling me, 'You're doing a good job.' The baby never said it, and he didn't either." Carrie's friend Jan, 37, and a mother of two preschoolers, had a similar experience. "Any resentments I felt weren't aimed at my kids," she admitted. "They were aimed toward my husband, because he gets to talk to people."

We also discovered in our discussions with mothers the truth behind Kaplan's declaration that "motherhood is supposed to be serene, but mothering an infant actually gives rise to some of the most intense feelings of panic, fear, rage and despair that adults can have."[23] We found that although women point much of that rage at themselves and their children, they level a substantial portion of it at their spouses as well. "I have a lot of anger, and it's an effort not to direct that to my children" said 37-year-old Kathy from Minnesota. "I think that I turn a lot of it inward and, consequently, it has more of an effect on my husband."

According to a study reported in the *Journal of Personality and Social Psychology*, it is the disparity in the division of labor that occurs after the birth of a child that causes women to experience a decline in marital satisfaction. "The performance of the bulk of the domestic chores at a time often experienced as physically and emotionally draining may lead to negative feelings on the part of new mothers toward their husbands," concluded the study.[24] Researchers found that the most dramatic differences occurred in the area of child care. Relatively few of the women in the study expected to be doing much more of the child care than their husbands and were very disappointed when they ended up doing far more than what they considered their fair share. More than 40 percent of the women reported a large discrepancy in child care division of labor. The researchers were puzzled by what they called the women's "unrealistic expectations" about their husband's contributions. They surmised that perhaps women have such high expectations because they had failed to talk about child care responsibilities with their spouses prior to giving birth.[25] We found this to be true in our studies as well.

In 1978, Jane discovered that women didn't expect much help from their husbands. However, women in the 1990s do. But the wrinkle is that in today's high-pressure economy, many men are working long hours or two jobs just to make ends meet. Despite a tremendous shortfall of time and energy in the spousal arena, women still wish that their husbands could be there to offer them physical and emotional support. There's powerful evidence to suggest that such support can have a marked effect on the well-being of women who are mothers. In a study outlined in the April 1992 issue of the *American Journal of Orthopsychiatry*, it was reported that the single, most important factor contributing to a woman's sense of overall satisfaction with her role was whether her husband supported her in how she chose to mother her children. "The only consistent correlations over time involved the mothers' satisfaction with the support they received from their spouses for their child care decisions and arrangements,"[26] concluded the authors. Another facet of the study that supports Dewald's point of view is the fact that none of the at-home mothers who participated spoke positively about the support of friends or family members for being the child's primary caregiver. In fact, the opposite was true—the women received virtually no support from others in their decision. Noted the researchers: "The image of a group of mothers sitting on the kitchen floor or at the neighborhood playground, caring for their children while giving and receiving support from each other for their child care responsibilities appears to be unrealistic."[27]

On the spiraling, downhill cycle that is The Mother Crisis, "Lack of Support" represents a pivotal point. For it's here that women either begin their plummet into the final stages of the crisis—"Unmet Needs," and "Loss of Choice"—or make an attempt to search for support in new and inventive ways. Most of the women in the 1970s study fell into the final stages of The Mother Crisis unimpeded. Most of the women interviewed in the 1990s reached out for help from one another before the fall. In a stirring attempt by women to fix what's wrong by themselves, they formed "mothers' clubs." I strongly believe that these groups have saved thousands of women from drowning in a full-blown Mother Crisis. But I also believe that it will take a lot more than women helping women to obliterate The Mother Crisis completely. It will take changes in the way women, men, and our culture view family life as a whole. By refusing to acknowledge that mothers have needs like the rest of the population, society loses a significant portion of productive citizenry to depression and despair. Carole, 29, from California, lost herself during the postpartum period while following her pediatrician's advice.

"I had seven infections in six weeks' time, and I just felt like a basket case," she recalled.

> I was crying all the time and the doctor would say, "You need to sleep more, you're not getting enough sleep and that is why you're getting the infections." But the pediatrician was saying, because my son was a premie, "You need to feed him every three hours around the clock. You set your alarm clock night and day and you feed him every three hours."

Because Carole was breast feeding, her health continued to decline. Not once did she consider supplementing or switching to formula entirely so that others could share the work load. Clinging to Dewald's "frontier mentality," she chose to tackle the job alone.

Christi, an overwhelmed mother of two from Charleston and a member of FEMALE, recognizes the value of a support group, which, to her, has, become a lifeline. "Just knowing that you're not alone out there—that is something that moms, that women, deserve and need. Not to have that is so awful; when you don't have it, you feel so low." In a few choice words, this young mother described how The Mother Crisis felt to her:

> When you have friends in your life there is joy, there is compassion and concern, there's a giving and receiving of love. When that is absent, you feel sad or unlovable, like nobody cares about you, like something is wrong with you. If you reach out [to someone] and they do not encourage your friendship, you wonder what is wrong with you, and that is scary. When that would happen, I'd go into a depression.

Women who adhere completely to the myth that Good Mothers must stay home full time are in the gravest danger of plunging into the final stages of The Mother Crisis—"Loss of Choice," and "Loss of Self." Their self-perpetuated guilt over leaving keeps them stuck in a world where options are few. Even mothers who make a last-ditch attempt to abandon the myth often sink deeper, for society offers few incentives to women wanting to leave their children to pursue other interests. In a July 1994, article that appeared in *Parents Magazine*, a writer explains why:

> To ensure equal treatment in the workplace of professional women who have children, there must be an explosion of two persistent myths—that these women have a poor work ethic … and that as long as mothers work, they are harming their children's opportunities for educational and, therefore, future professional success.[28]

Taken together—society's depreciation of the mother role, its tendency to discourage mothers from working outside the home, and the fanciful myths that prevent mothers from feeling good about themselves—the three main factors that perpetuate The Mother Crisis are overwhelming indeed. I believe that the best effort of everyone who cares about the well-being of our nation's mothers is required to shatter the myths and the attitudes that beat these women down. But if the obstacles to healthy motherhood are tackled one by one, women will have a good chance at overcoming them.

# Solutions ❧

# *Bridging the Gap* ❧ *Putting an End to the* Mommy Wars

*A**ll mothers are working* moms. Whether they spend each day doing laundry and changing diapers or punching a keyboard and a time clock, all women with children work hard every single day of their lives. Both sets of women—those with outside jobs and those who are homemakers—face the same day-to-day challenges of child rearing. Both sets of women know what it's like to be up half the night with a sick child and show up for work the next day. Both sets of women understand that Mom never gets a day off. One topic that's been given its fair share of ink is the so-called "Mommy Wars." It's the unnatural divide between mothers who have outside jobs or careers and mothers who have chosen to stay home with their children. Women who participate in the Mommy Wars arm themselves with barbs about those on the other side. Each side views the other as the enemy. It's an ugly, unproductive, totally unnecessary war in which women are both the warriors and the casualties. Both sets of women love their children. If mothers everywhere share in the same struggle known as parenting, then why are they battling?

## MOTHERHOOD MYTHS FUEL THE MOMMY WARS

I believe that women who enlist for combat in the Mommy Wars are the same women who tenaciously embrace motherhood myths. These are women who tailor their own lives according to the myths with which they most identify, and who expect other women to do the same. The majority of the at-home mothers we interviewed in 1995—most of whom had the Good Mother as their mentor—aimed right at the hearts of career women every chance they got. Admittedly, we gave them the perfect opportunity. One of the questions we asked them was "What do you think of mothers who work outside the home?"

"I'd rather get a dog if I didn't want to get intimately involved with my kids," declared Jamie from Minnesota. "There's this whole idea about quality time, which I think is real hokey." This woman not only assumed that mothers who work at outside jobs aren't intimate with their children but also condemned them for choosing a lifestyle that's different from her own. Her comment is both judgmental and presumptuous—the product of a value system that is, for the most part, myth-based. Since Jamie had no tangible knowledge of what it's like to be a mom with an outside job, her judgments could not be fact-based. Consequently, she arrived at the following faulty, albeit understandable, conclusion: "I think that ... not having any child care responsibilities would probably mean not having an intimate relationship with them," she said.

Jan, from California, makes impossible assumptions about the time "working" mothers spend with their kids. She uses the Good Mother ideal to chastise mothers for leaving home to work:

> [Mothers who work] don't spend but four or five hours max
> with their kids during the week. I feel like, unfortunately, that
> is what's wrong with the kids in our country, that women
> cannot, a lot of times, stay home. We need to do something so
> that they can if they want to, because that is the most impor-
> tant thing they're going to do.

Most of the women felt that working mothers were selfish
and did not value their children, that those who worked because
they wanted to—and not because they had to—didn't sacrifice
enough for their children. Many of them disguised their prejudices
by confusing them with the issue of child care—they spurned day
care centers for their deficiencies as a means of justifying their
disapproval. Such logic is tough to argue with, given that many
child care centers are indeed inadequate. But it's not honest. The
real problem that some at-home mothers have with working
mothers stems from their prejudices. They believe that mothers
who work outside the home are simply wrong for doing so. They
believe that if you must work to make ends meet, then you probably shouldn't have kids.

"I think a lot of women who choose to work aren't valuing
their children enough to make the actual sacrifice," claimed Mary
Beth, from Florida, "I feel like those mothers just don't get it,"
chimed in Dawn from South Carolina.

> I think the mothers who work—and I question whether they
> have to work in the majority of the cases, especially the
> people who live out in the suburbs in a big house, taking big
> vacations—I just think that it's too hard [for them] to give up
> their lifestyle for one thing. One woman I know—I could tell
> her kids were raised in day care from day one. And I saw how
> horrible it must be for those kids to be in day care, at least
> from the places I had experience with. You don't realize that
> there is absolutely no one on Earth that can love your kids like
> you do.

Connie, from Downingtown, Pennsylvania, made statements
that reeked of hostility and sour grapes:

> They [working mothers] complain to me how hectic it is, but
> they have more than me, so I know they could go without.

They just want the stuff, but then they act like they feel guilty. I think that you couldn't feel real guilty because you have a $30,000 car in the driveway and you go on these trips. I haven't been to Europe, and I don't go to Hawaii every other year. My kids haven't been to Disneyworld yet. I'm giving that up to be here.

Such comments illustrate the two blatantly judgmental ways that women restrict their own options, and those of others, once they become mothers. They label someone a Bad Mother for choosing to leave her children to pursue "selfish" interests or for not feeling the appropriate amount of guilt. They label someone a Bad Mother if the child care services available to her aren't up to par. The first accusation is myth-based in origin; the second merely blames women for the deficiencies of America's child care system. Women who work outside the home are expected to live up to the same Good Mother ideal that women who stay home strive to attain. If they don't, society works hard to deny them the right to earn a paycheck or to keep their children. Remember Marcia Clark? She fought hard to retain custody of her two young children during the O. J. Simpson murder trial. Career mothers function under a set of culturally imposed guidelines that is even stricter than that of their home-based counterparts. These impossible-to-achieve expectations are the seeds from which the Supermom myth sprouts, an image that a great many mothers with outside careers are driven by guilt to pursue. Most of them find out real quick, however, that to feel good about being both a mom and a career woman in a culture that expects perfection from both, is a fantasy. In *The Mother Puzzle*, author Judith Schwartz observes the following:

> After being taught in business dealings that we should al-
> ways strive for "win–win," we learn that when it comes to
> our own lives, the decisions are more like "either–or." We
> don't question the system but rather ourselves for not having
> strategically planned our lives better.[1]

Including herself among her readers, Schwartz admits, "We're afraid of children because we're afraid they'll curtail our options. Because we feel this way, we worry that we're selfish—the word other generations may use to describe our hesitancy about having children."[2] Women with outside ambitions apparently can't win—they're considered selfish if they have children and leave them; yet they're thought of as even more selfish if they pursue their aspirations and decide to have no children to leave! It's amazing to me that so many mothers are among the finger-pointers. In her characteristic no-nonsense style, Schwartz asserts that career women, like at-home moms, misdirect their anger at themselves and other women.

> Still feeling guilty that we could do what most of our mothers couldn't; still feeling the burden of having to prove our gender's seriousness and merit, we've scarcely allowed ourselves the luxury on being angry [at the system] when we feel we've been screwed…. We're at an odd juncture because neither working nor nonworking mothers are getting true support from the culture.[3]

Like Schwartz, I believe that our culture's refusal to accept women as individuals has pit one woman against another.

> Society's failure to support women has thrown us in upon ourselves, leaving us preoccupied with our own lives, with little energy left to raise questions and make demands on behalf of women as a group…. We accept society's definition of the problem rather than tackle the real problem—that our economic structure is incompatible with raising children.[4]

Tina, a 32-year-old mother of three from Downingtown, Pennsylvania, thinks that people who strive for material wealth should not have children at all. "I just think people have children for the wrong reasons," she said.

> If you are going to live in a $400,000 house, you need two incomes for it. I don't think it works for folks to drop kids off at day care at six in the morning, pick them up at six at night, and put them to bed at seven so you can have them up at five thirty. I don't have anything against them as individuals—I would never attack them personally—but I just don't think it's healthy for the children.

Dawn, also from Downingtown, echoed her friend Tina's opinion:

> If you are going to have kids, then raise the kids. Don't have the kids and give them to somebody else. If you can't afford to stay home to raise the kids, don't have them. They don't let you take a car and when you can afford it you pay for it. That pretty much says it in a nutshell. I get really aggravated, because I feel like it influences my life, too. I can't afford anything either because so many people having two incomes drives all the prices up.

Dawn said she's angry over high prices. I think she's angry over the fact that some women suffer less guilt than she when they leave their children, that guilt doesn't tie them down. I also think that Dawn—and other at-home moms who strike out at working mothers—probably suffer some regret over their choice to make the ultimate sacrifice. Notes author Terri Apter in her book *Secret Paths: Women in the New Midlife*:

> Women often engage in enormous efforts to control the regret they are inclined to feel. These efforts are special to women because society is far less friendly to them than it is to men in providing ready-made patterns to accommodate their different needs for love, family and personal development.[5]

## WOMEN ARE DIVIDED BY STEREOTYPES OF WORKING AND AT-HOME MOMS

In a 1990 reader's poll, *Parents Magazine* explored the nature of the split between at-home moms and working mothers. Researchers found that women on both sides were highly critical.

> Unfortunately, both working mothers and mothers who stay home may be so wedded to their choice that they are suspicious and critical of each other. Working mothers feel that they are accused of deserting their children in order to have nicer clothes or a bigger house, while those who stay home resent the assumption that they do nothing all day but watch soap operas and eat bonbons.[6]

According to author Ingrid Groller, who reported the study in the article, "Women and Work,"

Working mothers and at-home mothers have more in common than either group realizes. Both work very hard—and make personal sacrifices—to do what they think is best for their families. But it's clear, too, from the responses we received that society still has a long way to go before all mothers—whether they pursue a career or stay at home—get the support and reassurance they need.[7]

Researchers concluded that as more and more women with young children entered the workforce, two different doctrines regarding a woman's place have sprung up. One dictates that a woman should be home with her children, the other, that a mother has every right to pursue a career outside the home. They discovered that the Mommy Wars seem to start with both working mothers and at-home mothers on the defensive, since only a little more than one-third of each group think that they are supported by the other side. They also found that working mothers aren't nearly as critical of mothers who stay home as those mothers seem to assume. Actually, a majority of working mothers admire at-home moms. When asked to characterize their attitude about at-home mothers,

- 56 percent of working mothers said they admire them;
- 40 percent envy them;
- 8 percent are critical;
- 24 percent have no opinion.

Those who admire at-home mothers cited two primary reasons: "It's difficult to be home with children all day; and they are putting their children before financial concerns."[8]

Working mothers from the *Parents Magazine* study were considerably kinder to at-home moms than the at-home mothers in our study were to working mothers. The fact that so many of the women we interviewed in 1995 were highly critical of working mothers is extremely relevant, suggesting a return to a 1950s-era mode of thinking that promoted domesticity as the only proper role for women. Unfortunately, this type of thinking reinforces the very stereotypes that keep women divided.

In a nineties-something article by writer Lynn Darling, Leon

Hoffman, M.D., director of the Parent–Child Center of the New York Psychoanalytic Society, outlines the elements that provoke the Mommy Wars:

> To some extent ... we're paying the price of diversity. In past generations, parents made their decisions about what was best for their children within the confines of a family community that reaffirmed their ways of doing things. Now parents who have chosen lives very different from their own parents' look elsewhere for reinforcement ... and there's a constant need to model yourself on what others are doing, a constant comparing.[9]

Given the confusion, it's clear that society is still at great odds over this issue. Women are confused and unsure about themselves. So they cling insecurely to the myths and stereotypes that divide them and keep them from any real understanding of one another.

According to Mothers at Home, a northern Virginia group that encourages career women to take time off to raise children, the stress of the Mommy Wars is secondary to the inner tension women feel in determining how their children will be cared for. Noted an organization spokesperson in a newsletter of the same name:

> It is the exhausting inner turmoil they suffer as they weigh their alternatives. Pulled one way by an intense social and economic pressure to work and pushed another by a dawning realization that they are truly needed by their children, many of them wander in and out of the work force—seeking support from society, support at work, then at home—only to find it severely lacking in either place.[10]

One of the main reasons that women are confused and divided about mothering styles is that society is confused and divided, too. In the past several decades there have been scores of studies undertaken to find out whether nonmaternal child care is detrimental to the mother–child relationship. Until recently, the jury was still out. On April 20, 1996, the most far-reaching and comprehensive study done up to that date was released, reporting that using child care does not affect infants' trust in their mothers.

The 1996 study, sponsored by the National Institute of Child Health and Human Development, part of the National Institutes of Health, was designed to address one of the most emotionally charged issues in society today: Does a mother put her child at risk by working outside the home? It reported that the sense of trust felt by 15-month-old children in their mothers was not affected by whether the children were in day care, by how many hours they spent there, by the age they entered day care, by the quality or type of care, or by how many times care arrangements were changed. Instead, what affected that trust was a mother's sensitivity and responsiveness to her child.[11]

According to Dr. Deborah Lowe Vandell, one of the 25 researchers on the project, part of what prompted the study were real worries that child care, in and of itself, is unhealthy. One message of the study, however, was that if the quality of the interaction with the mother is sensitive, then the child is likely to develop a secure relationship with her.[12] Because it wasn't possible to poll the women in our second study about the contents of this report, I don't know whether its conclusions affected their opinions of mothers who work. One can only speculate that it might have softened them a bit.

## AT-HOME MOMS ARE THREATENED BY MOTHERS WHO WORK OUTSIDE THE HOME

In her book *Hard Choices: How Women Decide about Work, Career and Motherhood*, author Kathleen Gerson says working mothers are sending a confused society a message about women's dichotomy:

> This growing group of non-domestic women represents a kind of quiet rebellion against the continuing dilemmas and contradictions of women's place. These women are to some extent on strike against a set of structural arrangements that provides meager social supports and rewards for child rearing and a set of beliefs that pits the interests of the mother

> against the interests of the child. As long as child rearing remains an undervalued occupation ... a sizable proportion of women will reject full-time motherhood in favor of more highly rewarded alternatives.[13]

Gerson's view might explain why working women have a fairly high regard for at-home moms. It might also explain why at-home moms, many of whom feel abandoned by women who leave home for work, are angrier, more critical, and judgmental. After talking to scores of women who've chosen child rearing as their livelihood, I fully understand this tendency. Many at-home moms are clearly threatened by women who have overtly rejected the lifestyle that they have committed themselves to with great passion and zeal. They take the decision that working women have made personally, as if these women were telling them, "What you do isn't good enough for me." As a result, they focus more on working moms than they do on themselves and are quick to blame and condemn.

"I have a twisted feeling about mothers who work," admitted Kathy, a mother of two from Charleston, South Carolina.

> We have two neighbors who work. One has to leave at two each day to pick up the baby-sitter; the family never sits down together for a meal. The kids don't have a schedule. They are up and down, up and down. Across the street, this mother picks up her child at four, but I feel sad that she doesn't get to see what her daughter is doing all day and be there.

Sue from Maryland, rebukes working moms for putting money ahead of their children. "I think a lot of it's more greed than need; I don't know. If it's part-time, it's okay," she relented, "but I really think you have to be [home]."

Many of the at-home moms we spoke to projected their own feelings and fears onto working mothers. Noted Kami, from Nebraska:

> I know that no matter how much a woman says, "I can't stay home with my kids," or whatever, that there's a tug at her heart that she would rather be there. I know that so many people who have had their children abused and found out

later have felt horrendous guilt for leaving them in the care of someone else.

For Ginger, a mother of four from Texas, it was easier to project her own pain onto working mothers rather than face it head on. "I've had days, literally, where I was on my knees crying with spilled food all around me," she said.

> I didn't know what I was going to do when I was in the emergency room two nights ago with a migraine. I mean, it's hard, but I still feel sorrier for her [the working mom] because I wouldn't take anything for maybe a smile or an unexpected wrap around the back of the legs, you know, a hug. And I just look at them and I know that deep inside they hurt unless they're just extremely hardened or something. They've got to be a little hurt inside because they're not at home with their kids.

Other moms were clearly jealous of women whose paychecks earned them a higher standard of living. "One of my best girlfriends is an attorney and she's told me, 'I wish I could do it, but I can't.' But she lives in a $250,000 house," lamented Anne from California. "She could do it [stay home] if she was willing to live in my condition, in a $100,000 house or whatever. She could live this way, but she chooses not to."

Kitty, a mother of two from Charleston, paints all professional women who have children with the same discriminating brush. "There are those people, maybe in high-power professions—attorneys and stuff, who have nannies that raise their children. I'm saying there are people who have children because that is what they are supposed to do, but they don't really care who is taking care of them and what they are doing." Kitty, in fact, had a nanny of her own for a year. And she experienced a tremendous sense of loss over not being home with her child. "The nanny was seeing everything I should have been seeing," said Kitty. "She saw the first crawl; she saw the first walk."

I believe that the women who object the loudest to working moms are those who are the most insecure in their roles. Plagued by doubt, fear, jealousy, and Good Mother idealism, they're more easily threatened by women who view the mothering role differently; hence their self-righteousness. The mothers in our study send the message that women are supposed to choose roles—not juggle them.

"I feel that mothers who work outside the home have to make a choice," said Vicki, a mother of two from Silver Spring, Maryland.

> I think it's sad; I think they have their priorities all mixed up. Also, I feel some hostility, because I think it's a societal problem. People have to leave their children with underpaid day care workers who are not that focused on their child's desires, and I think the message to their children is that they are not that important and what they are doing outside the home is more important. They see their kids on weekends and evenings. I do not call that parenting.
>
> I think one parent needs to devote time to their children so they feel that emotional attachment and feel they are important. We have all these middle-class, educated parents that feel they have to live up to their homes or they are not intellectually stimulated enough. I've been a journalist and a lawyer, and I find that the guiding and development of my children is very interesting. There is a challenge every day; it is an intellectual challenge. It does not belittle the people who raise children! I could go on about this!

Gaye, a mother of two and a former sales executive from Hawaii, embraces a similar point of view:

> There are a lot of women who have to work outside the home for financial reasons, but I also think there are a lot of women who don't have to, and I think they are copping out. Some people are never satisfied; they just want more money to do things. I mean how much is enough?

Vicki, who considers herself a feminist, thinks working mothers look down on the work that at-home mothers do. "The negative message of feminism has been, in some ways, that the things that women used to do were not valuable, that we should try to become more like men, and that going out in the world and earning a paycheck is more important than staying home," she said.

## *MOTHERS MUST UNITE*

A big part of the split between mothers who work at paying jobs and mothers who don't is due to society's need to classify women into two distinctive "types." Explains author Kaplan,

> Females have been placed in a dilemma through most of their development because of two sets of labels provided by society: the seductive–submissive–admiring–compliant kind and the powerful–bitchy–castrating kind. It is hard to imagine that anyone would want to be classified either way. However, society has classified a narrow band of behavior acceptable for females.[14]

When women get typecast, they get defensive, regardless of which camp they fall into. After all, it's uncomfortable to squeeze oneself into a mold that's six sizes too small. Attempting to do so makes a woman less sure of who she is and, consequently, more defensive. If women were encouraged to shape their own selves—and their own destinies—they would feel much better about who they are and less likely to attack one another. Notes Kaplan,

> The more secure we are about who we are, the less we are shaken by encountering someone who is different from ourselves, and the less we panic when confronted with new possibilities and choices that we had never before considered.[15]

I agree with Kaplan that women need to bridge the gap between them. Before that can be done, the notion that one's behavior should be determined by one's sex needs to be abolished. Women also need to become as strong and self-sufficient as they can be and make attempts at things that go beyond myth and tradition. Furthermore, adult women should share their experiences to strengthen one another rather than condemn. They need to accept, even celebrate, each other's differences, and to acknowledge individuality as a good thing. More importantly, women must develop themselves fully to obtain the self-esteem necessary to feel secure about themselves. They need to abandon stereotypes and think for themselves. It's the lack of a secure sense of self that prompts women to compare themselves to others.

The women in our study who criticized working women the most did so to give themselves a boost in self-esteem and to reassure themselves that the choice they made was the "right" one. The interview groups that we conducted inspired women to open up just enough to begin to understand the differences among them. But that was usually the extent of their progress. The majority of the women had notions about mothering that were so firmly rooted that they ended up in self-righteous idealism. For women to truly support one another, this type of thinking must stop. If women are to free themselves from the absolute demands of child care that become the catalyst for The Mother Crisis, they must adopt a live-and-let-live attitude among themselves that will allow them to connect as partners with a shared sense of responsibility to their children, themselves, and each other. Otherwise, nothing in society, or within our own families, will change. Choice without guilt won't be an option. Role overload will persist among women with children. Stress levels among working moms and at-home moms will continue to climb, because if women don't give themselves permission to choose their own destinies, how can they expect their husbands, their mothers, their employers, their government, to offer consent through support? To my delight, however, a few of the 1990s moms were pro-choice on the question of whether a mother should work.

"I support a variety of options. I mean, any of us who are at home are only one husband away from being out in the workforce through divorce or death or whatever," noted Jan from California. "I definitely do not get on the soap box that the best thing for your child is to stay home," echoed Charleston-based Brenda. "I think the best thing is whatever makes the mom feel fulfilled." Kerry, from Oshkosh, Wisconsin, is untypically empathetic:

> I think it's great that other women can work outside the home—a lot of people need to do it. I feel lucky that I don't need to work outside the home. Everyone makes sacrifices— I've made a lot since I've been home. The working mother has no one to take her kids to the doctor when she's sick. I can just pick up my kids and go. And I know they must feel guilty taking off work when they're supposed to be doing a job.

Sarah, a Texas mother of three, acknowledges that different women need different arrangements. "For some people, I don't think they would be happy staying at home. And if you're not happy with yourself, you're not going to be a good mother. Maybe sending their child to day care is the best thing for one person. But for me, staying home is best." The sentiments of these few women offer a ray of hope that one day soon all mothers will have the same compassion for each other that they have for their children, and unite.

## THE WORK–FAMILY DILEMMA

Despite our culture's obsession with perfection, one "right" way of parenting has yet to be identified. Consequently, we have also failed to determine which is the "right" way to mother a child—perhaps because there isn't one. The 1996 study by the National Institute of Child Health and Human Development (NICHD) was of interest to those who still seek perfection, mainly because it named sensitivity as the key to good parenting, dismissing the notion that a "right" or "perfect" method of parenting even exists. It also renounced the importance of a variety of child care factors (e.g., number of hours spent in day care, age of entry into child care) in terms of the well-being of the child, suggesting that much of the debate over such factors is irrelevant. Yet the debate is still on over whether a mother who works is somehow harming her child.

Women are still confused over their destinies and their choices. The two issues are intricately intertwined. If all at-home mothers woke up one morning and decided to go out and get a job, at least half the books on parenting would immediately become obsolete. Whether women choose to work affects the debate over which parenting method is best, just as the debate over which parenting method is best affects whether women choose to work. Right now, a great number of women let the parenting experts make their career and childbearing choices for them rather than making their own choices based on their own unique individual needs and desires. Morin Davis suggests that women's role confusion contributes to this inability to make strong decisions, that women experience a split within themselves that perpetuates the split among them. Women who work and bear children often lack confidence in their own decisions because they think they have to choose which self is going to operate in the world—the mother self or the professional self.

"Women have to be able to recognize that there are two different ways of being in the world. That as the mother it's okay to be nurturing, to be needy, and that, as the career woman, it's okay to be assertive, striving, creative and so on." One mothers' support group contributes to this role confusion by standing on high moral ground under the guise of individual acceptance. While making impressive attempts to pull working mothers into its fold, the La Leche League, a conservative organization begun in the 1950s to promote breast feeding and the value of maternal nurturance, has nevertheless failed to conceal its disapproval of them. In a 1993 study of the group, Linda M. Blumand and Elizabeth A. Vandewater of the University of Michigan discussed how the League has responded to mothers' increased employment through the years and how its maternalism meshes and competes with feminist discourses. The researchers found that throughout the 1970s, the group largely ignored working mothers, but by 1981, had issued a clearly negative response. That year's League manual included the following: "Our plea to any mother who is thinking about taking an outside job is, 'If at all possible, don't.' "[16] By 1987, however, the League was distributing a positively worded book for working mothers, softening previously negative sentiments and addressing the needs of mothers who had to work.

According to Blum and Vandewater, the official League stance for the 1990s regarding nursing mothers who work strives for a nonjudgmental tone, but it is far from approving. "Much of the ambiguity in the League's stance centers on the interpretation of choice, lack of choice, and the legitimacy of women's different choices,"[17] they wrote. One of the books published by the League, *Of Cradles and Careers: A Guide to Reshaping Your Job to Include a Baby in Your Life*, states that it is every woman's right to determine what is right for herself and her family, yet contradicts the statement several pages later by declaring that to put a baby on the back burner to pursue a career is "to tamper with one of the most fundamental and basic elements of human nature."[18] Although the League of the 1990s emphasizes acceptance of all mothers, it also implies that many employed mothers are motivated by materialism and don't really have to work. The researchers concluded that the League's self-help approach masks the needs of mothers and children for greater social services and public entitlements. None of this is the least bit encouraging to the woman who is looking for acceptance of her decision to combine motherhood with a career.

Women should choose lifestyles that best suit them individually and tailor their approach to mothering according to their own individual value systems. But this is extremely difficult today, given society's reluctance to support such independent thinking and action among women. However, it is a critical first step in changing the way society views mothers. Once women demand the right to a self-determined life along with a cultural value system that supports it, things will begin to change. But until that happens, all mothers—whether they have to work or not, whether they choose to work or not—will be torn apart by guilt, a guilt perpetuated by a society that obliges women alone to take care of the children. One library search that I did unearthed more than a dozen books counseling working women on how to juggle their worldly and domestic duties. All of them approached the problem under the assumption that it was the mother's job to make sure the family was okay while she worked. Each book outlined, in myriad fashions and forms, how a working mother could budget her time better, streamline domestic chores, secure quality child care, squeeze in family time, schedule in romance, and still find time for a manicure, if only she was better organized! Terri Apter, author of *Secret Paths: Women in the New Midlife*, spoke with many professional women—all mothers with young children—who were attempting to do just that.

> They often sustained themselves with the belief that things could be better, even perfect, if only they were better orga-

nized, or had more energy. Though they observed, and resented, and resisted external constraints, their commands
were directed within.[19]

As a professional woman and mother of two young children
myself, I know that beating oneself up for not being better organized is counterproductive. Getting organized often takes just as
much time as role juggling. Even delegating is often a chore. What
if moms were to delegate the delegating? Give the job to their
spouses instead? The move would no doubt spawn a new generation of self-help books for men. One could be entitled *Daddies on
the Home Front, Coping with Domestic Equality*.

According to Friedan, such action is absolutely necessary if
women are to have real choices. "The second stage [of the women's
movement] may not even be a women's movement. Men may be
at the cutting edge of the second stage."[20] There must be government action as well, she says. "The United States is one of the few
advanced nations with … no national policy to provide child care
for those who need it. So the question [of whether to work or not]
is still treated as woman's 'choice'—if she 'chooses' to have a
child, it is her responsibility to take care of it."[21] Friedan admits
that she does not envy young women who are facing or denying
the agonizing "choice" that feminists won for them. "Because it
isn't really a free choice when their paycheck is needed to cover
the family bills each month, when women must look to their own
jobs and professions for the security and status their mothers once
sought in marriage alone."[22]

For most women today, particularly mothers, choice is a
double-edged sword. But it doesn't have to be that way. Like
Freidan, I want women to have the freedom to choose without
penalty, the freedom to choose without guilt.


## STOP FIGHTING ABOUT CHILD CARE AND FIGHT FOR IT!

Much of the discord between mothers would vanish if high-
quality child care were readily available and affordable through-

out the United States. Despite the fact that they condemned working mothers for placing their children in the care of others, the majority of the at-home moms in both studies placed child care first on their wish list. It's ironic that in one breath they damned women for using child care, substandard or not, but in the other, admitted that they yearned for it themselves. Most of the women didn't even recognize the contradiction. Perhaps that's because behind the idealism of the mothers who regard all child care as a cop-out is fear. Many are simply terrified that some harm will befall their children while they're in someone else's charge. It's a natural fear made worse by today's headlines. There is no shortage of news stories about baby-sitter abuse and neglect. Still, many mothers have to work to meet their financial obligations. Like at-home moms, they, too, suffer from fear and guilt. But these mothers don't have a choice. They must use outside child care, however imperfect it might be, then bear the brunt of "Bad Mother" criticism. As responsible parents, their challenge is to secure the best child care available within their means. In America, however, best doesn't necessarily mean adequate. But this sad state of affairs is not the fault of women. It's the fault of a society that does not put families first. This is not the inevitable affliction of an imperfect world. It's the logical result of a system that values its Gross Domestic Product (GDP) more that the well-being of its families, of a system that underpays people who care for children. Mothers don't have these fears in a society that regards child care as a mutual responsibility.

In a 1989 trip to France, First Lady Hillary Rodham Clinton saw firsthand what happens when a country makes caring for children a top priority. In her 1996 book *It Takes a Village, and Other Lessons Children Teach Us*, she reports:

> In France, there is a national consensus that the child care system should not just warehouse kids but prepare them for school and for life. Preschool teachers and directors have the equivalent of a master's degree in early-childhood and elementary education.[23]

French preschool programs for 1½ to 6-year-olds are universal, free, and cover just about all children whose parents want them to attend. According to Clinton, the quality of care is so high that even mothers who do not work outside the home choose to send their children to these government-subsidized centers. In France, three out of four home providers are licensed, and the law limits the number of children they care for to three per home. The incentives to get licensed are substantial: employee benefits, regular mailings of up-to-date information from the government, and periodic visits from a specially trained pediatric nurse.

"Do I believe the French love their children more than we do," asks Clinton. "Of course not.... What I do believe, however, is that the French have found a way of expressing their love and concern through policies that focus on children's needs during the earliest stages of life."[24] During her stay in France, the First Lady spoke with several political leaders, from Socialists to Conservatives, asking them how they managed to transcend their political differences to agree on the issue of government-subsidized child care. "How can you not invest in children and expect to have a healthy country?" was the reply she heard over and over again. Many European countries make a generous investment in their children. While the United States finally passed a bill that allows 12 weeks of unpaid maternity leave, these countries' policies put us to shame. In Finland, for example, women get 35 weeks of maternity leave at full pay; and in Sweden, 38 months at 90-percent pay. France grants women 16 weeks of maternity leave at 90-percent pay. In Germany, women receive 18 months of maternity leave and in Hungary, up to 3 years.[25]

At least four European nations offer benefits that assist working parents in managing their work and family responsibilities. For example, Sweden permits parents to reduce their hours to six per day until the child's eighth birthday (without pay). Sweden, Germany, and Hungary provide paid leave so that parents can care for ill children at home. If space in publicly funded day care programs are limited, France and Germany give priority to working parents.[26] Most countries' specific child care and family policies were designed either to promote maternal employment by assisting mothers in balancing home and working life or to increase fertility by reducing the costs of raising children. Sweden is unique in that it enjoys both a high female labor force and relatively high fertility. In the 1994 report, *Recent U.S. Child Care and Family Legislation in Comparative Perspective*, it's noted that Sweden's policies cover the five major areas of support: a system of subsidized high-quality public child care; support for families with children via the child allowance; an extensive system of parental insurance benefits for employed parents, including maternity and parental leave, cash benefits, leave for contacts with school or child care, and the right to a reduced work schedule upon return to work. The quality of subsidized programs is quite high, and Swedish parents have considerable choice over how they will care for their children. "What is unique about Sweden's policies is their emphasis on equalizing the roles of men and women through individual taxation policies and parenting policies for men," note the authors.

The authors emphasize that the United States, unlike Europe, has never held the explicit goal of promoting female employment. Although the United States has provided public education almost since its founding, only during the past two decades has publicly funded kindergarten become universal. There has been little movement toward public responsibility for preschoolers except in the case of disadvantaged children. Legislation enacted in October 1990, marked the first real expansion of public support for child care and preschool programs in the United States. New grants to states to fund child care assistance for low- and moderate-income families, and refundable tax credits for low-income parents were authorized. The bill also expanded Head Start, the major early educational program for disadvantaged children. Prior to the passage of the 1990 legislation, the majority of child care subsidies, through the tax code, were received by middle- and upper-income families. Benefits that would help parents manage work and family responsibilities are offered at the discretion of employers.

*SUPPORT FOR WOMEN WILL HELP END THE MOMMY WARS*

The United States' refusal to adopt comprehensive family support policies keeps this country from realizing its full female and, therefore, human potential. The best family support programs are those, such as Sweden's, that enable both parents to retain their livelihoods and to take time off to actively parent without being punished for it economically. In Sweden, says author and psychologist Penelope Leach, parenting (by fathers as well as mothers) is considered to be something children need, and the arrangements for parent care are organized as children's entitlement rather than for parents to use on their behalf. Day care, for example, receives direct public funding, so that it benefits all children rather than operating selectively, as the cash and tax benefits offered to parents in other countries, including the United States, so often do.[27] Only when U.S. businesses are directed by the government to support both maternal employment and paternal involvement at home will women have real-life options. Only when women stop decrying one another for pursuing such options will they be able to team together to lobby for more of the same kind of support. Were they to risk starting a dialogue, both camps of women—working moms and at-home mothers—would realize that they have more in common than they previously thought. At the very least, such a dialogue would strip away the fear and suspicion that cultivate existing stereotypes and create an opportunity for mothers to identify and champion their common cause. When I had my first child, Nicholas, in 1992, I helped start up a mothers' club in Windward Oahu. Our goal as founders was to build a loosely organized group that would serve as a support system for mothers of young children. We fashioned a set of guiding principles designed to foster a sense of unity and community. It didn't work. Members quickly separated into cliques. The "playgroup" clique consisted of moms who stayed home with their kids. The "professional" clique consisted of mothers with outside jobs. Women segregated themselves, even when they had the forum to unite. The group atmosphere deteriorated, with gossip and competition replacing nurturance and support. Members' individual traits were criticized rather than revered. Underlying much of the fray were accusations that this woman or that woman wasn't a Good Mother because ... you name it. As a result of such character assassination, this group now struggles to survive. If you are a mother, I implore you to move beyond this type of behavior so that you, and others like you, won't have to struggle so hard to survive.

## CHAPTER 9

# A Mother's True Worth ⌘ Conquering the Paradox of Motherhood

*If the hand that rocks the cradle rules the world, how come that hand's owner can't even collect minimum wage?[1]*

*A*lthough it happened more than 10 years ago, I can remember the conversation with my former husband like it was yesterday. It went something like this: "Joe, I really think it's awful when a couple divorces and the husband refuses to give his wife alimony because she didn't work while they were married." His response: "I don't think it's awful. I think it's fair. I mean, she didn't make any money, so why should she get any? All she did was take care of the house and the kids." His words shot through me like a knife. This was a man with whom, for five years, I had been trying to have children but couldn't. It was in that single, potent moment that I knew how fortuitous unexplained infertility could be. I also knew that I could no longer live with this person. The man with whom I had chosen to spend my entire life valued only that which could be measured in dollars and cents. And he had an extremely low opinion of the traditional definition of "woman's work." This conversation took place in 1983. Joe was 29 at the time; I was 27. In the 14 years since then, I have met many men of all ages—and a few women—who feel the same as Joe does. For many of those years, I believed that they were right—that "woman's work" was insignificant. This was true despite the fact that my Roman Catholic upbringing taught me that motherhood was a woman's highest calling. The paradox was evident to me at an early age. What I couldn't figure out, however, was why I got scared every time I thought about becoming a mother. In retrospect, I know that, despite the myths of my upbringing, I was mindful of the truth—that motherhood was regarded as a second-class job. I had spent many years observing other women, friends who had become mothers at very young ages. What I saw scared me. I began to equate motherhood with powerlessness, for that's how many of these young mothers appeared to me. Saddled with the sole responsibility of caring for their children, they had few life options open to them. Their lives were over, it seemed, before they had even begun. It never occurred to them to challenge the idea that raising the kids was a job they should do alone, without spousal or community support. They lacked power, and they lacked choice. That's the main reason I identified so strongly with the feminists of the time. I wanted my fair share of both. So I sought it the way most feminists did, by seeking power through the patriarchy—through the workplace, where a price tag was hung on your time and your skills. I gained a great deal in my struggle for a sense of personal power. But I lost a great deal, too. For a solid decade, I ignored the fact that, as a woman, and a potential mother, I had intrinsic value, that my value wasn't dependent on the the size of my income or on how well I wrote my last story. I internalized one of the main canons of the patriarchy—that you are worth only as much as you earn. My self-esteem was derived entirely from external sources. It's a way of thinking that serves no purpose once you become a mother, as I found out quickly in 1992, when I became one.

*RECLAIM YOUR POWER*

Many of us are shocked by the real impact that the paradox of motherhood has when we first assume the role. I was. If your goal is to escape the confusion of its contradictions, you need to know that doing so is totally up to you. You must realize that you can be passive no more. Once you've made a commitment to yourself to be honest, your self-esteem will begin to grow. Then you will be ready to seize back your power. You will understand that the pedestal upon which society places its mothers only gives women a false sense of power. Having real power means having the freedom to choose how you live, outside the constraints of mythical expectations. Once empowered, you will know the joy of pursuing your own dreams, of nurturing your interests, of loving yourself. Because you are honoring yourself, your love and compassion for others will grow. You will no longer resent the demands that your family makes on you, because you will have taken the time to attend to your own needs. Reclaiming your power begins with healthy self-esteem.

*VALUE YOURSELF AND OTHERS WILL VALUE YOU, TOO*

The core of The Mother Crisis is a Loss of Self. Women who decline into this stage suffer from a complete loss of self-esteem. We don't know for sure whether the women in our study who dipped this low lacked self-esteem from the onset or whether they had it and then lost it after becoming mothers. We do know that our samples consist of women who appeared to possess some measure of self-esteem, due to the fact that they were relatively successful on an educational, financial, and material level, or otherwise. Since our samples consist of women cut from a cross-section of middle-class America, with backgrounds that offered them ample opportunity to succeed, most of them expected to do so. Yet the majority of the women from both generations began to feel bad about themselves soon after becoming mothers. Striving for perfection, they were ashamed when they couldn't attain it.

They felt guilty about not achieving an ideal, something they felt they were quite capable of accomplishing.

Since The Mother Crisis is about losing one's self-esteem, then a woman's way out of it is to rebuild her tattered self-image. She's got to somehow become okay with herself as a mother. The first step is for her to banish all mythical ideals from her consciousness and to discover, or rediscover, her own intrinsic goodness. This is no easy task for most women, but it can be done. Women are culturally conditioned to rely on the opinions of others to feel good about themselves. In the isolation of motherhood, there is no such feedback. Lacking the necessary external strokes, a woman must learn to rely on herself. Our travels across America proved that more and more women are doing so, and finding out for themselves that generating positive self-esteem is an inside job. In his book *Honoring the Self, Self-Esteem and Personal Transformation*, psychologist Nathaniel Branden offers a blueprint for success. I urge all women on the brink of motherhood to follow it. One of the first points that the author makes is that to judge oneself by the standards of another is subversive to healthy self-esteem.

"Since we are social beings, some measure of esteem from others is necessary, but to tie ourselves to the good opinion of others is to place ourselves at their mercy in the most humiliating way,"[2] says Branden. Many of the women in our samples who experienced The Mother Crisis were enslaved by the standards of others regarding motherhood—standards that were completely unrealistic. Many more of the women were defeated by mythical standards that they had internalized as their own. Branden says there are several building blocks to positive self-esteem, but that the central pillar of esteem is a commitment to awareness, or "the will to understand."[3] Persons must have a real desire to know themselves and the truth before any real construction can begin. As indicated by the title of this book, a crisis is actually a crossroads, a turning point. Women in The Mother Crisis have reached a fork in the road but haven't chosen which avenue to take. The path to awareness is one choice. The other road is a dead end. According to Branden, it's easy to deceive oneself about the actual sources of positive self-esteem, because people often associate it with the end result of whatever they are pursuing, such as knowledge, success, fame, or the admiration of others. Individuals who fall into this trap of self-deception live lives that are totally performance-based. "Perform well and you will be valued" is their credo. It's a common Western belief, but one that simply cannot work in the context of motherhood, by virtue of the fact that there is no realistic definition of the role. All mythical definitions rely on the attainment of perfection. To gauge one's success on whether one attains an unattainable goal is to set oneself up for failure. Yet this is what women across America have done, resulting in a collective loss of self-esteem that's nothing short of devastating. As women support one another as mothers, there will be a collective recovery of self-esteem that's every bit as dramatic.

Another mainstay of positive self-esteem, says Branden, is "the will to be efficacious" in which an individual refuses to accept helplessness as her permanent condition.[4] "All of us know times of bewilderment, despair, and a painful sense of impotence or inadequacy. The question is, do we allow such moments to define us?"[5] he asks. The women who sank into the final depths of The Mother Crisis allowed their despair to define them. They accepted their loss of choice instead of rebelling against it. These women must seek the will to reject helplessness, if they are to break free from the painful cycle. Only then will they have the strength to see beyond their pain. Explains Brandon,

> We can feel temporarily defeated without defining our essence as failure. We can allow ourselves to feel temporarily hopeless, overwhelmed, while preserving the knowledge that after a rest, we will pick up the pieces as best we can and start moving forward again.... Our concept of self can rise above today's adversity.[6]

Women in the core of The Mother Crisis can, and must, convince themselves that they can.

Another key pillar of healthy self-esteem is independence. There is a great distinction between individuals who try to understand things for themselves, think for themselves, and judge for themselves, and those who expect others to do these things for them. According to Branden, "We can either exercise our own mind or pass on to others the responsibility of knowledge and evaluation and accept their verdicts more or less uncritically."[7] The majority of the women we spoke to in the 1995 study viewed themselves as independent thinkers. And they were, except where motherhood was concerned. Few of them ever really challenged their own preconceptions or those of others about the role before assuming it, as a truly independent thinker might do. Instead, they recycled the opinions of others and age-old myths, until they became values that governed their lives.

Hearing this interpretation, I'm sure many of these women would scream, "Foul!" Mainly because, on the surface, it appeared that they had scrutinized their beliefs about motherhood. But we dove beneath the surface during our interviews, where the truth lay naked and exposed. Most of these women only thought they had examined their ideas about motherhood. But through discussion, we discovered that they had merely rationalized a value system that had been spoon-fed to them by their culture, by their parents, or both. Many could not admit to this ideological dependency. They denied it. These were the women who seemed to be in the most pain. But many others could, and did, admit to it, usually the most outspoken among them. It soon became obvious that the ability to think independently kept many a woman from sinking too deep into The Mother Crisis. This was one of the main distinctions between the 1990s women and the 1978 respondents. Consequently, fewer 1990s women suffered a complete Loss of Self. Despite their tendency to deny the negative aspects of their mothering choices, today's women are more independent and possess more of the skills necessary to challenge the tyranny of Good Mother idealism. I think they have a good chance at putting the cycle of The Mother Crisis to rest.

According to Branden, the desire to see things as they are—to "honor reality"—leads to another aspect of high self-esteem—integrity. We have integrity when we demonstrate our values through our behavior. Herein lies one of the main stumbling blocks for women on the path to The Mother Crisis. They cannot demonstrate their values through their behavior, because their values include goals that are impossible to attain. Unable to meet these goals, they choose to label themselves failures rather than to re-examine their standards. The result? Loss of integrity. It's a self-destructive choice that eats away at self-esteem. Says Branden,

> Once we see that living up to our standards appears to be leading us toward self-destruction, the time has obviously come to question our standards, rather than to simply resign ourselves to living without integrity. We must summon up the courage to challenge some of our deepest assumptions concerning what we have been taught to regard as good.[8]

On that note, I suggest that if you are a new mother who feels guilty about not being able to live up to an ideal, STOP! Then ask yourself whose standard you are trying to live up to. What image of the Good Mother do you carry in your head? Get specific. What does your Good Mother do that you cannot? Does she bake home-made bread and produce laundry that's wrinkle-free? Or does she pack a briefcase in the morning and lunch boxes at night? Once you have a true mental picture of the standard you feel you are not living up to, you'll be able to determine whether it's appropriate according to your own individual wants and needs.

All this discussion leads us to what Branden calls the profoundly important assets of self-responsibility and self-acceptance. Both play crucial roles in esteem building. "Avoiding self-responsibility victimizes us with regard to our own life; it leaves us helpless,"[9] he says. A woman in the throes of The Mother Crisis believes that she is helpless, that she cannot escape her situation. She may even wonder how she got there. The resulting powerlessness puts her between the proverbial rock and a hard place, where she is unable to live up to her value system yet unable to challenge it. But to escape, she must. It's a frightening proposition. We saw the fear in the eyes of many women in our discussion groups, the fear that arises when the truth threatens to rear its forbidden head. Before a woman can begin to grow and change, she must also learn self-acceptance. Says Branden,

> I can accept that I am who I am, that I feel what I feel, that I have done what I have done—if I can accept it whether I like all of it or not—then I can accept myself. I can accept my shortcomings, my self-doubts, my poor self-esteem. And

> when I can accept all that, I have put myself on the side of
> reality rather than attempting to fight reality. I am no longer
> twisting my consciousness in knots to maintain delusions
> about my present condition.[10]

Self-acceptance clears the road on the journey toward positive
self-esteem. If a woman in The Mother Crisis can pierce the denial
that supports her delusions, see herself for who she is and assume
responsibility, then she will be able to break free. I have no doubt
that most women, given the proper support, can do this, for I've
met some who were well on their way. Before women can expect
society to value them as mothers, first they must value themselves.
Only then will they have the confidence to demand what they
need from our culture. And only then will society be compelled to
deliver it.


## LETTING GO OF GUILT

> *Guilt is the prosecutor who knows how to make every victim feel like*
> *the criminal. She follows the scene of doubt and self-hatred to its*
> *sources. She will not tell you what you have done wrong. Her*
> *silence is brutal. Her disapproval surrounds you in an envelope of*
> *cold nameless terror.*[11]

Guilt is not only the prosecutor, it is also the precursor to the
bottommost rungs of The Mother Crisis, the pivotal point between
self-destruction and self-reliance, if you will. If a woman is to
prevent her own descent into The Mother Crisis, or climb her way
out once she's in, she must recognize how utterly self-destructive
guilt can be. She must just learn how to put it in its rightful place
before it overcomes her. Although it's true that legitimate guilt has
a necessary role in every person's life, wrongful guilt does not.
The type of guilt that most mothers feel is as criminal as any thief,
for it robs them of their souls, beginning with their self-esteem.

According to Branden, the essence of guilt, whether major or
minor, is moral self-reproach: "I did wrong when it was possible
for me to do right."[12] Since the guilt that most mothers feel involves doing wrong when it was impossible for them to do what

they believed was right, it cannot be legitimate. In her book *Guilt Is the Teacher, Love Is the Lesson,* Dr. Joan Borysenko links guilt to every person's struggle for self-esteem. Healthy guilt, she says, deepens self-respect. It's a process of taking responsibility for behavior that goes against our convictions, followed by self-inquiry and letting go of the past. It deepens self-knowledge and nurtures compassion, empathy, and spiritual growth. According to Borysenko, this process teaches forgiveness. "Forgiveness creates a shift in perception that permits us to see our mistake as an opportunity to learn rather than as proof of how 'bad' we are," she explains.[13] Women stuck in The Mother Crisis are not dealing with healthy guilt, however. Theirs is of the unhealthy variety, as described by Borysenko:

> In the state of unhealthy guilt, it is not the omission or commission of a specific act that triggers remorse. Instead, we live in a constant state of diminishment regardless of what we do or don't do. This painful state of being in which we feel defective, phoney, flawed, or unworthy is called shame.[14]

The women who were in The Mother Crisis were ashamed of who they were. They believed that they were not good enough. "Taking on more than any human being can reasonably accomplish is a common characteristic of unhealthy guilt,"[15] explains the author. These women had nothing to be ashamed of, of course, but had not yet come to that realization. In many respects, women in The Mother Crisis are the keepers of their own prisons. They think and behave in such a way that keeps the gate locked. Regaining self-esteem puts the keys in the hands of the prisoner. In her book, Borysenko lists twenty-one expressions of unhealthy guilt. If you think you might be falling in The Mother Crisis, a brief look at a few of them should help you see how you work to push yourself down. Do you:

- Always apologize for yourself?
- Worry about what other people think of you?
- Never set aside time for yourself?
- Compare yourself to others?
- Try to do things perfectly?

- Worry about being selfish?
- Refuse to ask for or accept help from others?
- Have trouble saying "no"?

If you can see yourself in any of these dispositions, you are a person who has a need to overcommit. "This habit, a major cause of stress, is fed by the difficulty we have in saying no—both to our own needs to achieve and to other people's expectations of us,"[16] says Borysenko. Women overcommit to prove their worth. In reality, they're only avoiding the pain of their feelings, the anxiety that inevitably surfaces when they are alone without distractions. The women we met who were in The Mother Crisis worked very hard at proving their worth. They simply weren't aware that they didn't have to.

The same guilt that Borysenko calls "unhealthy," author Melissa Gayle West labels "false." "It's the result of a lie we have been told about how to be a mother."[17] West says that our culture feeds the guilt that mothers have by telling us we must always be there for our children, no matter what. "We simply cannot be there for them one hundred percent of the time, and we become ill as mothers when we swallow the poisonous belief that we must do so."[18] To get out of The Mother Crisis, a woman must learn that she can love her children and love herself at the same time. "Love has many faces, including at the appropriate time, one that says, 'No, I can't be there for you right now.' "[19] notes West. It's okay. Some of the women got angry when we asked them to examine their belief systems. They were clearly threatened by the request. Branden offers an explanation for this reaction in terms of the guilt that mothers feel. "Sometimes professions of guilt are a smoke screen for disowned feelings of resentment.... I am afraid to acknowledge how angry I am over what is expected of me."[20] So it's easy to see how destructive illegitimate guilt can be. Women must take responsibility for their feelings and learn how to distinguish between the healthy guilt that serves them and the false guilt that does not, for deciding to do nothing at all is the final threat to self-esteem, notes Branden.

"Passivity—the abdication of the responsibility of action—is the ultimate enemy,"[21] he declares. I urge all women who expect to be mothers soon to heed the wise doctor's words. Hold on to your sense of independence; remember that you alone are responsible. And to mothers who feel themselves faltering, get some support, join a mothers' club, talk to someone about how you feel. Honor your feelings; accept them. Be honest about what's bothering you most and figure out what you need to feel better. Take that first step out of the darkness of self-deception and into the warm glow of insight.

Our culture dictates that women should always be there for their children. It also commands them to "bring home the bacon and fry it up in a pan." It doesn't say a whole lot about relaxing by themselves or with other adults. The typical working mom today is always on the move, running from work in the morning, to school in the afternoon to pick up the kids, then back home, where she spends the remainder of the evening entertaining her children, oftentimes out of guilt. If you think that mothers who stay home experience less guilt, go back to Chapters 3 and 7. The widespread belief that the more one does for one's children the better a parent one is can undermine your marriage, or your sense of self, as quickly as termites do your house. North Carolina–based psychologist John Rosemond says that the concepts of "working mothers" and "stay-at-home moms" compel women to stop being wives once they have children. According to Rosemond,

> Their husbands then fall into line by becoming fathers, first and foremost; and that, kids, is the story of how parents— especially the female of the species—are now synonymous with servants and how the marriage has become the American Family's Cheshire Cat—now you see it, now you don't.[22]

Rosemond recognizes that there's nothing new about mothers working outside the home. What is new is the guilt over doing so. The psychologist advises working moms to spend time with their husbands in the evening and let the kids entertain themselves. He speaks of his mother, who was a single parent for the first 7 years of his life and then married. "In neither situation did she come home from work thinking she owed him something," he says.

"Quite the contrary, she came home feeling—are you ready for this?—I owed her something! What a concept!"[23] By contrast, many of today's kids are growing up thinking their mothers are obligated to them because, in Rosemond's view, the mother–child relationship has been turned upside-down. As a result, today's child is at great risk of becoming a petulant, demanding, ungrateful brat. And the more demanding he or she becomes, the more likely his or her mother will feel that she is not doing enough. "And around and around they go, this co-dependent union of mother and child,"[24] says Rosemond. Too many mothers today are co-dependent; they rely on the happiness of their children to bring happiness to themselves. So they work extra hard at making their children happy. And they think that making their children happy means always giving in to their demands.

If a mother really wants to raise healthy children, she will stop putting her kids first and put herself and the marriage first instead. Rosemond even goes so far as to say that the belief that children require a lot of attention is false. "At best it's a misunderstanding, born of misguided idealism. At worst, and especially when it's handed down from a so-called parenting expert, it's a lie."[25] The real job of the parent is to usher the child out of her life, he explains. Children will grow up with healthy self-esteem if they are encouraged to be self-reliant. This they cannot do if they receive too much attention from adults. But showing your child that he or she needs to get a life can't be done unless you have one too. So, mom, if you want to end your guilt trip, take the next available off-ramp. Realize that what you already do for your children—feed, clothe, protect, and nurture them—is enough. Say "no" to your kids more, put your feet up, read a book, rent a video, play tennis, get a sitter, and go to a movie with your husband. Relax.

## REDEFINING MOTHERHOOD

No one knows more about being a mother than mothers themselves. So why allow others to define the role? If you're a mother and want to influence change, it's imperative that you take your motherhood experiences out into the world. If the true value of motherhood is ever going to be realized, mothers must do this. Dr. Dyanne Affonso, dean of the School of Nursing at Emory University in Atlanta, says,

> The reason we haven't properly defined motherhood is because we haven't been listening to women. Women are the experts yet we don't act like they have a valid experience. Motherhood is as women define it. They're the ones who live the role.

Developing your own definition of motherhood will take a great deal of introspection, but the outcome will be empowering. Afterward, you will have the confidence and wherewithal to speak your mind. Once our culture has a way of realistically defining motherhood, it will be better able to measure a mother's true worth.

The following exercises are offered to help mothers build their confidence so that they can develop their own definition of motherhood:

- Honor your feelings. Motherhood gives rise to intense feelings. They are not wrong.
- Talk about your feelings to your spouse, family members, and friends.
- Ask for feedback.
- Join a "Mom's" club.
- Do affirmations (e.g., "Motherhood is valuable work").
- Accept your own mothering style.
- Accept the individual mothering styles of other women.
- Go somewhere without the children at least three times a week.

Building one's self-esteem and rediscovering who one is is the only way out of The Mother Crisis. Once a woman is free, she is obligated to help other women who are stuck in the quagmire. She can do this by telling anyone who will listen her truth about motherhood, without guilt and without shame. She can overtly reject the myths that our culture uses to demean us. The Mother

Crisis is widespread in America. If a large-enough movement of women repudiates the ideals that cause mothers distress, there's a good chance that society will change.

## MOTHERS DESIGN THEIR OWN SOLUTIONS

Although a large number of the women participating in our 1995 discussion groups were guarded with their feelings about motherhood, the majority gave candid responses when we asked them what kind of societal changes they would most like to see. Virtually all the women were conscious of our culture's paradoxical treatment of its mothers. And they were acutely aware of their diminished status due to the fact that they were no longer in the workforce. The women offered a variety of suggestions on how society can better support its mothers. In an attempt to elicit freer responses, we asked them to describe what a perfect support system for mothers might look like. Weeser, from Applegate, California, said that the best kind of support would come from churches and schools. She contends that as long as women are expected to be caretakers for the entire family, including the husband, mothers are going to continue to burn out fast.

> A lot of women who have served their husbands and their children, and all of a sudden they decide, that's it, they can't do it anymore, and they're angry at their husbands because their husbands haven't done anything for them, and they've done everything for their husbands. The husbands can't figure out what's going on. But women get this idea in their heads that we're supposed to be there for everybody, and I don't know where we get that.

The solution to the problem, according to Weeser, lies in education. "I think the church could help husbands [change their expectations] by having seminars or parenting classes. School and colleges could help, too. We get training for careers, but where is the training for relationships, for marriage and raising kids?"

Weeser's friend, Kitty, proclaimed that the best support system is a woman's husband.

I think our husbands are the greatest resource but that we don't have them around too much and don't tap into them enough. We find out when we're gone that they can really do a lot. We complain that they sit around and watch TV, but when I ask my husband to do something, he'll do it. He's very willing to help, given the opportunity.

The response we heard most from the women, however, had to do with child care. Quality, subsidized day care tops the wish list of nearly every stay-at-home mom that we met. Even women who were dead set against mothers who worked outside the home were proponents for flexible, subsidized day care. "I think the perfect support system would be free baby-sitting—free community, superquality day care centers," said Barbara from Hawaii. "It would be nice to have a day care system where you can drop your kids off for an hour or so."

Elly, from West Palm Beach, Florida, said that government-subsidized day care would be society's way of saying, "We value you and want you to work, and we also realize that child care is a valid concern." Elly also believes that church and community groups could do more for stay-at-home mothers by providing programs that help them get together. Connie, from Downingtown, Pennsylvania, would like to see corporate America pitch in more:

It would be really great if there was day care in every single business out there, so you wouldn't be taking your children anywhere else while you're at work, and there wouldn't be thirty kids in two rooms. It would be free to the employees, so that when your kids are sick they wouldn't look at you like you were trying to get a day off work.

Helen, from Rockville, Maryland, would like to see a blend of the old with the new for today's harried moms. "If I could design a perfect support system for mothers, it would be a mixture of what I'm experiencing now and what my mother experienced when I was growing up," she said. Helen is a member of a mom's club, and her community has access to a Parent's Resource Center, a drop-in facility for parents and children. A recovering alcoholic, she also attends Recovery with Kids, AA meetings for parents with children. Helen says she gets tremendous support from the people in these programs. "But this is support from the outside community that I've had to seek out," she explained. "I've had to join organizations. My mother had her neighborhood as her support system. Some people had their families. She didn't. To me, the perfect support system would be a combination of all three."

Helen's friend Carrie, who has moved a lot due to her husband's job, had an extremely inventive response: "The ideal thing for a support system would be to get on the computer, punch in your problem, and have an answer come right to you—have a support unit come right to you—just like they do on the soaps, snap your finger and you cyberspace into the situation you need to be in." While zapping oneself into cyberspace is not yet within our means, today's modern moms are getting more and more help from computers. *USA Today* recently reported that, across the country, at-home moms—and some at-home dads—are E-mailing and using on-line chat rooms and bulletin boards to find support and parenting advice. The forums they are using, such as *Moms Online* and *Parent Soup*, are the inventions of their peers, at-home moms who have become entrepreneurs. Users report that the bond they have with on-line acquaintances is often stronger than their ties to ordinary friends. Cyberspace appears to be less threatening than ordinary face-to-face encounters.[26] E-mail is a tailormade solution for mothers like Carrie, who are forced to pull up stakes every few years. "When my husband last told me that we might have to move because of the job I thought, 'There goes my support system,'" she recalled. "I'd worked six years to get this support system worked up—friends, family, confidants, backup sitters, sitting co-ops, exercising routines, stroller hikes, finding kid-friendly areas to go to where I can breast feed and not have somebody gawking over me."

One Downingtown mom's picture of the perfect support system is a throwback to nineteenth-century domestic life, when mothers enjoyed the help of household assistants. "I just think it would be wonderful to have someone do the really thankless jobs like housework and cooking," she said.

Debbie, from West Palm Beach, Florida, claims that all mothers would benefit from a service that provides knowledgeable infant and child-rearing professionals on an on-call basis.

> The perfect support system would be that whenever you had a baby, the government would pay for a full-time nanny to come in. If you needed to go out, just ring up the nanny, or if you needed to lay down because you didn't feel well, there would always be someone that you could trust and who was well trained.

Katherine, from California, believes that women should receive Social Security benefits for the years they put into child rearing. Nearly all the mothers thought that paid parental leave by employers would make life easier for both parents.

Perhaps the ultimate mother's support fantasy, however, is what Bonnie, from California, dubbed "a friend with ESP. It would be this circle of people—like a mom and a husband and a friend—who would be able to read my mind and know what I need. It's so nice when people come up with it on their own." Although it's ludicrous the first time you hear it, the idea might not be so farfetched. If more people had a real understanding of motherhood, rather than a mythical one, mothers might indeed get more unsolicited, spontaneous support. In summary, the support that mothers want most consists of the following:

- Quality, subsidized child care
- Free marriage and parenting education
- Free Parent Resource Centers
- Child-friendly public environments
- Cultural support of breastfeeding
- Paid parental leave from employers
- Social Security benefits for parents who stay home to raise children
- Better postpartum care
- More spousal support

If enough of us work at it, theirs is a dream that might well come true.

## WOMEN NEED MORE POSTNATAL CARE

Before a mother can think about caring for her child, she must care for herself. The first weeks and months after childbirth—the postpartum period—is the biggest challenge for a woman, because the constant demands of a newborn tend to overshadow her commitment to her own physical and emotional well-being. In many cultures, women rally around the new mother to ensure that she takes proper care of herself and her baby. In the United States, however, new mothers are often isolated and alone. In America, childbearing has been medicalized. Having a baby is treated like an illness, rather than a rite of passage. Women are shuttled in and out of hospitals in an effort to reduce costs and released to a home where there is often little or no support. Affonso says that women won't get better postpartum support until attitudes change about the significance of childbearing.

> I think one basic key [to better support] is that society has to conceptualize childbearing as an important phenomenon in the advancement of health of the society. That it's not just unique to women, it's not just a women's problem or a women's issue. Right now in our country, after women have their babies they're literally on their own. We do not have rituals and metaphors and cultural beliefs ... that this is an important time in the entire social structure. If we believed that, we'd be rallying around pregnant women in a whole different way. We would have health policy and public policies. Other parts of the world culturally, have rituals and sanctions in the postpartum to rally around the mother and make sure she has rest and recovery, time and adaptation.

According to Affonso, America's health care system is not structured to address the needs of women, because it doesn't work at identifying them in the first place. "It's [structured] more like, 'I'm the professional so I'm going to tell you what you need,'" she explains.

As a health care expert, Affonso lobbies on the federal level for increased public support, but advises women themselves to seek support on the local level. "Right now we're trying to downsize government right? So looking for it at the federal level ain't gonna work," she declares.

> Besides, needs vary so much from community to community that the [federal] government has trouble [helping mothers] because they can't do something that would work across the board. Woman on woman is the best thing going right now, I think, because they live in a societal structure that doesn't support them in a general way.

In essence, Affonso is saying that moms should keep on doing what they've been doing, forming mothers' clubs, baby-sitting co-ops, and anything else that addresses their needs. In the future, these organizations could serve as models for the establishment of pubicly funded programs and institutions.

### *AMERICA MUST GIVE PARENTS MORE HELP RAISING CHILDREN*

It is one thing to wish for a support system. It is quite another thing to get it. Yet everything that surrounds us began with a wish, with a vision. Although they might not have known it, all the women cited in this book had a vision of what they wanted for themselves as mothers. I have merely helped them illustrate it. The picture is clear—mothers want an America that helps parents raise its children. I'm going to talk about how to realize such an image. Before this image can be physically created, however, the three main factors that perpetuate The Mother Crisis must be quashed. The preceding parts of this chapter addressed two of them: (1) society's paradoxical treatment of mothers, and (2) the fanciful myths that prevent mothers from feeling good about themselves. Now we'll take a close look at the third primary factor that works at pulling mothers down, that is, society's tendency to discourage mothers from working outside the home.

According to feminist law professors Mary Joe Frug and Joan C. Williams, there is fundamental attitude in our culture that sets mothers up for a lifetime of continuous child care: "Women assume that if they do not sacrifice, no one will, and men assume if they do not, someone else will."[27] Society discourages mothers from working outside the home, not because women are a better fit in the home or because their outside employment endangers children, but because America embraces the all-pervasive belief that taking care of children is primarily a woman's responsibility. Notes author Mary Frances Berry in her book *The Politics of Parenthood,*

> Fundamentally ... what is needed is an organized challenge to gender relations and patriarchy and an understanding that imposing child care responsibilities principally on one parent rather than on both is a deprivation of rights. The issue of child care is really an issue of power, resources and control among adults; it is not a battle over who is more suited for care.[28]

I agree with Berry's prediction that the restructuring of gender relations will occur only when enough women decide they want change. "Just as many women feared an Equal Rights Amendment because it seemed to threaten their idea of family relations and roles, many women are frightened of changing gender roles at home to relieve the burdens about which they complain."[29] She's so right. I can't even begin to count the number of women from our study who complained about role overload, yet at the same time found a dozen excuses for not asking for relief. If women truly want the same opportunity that men have at realizing their full human potential, they have to work at redefining motherhood first.

According to Berry, the child care and employment researchers in the United States approach the issue of child care by looking for ways to help mom with her "responsibilities." When they do this, says the author, "They're dismissing her rights as a person. The choices she makes about how to spend her time and what interests to pursue become automatically more constrained than those of fathers."[30] Women need to work for more sweeping solutions to the problem that move beyond the realm of helping Supermom put on her cape. These would include such things as giving tax credits to real estate developers to build affordable housing near the workplaces or to equip shopping centers, "green" areas, and other public environments with meal-preparation facilities. Women must urge Congress to adopt legislation mandating paid parental leave for employees and look for ways to have parenting sanctioned under the guidelines for receiving Social Security benefits. Currently, the amount of money a person receives upon retirement is based on his or her earnings over a lifetime. As a result of combining work and family roles, women are more likely than men to have years of no earnings or lowered earnings. Women are out of the labor force for close to one-third of their potential work lives, whereas men are out of the labor force for only 3 percent of their working years.[31] Since women's wages are lower than men's during their working lives, low wages, combined with more years out of the labor force, result in a diminished PIA ("primary insurance amount" in labor department jargon) for retired female workers.[32] It's time to stop penalizing women for staying home to care for their children and reward them instead.

Since it might seem unreasonable to lobby for tax relief and improved government programs at a time when the federal deficit is spiraling out of control, the going could get tough. But women are used to tough. And there are larger issues at hand that demand that society take a closer look at how America is taking care of its kids, such as the rising juvenile crime rate, domestic abuse, and other violent crime. These issues must be addressed first, and sending women home to the kitchen Donna Reed-style is not the way to make them go away. The responsibility for children must be shared, for all of society is the beneficiary. Sure, there's a social cost. But why must women continue to pay more than their fair share of the debt? In Frug and Williams's view, the labor system, as it developed during and after the Industrial Revolution, has adapted to modern conditions by exploiting employed mothers in nuclear families and impoverishing divorced women and their children through a lack of support.[33] Virtually all the studies undertaken to relieve the stress women feel in juggling their dual roles overlook race and class differences among families, the problems of female-headed households, and families who work on anything other than nine-to-five shifts.

In 1965, only 2.3 percent of children under age 12 were in day care centers. By 1971, less than 8 percent of white working women placed their children in day care centers, and almost twice as many black working women did. Child care advocates argued that there were not enough centers, but preference polls indicated that most parents did not want nonrelative care, regardless of its quality. Americans believed, as Jane's 1978 survey also reflected, that centers were for poor people or would interfere with child development. Nixon's veto of the December 1971, Comprehensive Child Care Bill dimmed the prospects for a national child care program in the near future. A strong coalition of labor and public interest groups had effectively lobbied Congress to win passage of the bill, believing that millions of mothers would benefit from the freedom of choice that it would win them. But this group failed to realize that its proposals were simply in conflict with prevailing conservative attitudes. Hostility to child care legislation erupted when Mondale introduced the Child and Family Services Bill of 1975, proposing subsidized development child care for non-welfare families, making it a middle-class issue. Critics claimed the act would injure the American family. It would, in fact, have injured the traditional "mom stays home" version of the American family, but it would have granted women more freedom as well.

By 1988, however, the status of women had changed dramatically. According to the Bureau of Labor Statistics, nearly 57 percent of married women living with their husbands worked full time. Most of these women had children under the age of 6. Middle-class America now needed help. Women's organizations began to downplay a concern for women's rights and build support for a national child care policy. Molly Yard, then president of the National Organization for Women (NOW), emphasized that NOW supported a national and universal child care policy, because child care made it possible for mother to enjoy other rights. NOW was concerned with women's individual rights, whether they had children not, and would support any child care programs that did not violate this principal.

Despite the fact that congress passed and President Clinton

signed the Family and Medical Leave Act in 1993, attitudes in America about gender roles remained, as they do today, largely the same. The only way to foster change is to begin thinking of children as the responsibility of both parents and society. One way to put this idea into action would be through divorce decrees, says Berry. "A court decree should require not just child support payments but burden sharing or shifting to take care of the children in order to impress upon the parties the seriousness of their obligations,"[34] she says. "The parent without custody should also be required to help with other chores that drain custodial parents of time and energy such as baby-sitting, transportation to doctor's appointments and other child care services or to school."[35] While Berry acknowledges that these arrangements will be difficult to implement, they are important ways to begin to change the thinking of parents. Until attitudes about gender-role change at the grassroots level, it's unlikely that national policies on child care and parental support will be enacted. Only when the idea that mothers at home with children and fathers away at work is no longer viewed as right, only when we stop thinking of government-subsidized child care as a welfare issue, will there be a large enough constituency in America to affect public policy. There is still a double standard in America regarding the child care needs of the poor and those of the middle and upper classes. Poor, single mothers are encouraged to go to work and leave their kids in day care, whereas well-to-do married mothers are encouraged to stay home with the children.

In the 1986 study, "A Lesser Life," by Sylvia Hewlett, it was suggested that motherhood supports such as those provided in Western Europe would truly liberate women.[36] The author praised the extensive government-funded child care system in Sweden as a model for the United States and urged women to demand a similar one in this country. But there's an inherent risk at doing so. The effort must not take place at the cost of defining women as mothers, not persons. Until quality child care is regarded in the United States as a childhood right rather than a parental luxury, no universal policies will be adopted.

*CONQUERING THE PARADOX*

Many times as I was growing up, I heard my mother say, "Motherhood is a thankless job." I didn't understand what she was talking about back then. Now that I'm a mom myself, I recall that she said it only on those days when nothing she did seemed to matter, when all her explaining, her discipline, and her efforts seemed completely ineffective. I understand what she meant today, because I have those kinds of days myself. It's a struggle for me to put into words exactly how I feel about being a mother. For one thing, I never really wanted to be a mother until I was 31 or 32 years old. It was then that I began to feel like I was missing something. I wanted to be a part of the life flow that surrounds us. Childless, I did not feel a part of it. Suddenly I felt the need to contribute to the future in a life-affirming, tangible way.

Since childhood, I had worked hard at developing my intellect. As an adult, I focused on goal-oriented activities that had little to do with my intuitive side. Motherhood changed all that. For 4 years now, I have been called on to be compassionate when I want to be demanding, to be patient when I want it done now, to be kind and nurturing when frustration threatens to overwhelm me. I have been challenged in more ways than I can count. But as a mother who loves her children, I have continually strived to do better. I have learned how to be process- rather than goal-oriented. I have learned how to trust my instincts. I have reached down inside myself on days when I feel empty inside to find a love so deep, so unconditional, that it scares me. I understand that the present moment is the most precious time there is and that children do, indeed, grow up fast. Yet I am also a realist. I know that I am not whole unless I am writing, that I would be spiritually sick were I to give up that part of myself for my children. Of course, my children need me, and I am there for them. I am there for them while I am working at my computer and while I am standing at the kitchen sink. They are in my heart everywhere I go, every minute of every day. They are my heart. I wonder what was there before they came along. Why can't society value motherhood? Perhaps because its power is so awesome, its influence so universal, its presence so primal that to do so would be too frightening. For me, the experience has been truly profound. Motherhood teaches me something new about myself each and every day. I experienced my own Mother Crisis in 1992. Today, I have abandoned the myths of motherhood so that I can know who I am. I know where I want to go, and I like who I am becoming. I know that, as a mother, I have tremendous wealth and worth.

If you or someone you know has succumbed to the paradox of motherhood, I hope this book will give you the courage to renew your strength and remember who you are. The paradox of motherhood is powerful. It deprives us of a sense of self by telling us who we are. It takes a tremendous act of will to resist it. But as author and teacher Dr. Wayne W. Dyer points out, true freedom comes from letting go of labels that identify us, of realizing that we are not what we call ourselves, how we look to others, what we think, or what we do. Rather, we are the silent observer that resides within. She is who you are. Sit in the dark and watch your children sleep, and you'll get to know her better. The paradox of motherhood must be quashed. Although each of us must work alone to cast it out of our own psyches, we can work together to banish it from society. If you're scared, take a deep breath, pray if you like, and get some support. Welcome other women on your journey to personal freedom. You'll know when you are ready. The inspiration will come from deep within, from your soul. Trust that inner voice. She is who you are.

## CHAPTER 10

# *Epilogue* ↫

*T*he following excerpt from my journal is a snapshot of how my own Mother Crisis began. As my second child nears her first birthday, I breathe a welcome sigh of relief and thank God that I never have to doubt myself again.

Dinnertime is the pits. Standing, standing, STANDING, in front of the sink while my mind frantically tries to shut out the screams coming from my ankles. First, I focus on the TV, the "Wheel of Fortune" spinning its red, green, and purple slices of pie. It becomes a blur as thick as the clouds of frustration that emanate from my neck, my shoulders, my teeth, my jaw, my fingertips as I wipe, rub, and scrub tiny bits of cheese that cling like Krazy glue to the dinner plate.

"Nicholas," I seethe, through clenched teeth. "Why must you do this every night?" Turning my gaze upward to what, before parenthood, I believed to be the most powerful being in the universe, I repeat the question. Then, I bend down and gently pick up my 1-year-old toddler, bringing his blustery red, tear-stained cheek close to mine, and say in a voice that's so calm it gives the entire scene a surrealistic edge, "Mommy needs to wash the dishes so I'm going to put Nicky in his room if he wants to scream, OK?" Wondering how I did that without my whole body exploding, I begin to move my feet.

I walk slowly toward "the room" and the playpen that it houses. Nick, with his straight mop of blond hair making him look every bit like a tomato with a hat, flips his decibel switch to panic level. I begin to quake all over, inside and out. Legs shaking, stomach churning, mind spinning to the tune of a thousand mixed emotions, I place my firstborn into his play-pen and walk away without looking back. All of a sudden the room is a cave, and I am the hungry lioness who's just left her cub to fend for himself alone in the dark while she hunts.

Tonight I am scavenging for a different kind of sustenance ... soul food. One moment with myself where I can find the emotional center which, before motherhood, was only a yoga class away. No time for stretches now, I think, plunging my hands into soapy dishwater. Five minutes later, I return to my den, where Nick stands dripping wet from a mixture of perspiration and tears. "What kind of mother are you?" thunders a voice that I didn't even know existed until last year. I pick up my son and hold him tightly at my breast. Nick's tiny head flops onto my shoulder; his chest heaving with huge sighs of relief. All frustration evaporates as I gently rock him back and forth.

Such is the ambivalence of motherhood.

# *Appendix* ↶

*PARTICIPATION CRITERIA*

Women who:

- Are 25- to 45-years-old
- Have some post–high school education
- Have two children with at least one 2- to 6-year-old
- Have a spouse with post–high school education
- Are unemployed outside the home

*QUESTIONNAIRE*

1. Were you employed outside the home before you had children? If yes, what did you do?

   1978   Yes: 68; No: 3
   Professions: teachers—31; nurses—9; secretary—14; business—3; health fields—4; education—2; other—4. Nurturing—65; Nonnurturing—6

   1995   Yes: 106; No: 3
   Professions: sales—10; management—16; business—19; teaching—15; health/beauty—11; nursing—6; journalism—4; flight/travel—3; engineering—3; design—4; secretarial—8; law—1; other—6

The results of both surveys, 1978 and 1995, will follow each question.

2. If previously employed, give two reasons why your work was worthwhile or two reasons why it was *not* worthwhile.

   1978   Worthwhile: 87%; Not worthwhile: 13%
   1995   Worthwhile: 95%; Not worthwhile: 5%

3. Did you aspire to a higher position?

   1978   Aspired: 23%; Did not aspire: 77%
   1995   Aspired: 50%; Did not aspire: 50%

4. Were you happy with your performance in that job?

   1978   Happy: 89%; Not happy: 11%
   1995   Happy: 96%; Not happy: 4%

5. List five words that best described you prechildren.

   1978   Positive: 74%; Negative: 19%; Uncommitted: 5%
   1995   Positive: 86%; Negative: 10%; Uncommitted: 4%

6. Who decided to have children?

   I _____
   My husband _____
   Both _____
   1978   Woman: 18%; Husband: 0%; Both: 81%
   1995   Woman: 15%; Husband: 1%; Both: 82%; Other: 2%

7. Give three reasons why you decided to have your first child.

   1978   Boost low self-esteem: 12%; Social pressure: 18%; Unplanned: 19%; Loved children/ready for family: 49%
   1995   Love children/ready for family: 43%; Social pressure: 3%; Biological time clock: 28%; Need to mother: 9%; Couldn't find work: 1%; Unplanned: 15%; Uncommitted: 2%

8. a. Who decided you would stay home with your first? (Check one):

   I _____, Husband _____, Family _____, Other _____

1978   Woman: 71%; Husband: 0%; Both: 28%
1995   Woman: 48%; Husband: 3%; Both: 38%; Family: 3%;
Other: 4%; Uncommitted: 6%

b. Why are you staying home with your children?

1978   It's my job: 9%; I want to for me: 22%; It's important
for them: 60%; Besides, I can't get that job: 7%
1995   It's my job: 26%; I want to for me: 19%; It's important
for them: 25%; Don't want others rearing them: 17%; Besides, I can't get that job: 10%; Uncommitted: 3%

9. Describe how you felt when you first became a full-time, at-
home mother (circle one of each pair):

| | |
|---|---|
| more bored | less bored |
| more free | less free |
| more lonely | less lonely |
| more boring | less boring |
| more happy | less happy |
| more satisfied | less satisfied |

you fill in _____

1978   More positive: 50%; More negative: 42%; Uncommitted:
7%
1995   More positive: 53%; More negative: 26%; Equally positive and negative: 20%; Uncommitted: 1%

10. Give three reasons for having second child:

1978   Companion for first/Always wanted two: 83%; Unplanned: 5%; Other: 8%; Uncommitted: 1%
1995   Companion for first: 31%; Always wanted more: 28%;
Didn't want "only" child: 24%; Unplanned: 9%; Other: 4%;
Uncommitted: 4%

11. Are you happy with your decision to stay home?

1978   Yes: 64%; Not happy, but my responsibility: 4%; Yes, but
…: 29% (Depends on the day: 4%); Have regular times away:
4%; Would like to return to career: 21%; Uncommitted: 1%

1995   Yes: 80%; Not happy, but my responsibility: 2%; Yes, but
…: 17%; Sometimes I'd rather work: 33%; I'm worried about
my career/future: 17%; I do it for them: 22%; This is very
difficult: 28%; Uncommitted: 2%

12. Who decided on the number of children you'd have?

1978   Woman: 25%; Husband: 4%; Both: 65%; Other: 4%
1995   Woman: 15%; Husband: 4%; Both: 70%; "God": 6%;
Other: 5%

13. Why have you continued full-time, at-home mothering?

1978   It's my duty: 14%; I want to for me: 47%; It's important
for them: 28%; I can't get that job: 4%
1995   It's my duty: 6%; I want to for me: 17%; It's important
for them: 58%; I can't get that job: 15%; Couldn't and work: 3%;
Uncommitted: 1%

14. List the tensions you feel in your role as a mother.

1978   Burden of total responsibility; making major decisions
for children; mother role vs. housekeeper; vs. wife; constant
demands on time, energy, sibling fighting; lack of time for self,
lack of intellectual stimulation; coming last after every one
else's needs met; ambivalence of too much of herself given vs.
not enough; feelings of inadequacy to fulfill expectations; concern with consistency and fairness with discipline.
1995   Not getting own needs met; lack of acknowledgment of
a good job; discipline and sibling problems; concerns over
relationship with husband; too much to do—feel like I'm
neglecting children and other responsibilities.

15. How do you get relief from these tensions?

1978   Talking to friends (incl. husband): 30%; Activities out of
home with children: 32%; Quiet time at home alone: 12%;
Crying, yelling: 16%; Uncommitted: 5%

1995   Talk to friends: 31%; Talk to husband: 15%; Take action (exercise, school, work, crafts, go out): 39%; Pray: 3%; No relief: 12%

16. Are there any joys in mothering? If so, identify them?

1978   They love and need me: 47%; Seeing them happy and succeed: 24%; Watching their growth and development: 25%; Uncommitted: 2%
1995   They love and need me: 52%; Seeing them happy and succeed: 22%; Watching their growth and development: 26%

17. Are you happy in your role of mother? Yes _____, No _____

1978   Yes: 67%; Usually: 28%; Uncommitted: 2%
1995   Yes: 85%; Usually: 15%

18. What word *most* describes your relationship with your children?
Friend _____, Nurturer _____, Teacher _____, Disciplinarian _____, Leader _____, Other _____

1978   Friend: 1%; Teacher: 18%; Leader: 2%; Nurturer: 28%; Disciplinarian: 4%; Other: 1%; Most: 14%; All: 28%
1995   Friend: 5%; Teacher: 8%; Leader: 1%; Nurturer: 42%; Disciplinarian: 5%; Other: 4%; Most: 24%; All: 12%

19. Do you seek your childrens approval? How?

1978   Yes: 43%; No, but …: 19%; No: 32%; Uncommitted: 6%
1995   Yes: 61%; No, but …: 17%; No: 17%; Uncommitted: 5%

20. Do you feel guilty about any areas of child rearing? If yes, which areas and why?

1978   Yes: 82%; No: 15%; Uncommitted: 2%
1995   Yes: 87%; No: 11%; Uncommitted: 2%

21. a. What kind of a mother do you think you are? Rate yourself on scale of 1 to 10 (10 being best in terms of your qualities as a mother).

    1978   Average rating: 8.3
    1995   Average rating: 7.8

    b. Are you: strict _____; permissive _____ (Check one)

    1978   Strict: 57%; Permissive: 18%; Flexible: 19%; Uncommitted: 4%
    1995   Strict: 45%; Permissive: 28%; Flexible: 25%; Uncommitted: 3%

22. What are the positive effects of children on your marriage?

    1978   Common bond with husband: 61%; Great enjoyment: 15%; Maturing with increased self-knowledge: 18%; Uncommitted: 4%
    1995   Common bond with husband: 71%; Increased love in family: 13%; Maternal maturation: 4%; Paternal maturation: 7%; Minimal positive effects: 3%; Uncommitted: 2%

23. What are the negative effects?

    1978   No time for me: 2%; No time alone with husband: 43%; Tension and conflict (money, discipline, expectations): 36%; Fatigue: 5%; No effects: 2%; Uncommitted: 5%
    1995   Loss of time with spouse: 27%; Increased conflict with spouse: 11%; Loss of time/increased conflict with spouse: 48%; Increased stress (time, financial, etc.): 6%; Too tired: 5%; None: 1%; Other: 2%

24. It's a general statement that the woman of the house is responsible for everyone's happiness and the meeting of their emotional needs. Do you agree?

    1978   Yes: 50%; No: 0%; Both: 50%
    1995   Yes: 64%; No: 28%; Both: 7%; Uncommitted: 1%

25. Who meets your emotional needs?

    1978   Me: 2%; Husband: 18%; Many (incl. friends, family):
    67%; Unmet: 8%; Uncommitted: 2%
    1995   Me: 5%; Husband: 22%: Many: 63%; Unmet: 6%; Un-
    committed: 4%

26. There's a saying that in all marriages, one loves more than the
    other. Do you accept this or not?

    1978   Agree: 22%; Disagree: 69%; Don't know: 8%
    1995   Agree: 35%; Disagree: 61%; Don't know: 4%

27. Do you think you're a good wife? (Rate yourself on 1 to 10
    scale, 10 being best.)

    1978   8.15 average
    1995   7.44 average

28. Rate your marriage (1 to 10, 10 being best).
    Before children _____
    After children _____

    1978   Average: Before children: 8.23; After children: 8.4
    1995   Average: Before children: 8.03; After children: 8.05

29. Having children affects every mother differently. How do you
    think you've changed emotionally since you've become a
    mother?

    1978   More mature: 36%; More anxious: 29%; More sensitive
    to others: 22%; Understood better by mother: 2%; No change:
    4%; Uncommitted: 4%
    1995   More mature: 45%; More sensitive: 14%; More anxious:
    31%; Less happy: 5%; No change: 2%; Uncommitted: 4%

30. What would you say about your intellectual development?

    1978   Up: 19%; Down: 50%; Same: 31%
    1995   Up: 52%; Down: 39%; Same: 4%; Uncommitted: 5%

31. Do you feel your husband is growing intellectually?

    1978  Yes: 92%; Not especially: 8%
    1995  Yes: 93%; No: 6%; Uncommitted: 1%

32. Do you feel left behind by him?

    1978  No: 66%; Yes, or sometimes: 33%; Uncommitted: 1%
    1995  No: 73%; Yes, or sometimes: 27%

33. If so, what are you doing about this?

    1978  Get involved in community: 11%; Plan school or work: 11%; Increase current events: 15%; Talk about it: 8%; Nothing: 54%
    1995  Plan future activities: 17%; Read: 10%; Take class: 10%; Volunteer: 4%; Help with husband's job: 20%; Nothing: 28%

34. Have your relationships with friends changed in quantity and quality since children?

    1978  Yes: 83%; No: 16%; Positive change: 69%; Negative change: 14%; Closest friend is also mother: 46%
    1995  Yes: 66%; No: 8%; Positive change: 14%; Negative change: 10%; Uncommitted: 2%; Of positive changes, 72% have formed closer relationships with other mothers.

35. Right now do you see your identity as coming primarily through your children or through your own accomplishments?

    1978  Self: 25%; Children: 44%; Both: 31%
    1995  Self: 11%; Children: 57%; Both: 31%; Husband: 1%; Uncommitted: 1%

36. How did having children change your self-image?

    1978  Feel more womanly: 22%; Increased self-knowledge: 14%; More confident: 19%; Positive change: 56%; Negative change: 36%

1995  More positive: 46%; No change: 6%; Negative change: 46%; Uncommitted: 2%

37. Many women experience what I call "The Mother Crisis." Are you the kind of mother you always thought you'd be?

1978  Yes: 68%; No: 23%; Uncommitted: 9%
1995  Yes: 52%; No: 44%; Uncommitted: 4%

38. If you've not, describe the difference:

1978  Better at mothering than expected: 11%; Thought I'd play more with the children: 15%; Less patient and competent: 74%
1995  Better at mothering than expected: 17%; Thought I'd play more with the children: 25%; Less patient and competent: 58%

39. How do you feel you display your push for independence?

1978  Plan career: 16%; Make major decisions alone: 29%; Get involved in community: 31%; Open hostility: 14%; Uncommitted: 10%
1995  Increase own interests/goals: 59%; Increased aggression: 11%; Nothing: 30%

40. Have there been any recent changes in your self-image?

1978  No change: 32%; Yes, positive: 53%; Yes, negative: 10%; Uncommitted: 5%
1995  No change: 31%; Yes, positive: 33%; Yes, negative: 28%; Uncommitted: 1%

41. If so, what are they? Open-ended, no statistics.

42. Do you have any goals for 5, 10, and 15 years? (Yes or no) 5 yrs. _____, 10 yrs. _____, 15 yrs. _____

1978  No goals: 25%; 5 yrs.: 30%; 5 to 10 yrs.: 7%; 10 to 15 yrs.: 11%; 5, 10, 15 yrs.: 25%

1995   No goals: 13%; 5 yrs.: 34%; 5 to 10 yrs.: 10%; 10 to 15 yrs.: 10%; 5, 10, 15 yrs.: 32%; 5 and 15 yrs.: 6%; 10 yrs.: 4%

43. What are they?

1978   Be a good mom: 16%; Volunteer: 7%; Return to school, work, career: 61% (incl. changing careers)
1995   Be established at home; in new home; financially secure; return to work/career; return to school; provide good education for the children; get back to self/husband; have children be independent; start own business

44. a. Are your plans for staying home with your children the same as when they were born?

1978   Yes: 60%; No: 35%; Uncommitted: 5%
1995   Yes: 67%; No: 33%

b. If changed, how?

1978   Feel need to work: 83%; Need to stay home stronger: 17%
1995   Return to work/school: 10%; Stay home longer: 23%

45. Compared to your life goals before you had children, are your life goals different now? How?

1978   Yes: 29%; No: 59%; No life goals: 10%; Uncommitted: 2%
1995   Yes: 51%; No: 47%; Uncommitted: 2%

46. If you knew then what you know now would you have children again? Why?

1978   Yes: 95%; Probably not: 5%
1995   Yes: 99%; No: 1%

47. Would you have as many?

1978   Yes: 76%; Yes, and more: 9%; Maybe less: 15%
1995   Yes: 76%; Yes, and more: 18%; No, less: 6%

48. If you were doing it over again, would you be a full-time, at-home mother?

   1978   Yes: 82%; Not sure: 3%; No, would return to work sooner: 13%; Uncommitted: 2%
   1995   Yes: 93%; No: 7%

49. If you could have a job (outside the home) tomorrow that is perfect for you, would you take it?

   1978   No: 43%; Yes: 52%; Would seriously consider it: 5%
   1995   Yes: 29%; No: 71%

50. What concrete suggestions would you give a dear friend to help her in coping with the problems of being a mother?

   Open-ended. No statistics.


*WOMEN IN THE MOTHER CRISIS*

1978—92% In The Mother Crisis (MC): 71 respondents
   No Mother Crisis          8%
   1 of 4 MC questions      19%
   2 of 4 MC questions      24%
   3 of 4 MC questions      17%
   4 of 4 MC questions      32%

1995—89% in The Mother Crisis (MC): 109 respondents
   No Mother Crisis         11%
   1 of 4 MC questions      23%
   2 of 4 MC questions      22%
   3 of 4 MC questions      20%
   4 of 4 MC questions      24%

# *Notes* ∽

## INTRODUCTION

1. Victoria Neufeldt, Editor-in-Chief, *Webster's New World Dictionary, Third College Edition* (Springfield, MA: G & C Merriam, 1988), 328.


## CHAPTER 1

1. Rhoda Metraux, ed., *Margaret Mead—Some Personal Views* (New York: Walker and Company, 1979), 14.
2. Maxine Harris, *Down from the Pedestal* (New York: Doubleday, 1994), 21.
3. Compiled by Bryan Holmes with the editors of the Viking Press and *Ladies Home Journal, The Journal of the Century* (New York: Viking Press, 1976), 33.
4. Ibid.
5. Barbara Ehrenreich and Deirdre English, *For Her Own Good: 150 Years of Expert Advice to Women* (Garden City, NY: Anchor Press/Doubleday, 1994), 29.
6. Ibid., 92.
7. Ibid.
8. Ibid., 115.
9. Ibid., 131.
10. Betty Friedan, *The Feminine Mystique* (New York: Dell, 1962), 364.
11. Compiled by editors of the Readers Digest Association, *Our Glorious Century* (Pleasantville, NY: Author, 1994), 48.
12. Ehrenreich and English, 131.
13. Ibid., 148.
14. Friedan, *The Feminine Mystique*, 85.
15. Benjamin Spock, M.D., *The Common Sense Book of Baby and Child Case* (New York: Duill, Sloan and Pearce, 1957).
16. Readers Digest Association, 260.
17. Friedan, *The Feminine Mystique*, 217.
18. Ibid., 16.
19. Readers Digest Association, 301.

20. Ibid., 261.
21. Friedan, *The Feminine Mystique*, 69.
22. Ibid., 72.
23. Ibid., 64.
24. Jane Howard, "Katharine Graham: The Power That Didn't Corrupt" [*Ms. Magazine*, October 1974], *The Decade of Women: A Ms. History of the Seventies in Words and Pictures*, eds. Suzanne Levine and Harriet Lyons (New York, Paragon Books, 1980), 40.
25. Suzanne Levine and Harriet Lyons, quoting astronaut James Lovell in [*Ms. Magazine*, September 1973], *The Decade of Women*, 35.
26. Ellen Frankfort, "Rosie: The Investigation of a Wrongful Death" [*Dial*, 1979], *The Decade of Women*, 137.
27. Gail Rock, "Same Time, Same Station, Same Sexism" [*Ms. Magazine*, December 1973], *The Decade of Women*, 156.
28. Gloria Steinem, "Introduction," *The Decade of Women*, 8.
29. Levine and Lyons, quoting actress Marlo Thomas, *The Decade of Women*, 39.
30. Andrea Dworkin, "Phallic Imperialism" [*Ms. Magazine*, December 1976], *The Decade of Women*, 114.
31. Levine and Lyons, *The Decade of Women*, 16.
32. Ellen Goodman addressing the Association of National Advertisers [November 1978], *The Decade of Women*, 163.
33. Phyllis Schlafly, quoted in "The Sweetheart of The Silent Majority" [*Ms. Magazine*, March 1974], *The Decade of Women*, 81.

## *CHAPTER 2*

1. Judith D. Schwartz, *The Mother Puzzle: A New Generation Reckons with Motherhood* (New York: Simon and Schuster, 1993), 117.
2. Ibid.
3. Shari L. Thurer, *The Myths of Motherhood: How Culture Reinvents the Good Mother* (Boston: Houghton Mifflin, 1994), 291.
4. Ibid., 287.
5. Ibid., 288.
6. Ann Dally, *Inventing Motherhood: The Consequences of an Ideal* (New York: Schocken Books, 1983).
7. Ken Tucker, "The Mother of All TV Mothers," *Entertainment Weekly*, (October 14, 1994).
8. Brenda Bankart, "Japanese Perceptions of Motherhood," *Psychology of Women Quarterly*, 13, 1989: 59–76.
9. Carol Dix, *The New Mother Syndrome: Coping with Postpartum Stress and Depression* (New York: Simon and Schuster, 1985) 9.
10. Ibid., 11.
11. Ibid.
12. Ibid., 13.

## CHAPTER 3

1. Paula J. Caplan and Ian Hall-McCorquodale, "Mother-Blaming in Major Clinical Journals," *American Journal of Orthopsychiatry* 55(3), July 1985: 349.
2. Ibid.
3. Ibid., 346.
4. Ibid., 246.
5. Ibid.
6. Ibid., 352.
7. Judith D. Schwartz, *The Mother Puzzle: A New Generation Reckons with Motherhood* (New York: Simon and Schuster, 1993), 48.
8. Ibid.
9. Ann Dally, *Inventing Motherhood: The Consequences of an Ideal* (New York: Schocken Books, 1983).
10. Betty Friedan, *The Second Stage* (New York: Summit Books, 1981), 56.
11. Sandra Scarr, *Mother Care/Other Care* (New York: Basic Books, 1984), 124.
12. Herta A. Guttman, "Autonomy and Motherhood," *Psychiatry* 46, August 1983: 231–232.
13. Faye J. Crosby, *Juggling: The Unexpected Advantages of Balancing Career and Home for Women and Their Families* (Toronto, New York: Free Press; Canada: Maxwell Macmillan, 1991), 95.
14. Guttman, "Autonomy and Motherhood," 233.
15. Friedan, quotations from early American feminists on the nature of the early American household, *The Second Stage*, 315–316.
16. Ibid., quoting psychologist Eric Fromm on the effect an unfulfilled mother might have on her children, *The Second Stage*, 316.
17. Ibid.
18. Ibid., quoting psychologist Abraham H. Maslow on his concept of self-actualization and how it pertains to women who cease to grow psychologically.
19. Ann Dally, quoting Juliet Mitchell on the danger of a mother's lack of autonomy, *Inventing Motherhood*, 172.
20. Ibid., 173.
21. Scarr, *Mother Care/Other Care*, 110.
22. Ibid., 119.
23. Carol Dix, *The New Mother Syndrome: Coping with Postpartum Stress and Depression* (New York: Simon and Schuster, 1988), 11.
24. Ibid., 7.
25. Dyanne Affonso, "Tough Times for New Moms," *Baltimore Times*, (October 10, 1995).
26. Ibid.
27. "*NBC Dateline*," NBC, (October 23, 1995).
28. Ibid.
29. Mary J. Levitt, Ruth A. Weber, and M. Cherie Clark, "Social Network Relationships as Sources of Maternal Support and Well-Being," *Developmental Psychology* 22(3), 1986: 310–316.
30. Scarr, *Mother Care/Other Care*, 139.

31. Ibid., 140.
32. Penelope Leach, *Children First* (New York: Alfred A. Knopf, 1994), 238.
33. Ibid., 236.
34. Ibid., 73.
35. Ibid., 238.
36. Scarr, *Mother Care/Other Care*, 43.
37. Friedan, *The Second Stage*, 23.


## CHAPTER 4

1. Sandra Scarr, *Mother Care/Other Care* (New York: Basic Books, 1984), 53.
2. Ibid., 20.
3. Ann Dally, *Inventing Motherhood: The Consequences of an Ideal* (New York: Schocken Books, 1983), 220.
4. Judith D. Schwartz, *The Mother Puzzle: A New Generation Reckons with Motherhood* (New York: Simon and Schuster, 1984), 58.
5. Betty Friedan, *The Second Stage* (New York: Summit Books, 1981), 92.
6. Ibid., 67.
7. Ibid., 86–87.
8. William Henry Chafe, quoting anthropologist Margaret Mead, *The American Woman: Her Changing Social, Economic and Political Roles, 1920–1970,* (New York: Oxford University Press, 1971), 100.
9. Jacqueline Shannon, "Can You Be Somebody and a Mommy Too?" *Cosmopolitan* (October 1994), 127.
10. Alice M. Atkinson, "Stress Levels of Family Day Care Providers, Mothers Employed Outside the Home, and Mothers at Home," *Journal of Marriage and the Family* 54 (ISSN: 0022-2445).
11. Betty Friedan, *The Feminine Mystique* (New York: Dell, 1963), 307.
12. Penelope Leach, *Children First* (New York: Alfred A. Knopf, 1994), 245.
13. Ibid., 245.
14. Scarr, *Mother Care/Other Care*, 210.
15. Scarr, 212.
16. Albert I. Rabin and Benjamin Beit-Hallahmi, *Twenty Years Later: Kibbutz Children Grown Up* (New York: Springer, 1982), 9.
17. Ibid., 7.
18. Benjamin Zablocki, *The Joyful Community* (Chicago and London: University of Chicago Press, 1980), 23.
19. Ibid., 19, "An intentional community is a group of persons associated together [voluntarily] for the purpose of establishing a whole way of life. As such, it shall display to some degree, each of the following characteristics: common geographical location; economic interdependence; social, cultural, educational, and spiritual interexchange of uplift and development. A minimum of three families or five adult members is required to constitute an intentional community."
20. Scarr, *Mother Care/Other Care*, 222.
21. Zablocki, *The Joyful Community*, 117.

22. Dally, *Inventing Motherhood*, 87.
23. Ibid., quoting Dr. John Bowlby's monograph prepared for the World Health Organization in 1951, 87.
24. Scarr, 210.
25. Ibid., 218.
26. Arnlaug Liera, "Mothers, Markets and the State: A Scandanavian 'Model?'" *Journal of Social Policy* 22 (ISSN: 0047-2794), July 93: 329.
27. Leach, *Children First*, 48.
28. Scarr, 222.
29. Ibid., 130.
30. Ibid., 131–132.
31. Ibid., 154
32. Ibid.
33. Dally, *Inventing Motherhood*, 259.
34. Ibid., 269.
35. Rhoda Metraux, Ed., *Margaret Mead—Some Personal Views* (New York: Walker and Company, 1979), 43.

## CHAPTER 5

1. Michelle Green, "The Best Revenge," *People Magazine* (October 2, 1995), 101.
2. Bud Collins, "Billie Jean King Evens the Score" [*Ms. Magazine*, July 1973], *The Decade of Women: A Ms. History of the Seventies in Words and Pictures*, eds., Suzanne Levine and Harriet Lyons (New York: Paragon Books, 1980), 69.
3. Suzanne Levine and Harriet Lyons, Eds., *The Decade of Women*, 18.
4. Sara M. Evans, *Born for Liberty: A History of Women in America* (New York: Free Press, 1989), 295.
5. Ibid., 288.
6. Ibid., 288–289.
7. Judith D. Schwartz, *The Mother Puzzle: A New Generation Reckons with Motherhood* (New York: Simon and Schuster, 1984), 72.
8. Maxine Harris, *Down from the Pedestal: Moving beyond Idealized Images of Womanhood* (New York: Doubleday, 1994), 8.
9. Ibid.
10. Christine Northrup, *Women's Bodies—Women's Wisdom* (New York: Bantam Books, 1994), 5.
11. Carol Tarvis, ed., *Every Woman's Emotional Well-Being* (Garden City, NY: Doubleday, 1986), 11–12.
12. Evans, *Born for Liberty*, 300.
13. Ibid., 301.
14. Paula J. Kaplan, *Between Women: Lowering the Barriers* (Toronto: Personal Library Publishers, 1981), 151.
15. Elizabeth Janeway, *Man's World/Woman's Place: A Study in Social Mythology* (New York: William Morrow and Company, 1971), 51.
16. Ibid., 151.
17. Schwartz, *The Mother Puzzle*, 76.

18. Harris, *Down from the Pedestal*, 21.
19. Kaplan, *Between Women*, 41.
20. Harris, *Down from the Pedestal*, 41.
21. Susan Faludi, "The War on Women: The Big Lie," *Detroit Free Press* (October 20, 1991), 6.
22. Ibid., 7.
23. Mona Charen, "The Feminist Mistake," *National Review*.
24. Kay Ebeling, "The Great Experiment That Failed," *Newsweek*.
25. Faludi, "The War on Women," 7.
26. Ibid.
27. Ibid.
28. Ibid.
29. Ibid.
30. James C. Dobson, "Questions," *Focus on the Family* (November 1995), 5.

## CHAPTER 6

1. Judith D. Schwartz, *The Mother Puzzle: A New Generation Reckons with Motherhood* (New York: Simon and Schuster, 1984), 33.
2. Susan Faludi, "The War on Women: The Big Lie," *Detroit Free Press* (October 20, 1991), 6.
3. Ibid.
4. Michelle Green, "The Best Revenge," *People Magazine* (October 2, 1995), 108.
5. Michele Cohen, quoting Jane Halpert, "Will Motherhood Cost You Your Job?"*Redbook* (May 1993), 84.
6. Ibid.
7. Deborah Swiss, Ed.D., and Judith P. Walker, *Women and the Work/Family Dilemma. How Today's Professional Women Are Finding Solutions* (1993).
8. Michele Cohen, "Will Motherhood Cost You Your Job?" p 84.
9. Elisabeth Badinter, *Mother Love: Myth and Reality* (New York: Macmillan, 1980), 246.
10. Ibid.
11. Ibid., 258.
12. Ibid., 307.
13. Elizabeth Janeway, *Man's World/Woman's Place: A Study in Social Mythology* (New York: William Morrow and Company, 1971), 26.
14. Ibid., 28.
15. Ibid., 34.
16. Sandra Scarr, citing research by Clair Etaugh on a predominantly negative attitude toward working mothers in the popular press, *Mother Care/Other Care* (New York: Basic Books, 1984), 8.
17. Badinter, *Mother Love*, 206.
18. Schwartz, *The Mother Puzzle*, 63.
19. Scarr, *Mother Care/Other Care*, ix.
20. Ibid., 5.
21. Ibid., 4

22. Schwartz, *The Mother Puzzle*, 51.
23. Ibid., 81.
24. Paula J. Kaplan, *Between Women: Lowering the Barriers*, (Toronto: Personal Library Publishers, 1981), 41.
25. Janeway, *Man's World/Woman's Place*, 37.
26. Ibid., 153.
27. Maxine Harris, *Down from the Pedestal: Moving beyond Idealized Images of Womanhood* (New York: Doubleday, 1994), 40.
28. Ibid., 35.

## CHAPTER 7

1. Melissa Gayle West, *If Only I Were a Better Mother* (Wahole, NH: Stillpoint Publishing, 1992), 42.
2. Ibid.
3. Ibid., 46.
4. Ibid., 47.
5. Ibid., 50.
6. Elisabeth Badinter, *Mother Love: Myth and Reality*, (New York: William Morrow and Company, 1971), xxiii.
7. Ibid.
8. Elizabeth Janeway, *Man's World/Woman's Place* (New York: William Morrow and Company, 1971), 9.
9. Terri Apter, *Secret Paths: Women in the New Midlife* (New York: W. W. Norton and Company, 1995), 82.
10. Lynn Darling, "What's Maternally Correct?" *Redbook* (March 1995), 126.
11. Darcie Sanders, "Those Myths about Stay-at-Home Moms," *Good Housekeeping* (August 1992), 1.
12. Ibid., 2.
13. Ibid.
14. Rhoda Matraux, ed., *Margaret Mead—Some Personal Views* (New York: Walker and Company, 1979), 27.
15. Janeway, *Man's World/Woman's Place*, 52.
16. Ibid., 54.
17. Ibid., 302.
18. Matraux, ed., *Margaret Mead*, 30.
19. Paula J. Kaplan, *Between Women: Lowering the Barriers* (Toronto, Personal Library Publishers, 1981), 162.
20. Ibid.
21. Ibid., 112.
22. Ibid.
23. Ibid., 55.
24. "Changes in the Marital Relationship during the Transition to First-Time Motherhood: Effects of Violated Expectations concerning Division of Household Labor," *American Psychological Association, Journal of Personality and Social Psychology* 55(1), 1988: 78–87.

25. Ibid.
26. Laurie Leventhal-Belfer, Phillip A. Cowan, and Carolyn Pape Cowan, "Satisfaction with Child Care Arrangements: Effects on Adaptation to Parenthood," *American Journal of Orthopsychiatry* (April 1992), 171.
27. Ibid.
28. "Don't Put Mom on Your Resume," *Parents Magazine* (July 1994).

## CHAPTER 8

1. Judith D. Schwartz, *The Mother Puzzle: A New Generation Reckons with Motherhood* (New York: Simon and Schuster, 1984), 42.
2. Ibid., 78.
3. Ibid., 42.
4. Ibid.
5. Terri Apter, *Secret Paths: Women in the New Midlife* (New York: W. W. Norton and Company, 1995), 94.
6. Ingrid Groller, "Women and Work," *Parents Magazine* (July 1990), 64.
7. Ibid.
8. Ibid., 66.
9. Lynn Darling, "What's Maternally Correct?" *Redbook* (March 1995).
10. "Mothers Speak Out on Child Care," *Mothers at Home* (November 1989).
11. A report, "National Institute of Child Health and Human Development, Infant Child Care and Attachment Security: Results of the NICHD Study of Early Child Care," *Symposium. International Conference on Infant Studies*, Providence, RI (April 20, 1996), 1–15.
12. *New York Times* News Service, "Trust in Mom Isn't Lost in Day Care," *The Sun* (21 April 1996), 7-A.
13. Kathleen Gerson, *Hard Choices: How Women Decide about Work, Career and Motherhood* (Berkeley: University of California Press, 1985), 219–220.
14. Paula J. Kaplan, *Between Women: Lowering the Barriers* (Toronto: Personal Library Publishers, 1981), 143.
15. Ibid., 153.
16. Linda M. Blumand and Elizabeth A. Vandewater, "Mother to Mother: A Maternalist Organization in Late Capitalist America," *Social Problems* 40(3), 1993: 287.
17. Ibid.
18. Ibid., citing "Of Cradles and Careers: A Guide to Reshaping Your Job to Include a Baby in Your Life," a publication of the LaLeche League.
19. Apter, *Secret Paths*, 19–20.
20. Betty Friedan, *The Second Stage* (New York: Summit Books, 1981), 28.
21. Ibid., 74.
22. Ibid., 73.
23. Hillary Rodham Clinton, *It Takes A Village and Other Lessons Children Teach Us* (New York: Simon and Schuster, 1996), 221.
24. Ibid., 222.
25. "Will Motherhood Cost You Your Job?" *Redbook* (May 1993), 84.

26. Sandra L. Hofferth and Sharon Gennis Deich, "Recent U.S. Child Care and Family Legislation in Comparative Perspective," *Journal of Family Issues* 15, September: 449–466.

27. Penelope Leach, *Children First* (New York: Alfred A. Knopf, 1994), 99.

## CHAPTER 9

1. Norma and Art Peterson, *The Unofficial Mother's Handbook* (New York: Penguin Books, 1989), cover.

2. Nathaniel Branden, *Honoring the Self, Self-Esteem and Personal Transformation* (New York: Bantam Books, 1985), 44.

3. Ibid., 45.

4. Ibid., 47.

5. Ibid.

6. Ibid., 48.

7. Ibid., 49.

8. Ibid., 53.

9. Ibid., 55.

10. Ibid., 59.

11. J. Ruth Gendler, *The Book of Qualities* (New York: Harper and Row Publishers, 1988), 25.

12. Branden, *Honoring the Self*, 60.

13. Joan Borysenko, *Guilt Is the Teacher, Love Is the Lesson* (New York: Warner Books, 1990), 27.

14. Ibid.

15. Ibid., 35.

16. Ibid.

17. Melissa Gayle West, *If Only I Were a Better Mother* (Wahole, NH: Stillpoint, 1992), 75.

18. Ibid.

19. Ibid.

20. Branden, *Honoring the Self*, 63.

21. Ibid., 70.

22. John Rosemond, "Parent Power," *Honolulu Advertiser* (May 27, 1996), B1.

23. Ibid.

24. Ibid.

25. John Rosemond, *John Rosemond's Six-Point Plan for Raising Happy, Healthy Children* (Kansas City: 1989), 8.

26. Karen S. Peterson, "Stay-at-Home Moms across Globe Form On-Line Bonds," [*USA Today*], *Honolulu Advertiser* (August 11, 1996), D10.

27. Mary Frances Berry, *The Politics of Parenthood: Child Care, Women's Rights, and the Myth of the Good Mother* (New York: Penguin Books, 1993), 39.

28. Ibid., 41.

29. Ibid., 40.

30. Ibid., 29.

31. Ibid., 41.

32. Eric R. Kingston and Regina O'Grady-LeShane, "The Effects of Caregiving on Women's Social Security Benefits," *Gerontologist* 33(2), 1993: 230–239.
33. Ibid.
34. Berry, *The Politics of Parenthood*, 39.
35. Ibid., 217.
36. Ibid., citing "A Lesser Life" by Sylvia Hewlett, 1986, 41.

# Index ♋